MY LIFE IN

BUSINESS SUITS,

HOSPITAL GOWNS,

AND HIGH HEELS

My Life in
Business Suits,
Hospital Gowns,
and High Heels

IN CONTROL, BEING CONTROLLED,
OUT OF CONTROL!

• • •

Tom LeNoble

 Opening Pathways

COPYRIGHT © 2026 TOM LENOBLE
All rights reserved.

MY LIFE IN BUSINESS SUITS, HOSPITAL GOWNS, AND HIGH HEELS
In Control, Being Controlled, Out of Control!
First Edition

ISBN 979-8-9932921-2-0 *Hardcover*
   979-8-9932921-1-3 *Paperback*
   979-8-9932921-0-6 *Ebook*
   979-8-9932921-3-7 *Audiobook*

LCCN 2025921214

Every storm runs out of rain.
—MAYA ANGELOU

. . .

*This book is dedicated to all who inspired me
to keep going...no matter the storm.*

Contents

Rita Dayworth, 1973

The Return of Rita

San Francisco, CA. October 2024. Evening.

My seventieth birthday party was about to begin, and I was nowhere to be seen.

This event had been in the works for four months, and everything had been arranged to perfection. The rooftop space above Market Street was a seamless mix of intimate and sophisticated. Fire pits cast a warm glow on the terrace and just enough heat to hold back the fall chill. The air was fragrant with the smell of flowers flown in from Maui, my second home. Framed pictures of my parents were displayed throughout the indoor bar area. Smartly dressed servers circulated with trays of champagne and canapés.

My guests had RSVP'd many weeks before, and since then I'd been teasing them with emails to get them excited for what was to come—and to stress the importance of punctuality. Tonight, even the known stragglers had arrived by 6:30 sharp, just in time to see the sun start to set behind the San Francisco skyline.

People had started murmuring about where I was, but with or without me, it was showtime.

My dear friend, the performer Misa Malone, stepped out onto the stage area and kicked off the celebration. The audience was captivated as she sang a selection of some of my favorite songs—a mix of standards and ballads from the '70s and '80s that we had chosen to tell a particular story: that of a person searching for love and happiness, and finally finding it within themselves.

I smiled to myself at the thought of my friends whispering to each other in disbelief that I would be missing such a special performance—in my honor! Some probably figured, *Oh, that's so Tom. He asked this wonderful woman to entertain us so he could be fashionably late and make an entrance.*

Well, they weren't wrong.

The moment had come. Misa reached the end of her final song, "I'm Here" from *The Color Purple*, and put her own spin on the lyrics:

> But most of all I'm thankful for
> Lovin' who I really am
> I'm beautiful,
> Tom is beautiful,
> And he's *here*!

As the guests applauded, the MC for the evening took the mic and announced: "Ladies and gentlemen...the incomparable *Rita*!"

Showtime!

· · ·

To the opening notes of Nancy Wilson's "Free Again," I emerged from the makeshift wings with my back to the crowd in a black silk number under a gold sequin duster, black elbow gloves, a cloud of red hair, long earrings grazing my shoulders, and black heels. When I turned around to lip-sync the words, "Free again, back to being free again / Back to being me again," the crowd reacted just as I knew they would.

It was good to be back on stage.

Only one or two friends in the room that night suspected that "Rita Dayworth" was going to make an appearance at my birthday party. (Rita hadn't been seen in at least thirteen years, but she never could resist an audience.) But many more in the crowd understood just how deeply that lyric—"Back to being me again"—resonated with me.

· · ·

In my seventy years, "me" has meant a lot of different things.

I've been the poor little boy who grew up in a shack with no refrigerator or hot water. The chubby, unathletic kid who didn't fit in anywhere and was teased for being a sissy. The churchgoing mama's boy on a path into the ministry because it seemed like the proper thing to do.

I've been the misfit teenager who found his tribe among the theater kids. The pothead college student who ditched the lecture hall for the lights of a drag bar.

I've been the gay man who lived the high life in the 1980s, until the AIDS epidemic came for those most dear to me. A "gray hair" who, at age fifty-three, had a front seat to the dawn of social media as one of the first one hundred employees at Facebook.

And I've been an HIV and cancer patient who was told no less than *three times* that I had only six months to live.

I'm still all those things.

And I'm still here.

· · ·

For a long time, I believed that all of those different "me's" needed to be kept separate. They were different roles to play that could not all be part of one being, like stages to pass through on my way to some predetermined destination. But the world has changed. More importantly, I have changed.

And on that October night, over five songs and five costume changes, I honored all of it. For those twenty-five minutes, even though I was so done up as to be unrecognizable, I bared more of myself to my friends than I ever have before.

Until now.

· · ·

This book is the unvarnished story of my life: the good, the bad, and the often outrageous. The wild childhood spent in poverty. The years of trying to hide in plain sight. The night I traded closeted shame for (extremely) public self-acceptance. The times I skated close to the edge, and the times I carried others through their darkest moments and out the other side.

And though I love a good story (the more scandalous the better), there's a deeper reason for wanting to tell mine.

I want to share all I've learned about resilience, acceptance, and intention to help you, the reader, push forward in your own life, past whatever is making you feel stuck—be it personal, professional, or spiritual.

Lord knows I've had to do it more than a few times.

So, to quote Ms. Nancy Wilson at the end of Rita's opening number:

Time to call up all the crowd
Raise the roof and shout out loud
Time to have a party.

ONE

Love Shack

EVERYTHING STARTED IN UNASSUMING LITTLE JACK-
sonville Beach, Florida. I was born in the fall of 1954 to Mary
and Vic LeNoble, six years and one day after my older brother
Victor Jr., whom I called Bubby. My childhood was not your typical
1950s *Leave it to Beaver*–style picture of American peace and prosper-
ity. Or maybe it was, but the poor version. We didn't have everything
we wanted growing up. But we had everything we needed.

Until I was about twelve, we lived in a dwelling that was known as
"the Shack"—even we called it that—down a little dirt road in what
seemed like the middle of nowhere. It had one bedroom, which I
shared with my brother and, for a time, my grandmother Minnie Ida,
who would tell me about the messages she received from the electric
fan. My parents slept in the living room, though by the time we got
up each morning, any evidence that it had served as their makeshift
bedroom had been magically whisked away.

The Shack had no refrigerator—my father was always hauling
in ice for the icebox—and no hot water. When it was time to cook
or take a bath, my father would heat up water in these enormous

stainless-steel vats the size of barrels that he'd heave on and off a heater. I can still smell the kerosene.

We did have an indoor bathroom, with a lovely claw-footed tub to boot. But the bathroom had no flooring. The old linoleum was cracked and pulled up in so many places you could see right through to the wooden foundation underneath. When it was time to bathe, my father would fill up the tub with water from the vat, and because hot water was such a precious resource, we would take turns bathing, one by one, topping it up with more hot water as it cooled. There was a definite pecking order, and being the youngest, I always had to go last. But everybody got to go first on their birthday.

· · ·

There was rarely a dull moment at the Shack; nothing was ever very predictable or conventional, but you don't realize that when you've got nothing to compare it to.

I was about five years old when we got our first car, a 1955 Oldsmobile gifted to my father by the construction company where he worked his whole life. My mother didn't know how to drive (not unusual for women at the time), so my aunt Jane tried to teach her. The car was a stick shift, and I remember hearing the two of them laugh hilariously as they hop, hop, hopped up and down our dirt road.

Mom never really got the hang of it, but that didn't stop her from driving. She would take me to school, and if she couldn't get the car into the right gear, or if the brakes were broken and we couldn't afford to get them fixed, she would just slow down as we neared the school and tell me to jump out as we passed. I would throw myself out of the car, and the Olds would roll on out of the school's circular driveway and down the road.

That said a lot about us, and about the way my future would unfold. Life at the Shack may have been a little rough around the edges, but it prepared me for tumultuous decades to come: I learned to be light on my feet, to keep my eyes wide open to what was going on around me, and to handle it all without a lot of muss or fuss.

No matter what happened, we learned to just keep going.

Mom and Dad

Mary and Vic LeNoble were deeply devoted to one another for their entire lives, though you would have never known it from the outside. Ask any of their friends, and they'd tell you they had no idea how those two stayed together, because they were always bickering. But that was just their dynamic. Underneath it, there was a very real bond between them, an understanding. They were partners. I could sense it when I was a child, even if I never once saw them kiss.

I do suspect there were fireworks when they first met, because they were both very good-looking when they were young. Dad was a man's man and very, very handsome—about six feet tall, blue-eyed, and always trim and tan from working outdoors. He used to tell people he was part Native American, or "Indian," as he said. I don't see how that could've been true, since both his parents emigrated to Florida from Germany and Austria, but I never challenged him on it.

Dad's parents had been quite wealthy and had enjoyed a very cultured life back in Europe. I remember thinking they sounded like something out of a storybook. His father, Richard LeNoble, was an artist, businessman, and scientist. His mother, Valeska Helena Frederica Schulte-LeNoble—we called her Ma—had been a ballerina and opera singer and could speak six or seven languages.

In the old country, Richard and Valeska had their own antique store and had lived in lovely homes. They came to the United States in 1905, opened a farm business in northern Florida, and built the first automotive garage in the Southeast.

For the first five years of my father's life, the LeNobles lived comfortably in a huge old house full of paintings, furnishings, and art pieces, on a farm bordering the St. Johns River in Jacksonville. And every day, Richard put the money that he made in the bank, but always kept five dollars on hand in case of emergencies. When the Great Depression hit, they were left with exactly that: five dollars. That was it. They sold their riverfront farm (which would be worth millions today) and moved into a small house in a neighborhood nearby, cramming it full of the pieces of their old life. Dad's parents had been elegant, successful people, and though they still had all these artifacts of wealth, they were now dirt poor.

Dad's life was forever changed. Richard was simply too shattered by the experience of losing everything and would never work again. He became abusive, and as an only child, Dad was the main target of his anger. I was terrified of my grandfather when I was little. But I was also scared of my father, so I never imagined Dad could also fear someone. Dad was very stoic, and it wasn't until I was in my forties that I would understand how much his father's treatment affected him and how it would color the way he related to Bubby and me.

Just as hurtful to Dad as the physical abuse, though, was the fact that my grandparents had a houseful of valuable possessions but would never think of selling them to get by. Instead, Dad would go out and hunt squirrels and other critters to barter for necessities and extra food to supplement what Ma grew in her garden. And when, as a teenager, he outgrew his last pair of shoes, Dad dropped out of high school because the family could not afford new ones.

Dad deeply resented his father for clinging to the past at the expense of his family and lived the rest of his life worried that disaster could strike at any moment.

· · ·

Like my father, my mother, Mary, also grew up always bracing for disaster. Mary was the middle child of Minnie Ida and Phillip, and was very pretty when she was younger, with blue eyes, beautiful fair skin, and dark hair that she would curl. Her older brother, Phil Jr., was a radio host and apparently had a promising career in television. But he was a terrible alcoholic, and Mom had to quit high school for a time to get a job and help put Phil Jr. through rehab. She was the savior and caretaker in her family, as she would go on to be in ours, always looking out for people. Part of that caretaking role meant that she would grow up to be the biggest worrier I've ever known.

Mom was raised a staunch Methodist and would go on to become a founding member of our local Methodist church. This was just one of the ways my parents were absolute opposites. My father set foot in church only five times—and one of those times, he was in a box. The other times were his wedding, our baptisms, and my mother's memorial service. People used to say, "If Vic LeNoble walks into church, watch the rafters because they're either going to fall down or he's there to fix them."

Know Your Role

The LeNoble household was somewhat eccentric, but when it came to family roles, Mom and Dad were a pretty traditional pair for the South in the 1960s. Mom cooked, cleaned, ran the house, and took care of me, Bubby, and Nana, with whom Bubby and I shared the Shack's single bedroom. Every month, she got an allowance from my dad for household expenses. I don't know exactly how much it was, but I know the amount stayed the same over their whole marriage—fifty years and no cost-of-living increase!

Once I started kindergarten, Mom began working full-time. I always told people my mother worked for the school board, implying that she was a teacher or administrator, but she was actually a lunch lady for twenty-eight years. In those days, the job involved running a real kitchen and cooking meals for the kids from scratch.

· · ·

Mom was totally devoted to us in the best way she knew how. For better or worse, in her mind mothering meant smothering; it was as if she was so profoundly scared of losing me or of my getting hurt that it drove everything she did. She fixated mostly on me and my safety because I was so dramatically different from my older brother. Bubby was quiet and shy, the consummate rule-follower, while I was rebellious and curious and didn't hesitate to jump right into things, often literally, resulting in many stitches and broken bones. I don't think Mom really knew how to handle my rambunctiousness. To have any peace of mind whatsoever, she needed to know exactly where I was at all times.

That's why I went to nursery school until I was about fourteen years old. There was a nursery near the elementary, junior high, and senior high school buildings where Mom worked and I went to school. I always went home from school with her, and when she got a job at a different school sometime during my junior high years, I would walk to the nursery school after school and wait for her to get off work and pick me up. I didn't question why I couldn't just walk home by myself, given we lived just eight blocks from the nursery—I was to go home with Mom, and that was that.

Her way couldn't have been further from what's known today as "free range parenting," a term which makes me think of my father, only he didn't do much actual parenting. I can still hear him scolding Mom to "just let the boy be" when she would fret over every little stumble or scratch. Because God forbid, I should grow up "soft."

Dad loved the outdoors and approved of my habit of exploring the woods and swamps all around Jacksonville Beach, and I'm convinced he enjoyed being out in the woods with animals—whether he was just observing them, bringing them home as pets, or hunting and skinning them—more than he enjoyed being with people. He was still a well-brought-up Southern man, so he was unfailingly polite to everyone, especially strangers—everybody loved Vic LeNoble—but he grew up having to fend for himself and be resourceful. That made him independent but also lonely and distant.

Dad never could get Bubby to go out hunting and fishing with him, so once I was old enough, he tried with me. When I was eleven, he took me out to the big sand dunes on the beach to teach me how to shoot a gun. He lectured me on safety and proper use and showed me how to load the pistol he brought with him. I can remember hating how it felt in my hand, but I aimed and shot like he had shown me. He laughed when I was stunned by the kickback. "You'll get used to that," he said. I could sense his disappointment when I handed the gun back to him and said, "I don't ever want to do this again."

Dad was always walking through the woods surrounding the Shack and would catch all sorts of animals that he would bring home to show us, then release. Our bathroom in the Shack had locks on both sides of the door—so you could lock people in as well as keep them out. My father was quite a trickster, and thought it was great fun to bring home a baby alligator or possum or maybe a horny toad from his long walks in the woods, toss it into the bathroom when my mother was in the tub, and lock it in there with her. I remember her screaming, and Dad unlocking the door to find Mom and this animal facing off with their backs to the walls, each one trying to get as far away from the other as possible. She would curse Dad in her church lady voice, but in the end, it always came back to: "That's just Vic." The woman was a saint.

· · ·

And yet, for as much as they appeared to drive one another crazy, there was no mistaking Mom and Dad's devotion to one another— especially when one of them had any sort of a health scare. Mom was a smoker, which I always found a bit at odds with her churchgoing ways. Other than her Winstons (and later her Pall Malls, then her Kents), her two cups of coffee every day, and a nap every afternoon, she had no real indulgences. But smoking was viewed differently back then. It was a sign of refinement—that you had "made it." So nobody gave her much grief about any of it because she was such a little angel and was always fluttering around, taking care of everybody.

At some point during my childhood, she had to have a hyster-ectomy. In those days, you went into the hospital the night before a procedure to get prepped and have a barrage of tests and X-rays. The next morning, the doctor marched into her room and said, "You can't have this surgery. You have spots on your lungs. You have to quit smoking right now, or you'll die!"

Her reaction was to say to my father: "Let's switch to a pipe."

Nobody brought up the minor detail that a pipe also involves tobacco.

My dad went out and got her the cheapest, more horrible corn-cob pipe he could find, along with the most disgusting tobacco. She took one puff, and that was the end of the pipe. Desperate to satisfy her oral fixation, she started chewing on practically everything in the house, so Dad bought her a box of straws. But it took her only a few days to get through them.

Finally, she discovered chewing gum. If we'd been able to afford stock in Wrigley's, our lives would have been very different. My father's days became about making sure Mom had enough Double-mint to see her through.

After a couple of months, the doctor reconsidered and decided she needed to have the hysterectomy even if she did have spots on her lungs. She went in the night before and again had all the tests and X-rays. In the process, they discovered that they had mixed up the original set of X-rays. The spotted lungs were someone else's.

"There was never anything wrong with your lungs," the doctor said.

Mom looked at my father and said, "Get me a cigarette."

"If you smoke again, I'll leave you," he said, without any hesitation. I'm sure he was bluffing. But she never did have another cigarette.

· · ·

Though it took him a couple of tries to finish high school (he went back once the shoe issue was resolved), Dad was a lifelong learner and incredibly skilled when it came to tinkering and working with his hands. He was always taking things apart and putting them back together, and he could fix anything, including electronic equipment of all kinds. He trained as a TV repairman back in the day of cathode-ray tubes and was a serious ham radio operator who helped with the city's emergency response whenever hurricanes knocked out communications. In my teen years, he became a deputy sheriff—a funny thing, given what I would get up to during those years. Dad read voraciously, mostly *National Geographic* and other magazines about the outdoors, animals, and mechanical subjects. I imagine his love of *National Geographic* was what led him to become a very good amateur photographer. I often wonder what he could have achieved if he'd finished school the first time, maybe even gone to college, and worked as something other than a laborer.

That's not to say he didn't have aspirations. That's one thing I've noticed about Southern folks—there's a touch of grandiosity to them. They have Big Plans, a sense that fame and riches, or at least a better life, could be just around the corner.

That was certainly true of my father. His Big Plans were all focused on building my parents' dream house. Sometime in the early 1950s, when real estate deals were often done on the basis of, "Give me fifty dollars now and maybe some more later," my father had acquired five lots for a total of three hundred dollars. My grandfather built the Shack on one of the lots and kept the adjacent one empty. Two doors down from us was a larger house built by a Navy doctor. When I was about twelve, his family was transferred, and Dad bought that house rather than try to expand the Shack to accommodate us all. By that point, my grandfather had died, and there was no way we were going to fit *two* little old ladies in that bedroom with me and Bubby. He bought the house around Christmastime and surprised us all by hanging the keys on the Christmas tree. We all moved into the doctor's house with Nana, and Ma took over the Shack.

On the three lots across the street, my father was going to build a huge house with fig trees and a pool. I learned later that he'd even drawn up plans for it. I think in his mind's eye, Dad envisioned something like Tara from *Gone with the Wind*.

When we complained about the heat in summer, Dad would send us across the street with shovels and tell us to start digging the pool. But when his mother got sick and needed professional care for the rest of her life, the money for Tara was reallocated. Later, when my mother got sick and we needed even more money, Dad sold those three lots. He had had prostate cancer and gone into remission by that point, and he wanted to ensure that my mother had enough money in case he went first. So, the Big Plans had to change.

Ultimately, it was another one of those losses that they were always preparing for. Later in life, I was able to see how much he pushed away these disappointments, personal and professional, and just got on with life. But I know he felt them.

· · ·

I don't think Dad knew what to do with a lot of emotions when they got to be too much. He may have been a little depressed and a bit repressed on top of that. My mother, who was never rattled by much (except the occasional possum in the bathroom), didn't really allow a lot of anger or depression to be expressed at home. In her mind, there was always someone who was worse off so we should be grateful for what we had, meager as it sometimes was.

Then there was also that great Southern tendency to want to save face: When you had a problem, or you were feeling down, or you were too overwhelmed by emotion, you didn't let it show. And so, we grew up absorbing the lesson that how you presented yourself was often more important than whatever trouble was going on inside.

Regardless of his stoicism, Dad was quick to anger. And when I got a little older and started testing boundaries, Dad became the disciplinarian. The one time I faced off against my father, at maybe eight years old, I got a spanking with his belt. I don't know what came over me, but I laughed at him as he was giving me a serious talking to.

Well, that did it. He probably considered a belt to be no big deal because *his* father had knocked him across the room with a closed fist. But Mom intervened and put a stop to that kind of punishment right away. The Shack was tiny, and I was never shy about eavesdropping, so I overheard their whole conversation as I was crying in my bedroom after my spanking. She told him in a very quiet, steely voice that if he ever used his belt again, she would leave and take us with her.

Luckily for me, Dad devised a new punishment that didn't involve me taking a beating of any kind. Whenever I did something wrong, I had to write ten thousand times, "I, Thomas LeNoble, promise to mind my parents, elders, and brother, or my daddy will give me the worst whipping of my life."

This punishment was meted out frequently and took so much time that some days I couldn't do anything other than go to school, do my homework, and keep writing until I was finished. I'd wake up, write, eat breakfast, write, go to school, come home, write, eat dinner, and write.

It was agonizing—until I discovered the magic of carbon paper. I whipped out my ten thousand sentences in no time and proudly presented them to my father. Much to my dismay, Dad saw right through the ploy and ripped up the papers before my eyes. But he did cut the quota down to five thousand to reward my creativity. I learned later that he chuckled to himself for hours about my cleverness.

When I was in my thirties, I got a letter from my dad in the mail that included a paper covered with, "I, Thomas LeNoble, promise to mind my parents, elders, and brother, or my daddy will give me the worst whipping of my life." It was signed by me and dated 1966. I discovered later that he had saved not only those papers but every Father's Day card and letter I'd ever sent him.

· · ·

Dad and I didn't have a bad relationship; we just had almost nothing in common. From a young age, I felt that I was different from him, and I think I was a little afraid of not pleasing him. He didn't spend a lot of time with us as it was, didn't play with us when we were very small, and my mother once told me that he wouldn't hold us when we were babies because he was afraid he'd hurt or break us. He adored his mother, but growing up as an only child with the kind of father he had, he just didn't have a good role model. It wasn't until later on, when I saw everything that he'd saved from my childhood and when he and I grew very close after Mom passed away, that I realized how much he'd been affected by his relationship with his father.

Even when I was small, I knew I was loved and supported by my parents. But it was never something we talked about day to day. It was all part of that Southern way of not showing "too much" on the surface.

Even inside your family, some things were simply not to be discussed.

I think this—in addition to the six-year age gap and our very different personalities—created a distance between me and Bubby as well. We were both gay and, in a funny way, that too kept us apart. We didn't even know what "gay" was back then, really; we just knew that there was something about being a "fag" or a "sissy" that was wrong, and the family was the last place you wanted to talk about, let alone acknowledge, being one of those things—even to your sissy brother.

Bending the Rules

Finding little loopholes and ways around rules was something that I would become particularly good at. I think some of that came from the Southern culture I was steeped in, where we liked that there were rules to make everything run smoothly and let everyone know what was expected of them. And as long as everything looked the way it was supposed to and no one was too brazen, we wouldn't ask too many questions beyond that.

Before my parents were married, Dad had a little side business making moonshine. His moonshine had a special flavor and color because he used apricots and oranges in the distilling process. That attracted a high-end clientele of doctors and lawyers, and he knew he could charge them more.

No one in our family really drank. When it came to the moonshine, my mother objected to the illegality of it all, but she was more opposed to the alcohol—she had seen it destroy her brother's life and alter hers by extension. Once they married, the tacit agreement between Mom and Dad was that the moonshine would remain completely out of sight and out of mind.

So Dad kept his little still hidden out in the woods, and everything was going along nicely until one day, a customer came to the door, drunk. Mom ran him off and told my father that night, "It's me or the moonshine."

"Okay. Follow me," he said.

He led her out into the woods where he'd hidden all his glass jugs, poured them into the ground, looked at her, and said, "There's your answer. But we'll be poor forever." With that, he turned around and walked back to the house.

I wouldn't say they were poor forever. They were able to raise us and send us out into the world to live our own independent lives, which made them very, very proud. But, consciously or unconsciously, nobody in the LeNoble family believed we would ever have any money.

It was part of that shadow that followed them their whole lives:
You can hope for and work toward a better future, but you
never know when the rug will be pulled out from under you.

I came to think of it as The Moonshine Curse.

Even after Dad stopped making moonshine and the poverty curse was in place, there always seemed to be just one last jug somewhere out in the woods. We all knew about it but pretended not to.

On holidays, we usually entertained my uncle Jack and aunt Ginny, who would bring her famous potato salad, the best potato salad ever made by human hands. Uncle Jack was often already drunk when they showed up. Mom's aunt Phyllis would usually be there, too. She was about five feet tall with flaming red hair and in her youth had been Miss Jacksonville Beach. She always wore enormous hats because, God forbid, she should get a freckle.

We would have our holiday dinner, and afterward, the adults would have coffee with dessert. Right before the coffee was served, my father would disappear for a minute or two. I learned later that a little bit of moonshine would mysteriously appear in everybody's coffee—except my mother's.

After that, the evening usually picked up a bit. Aunt Ginny and Aunt Phyllis would play their ukuleles and sing, and Mom would join in. As the singing got louder and more raucous (God knows what the proof of that moonshine was), Mom would get quieter and quieter and start to become visibly annoyed. She'd stop singing and retreat to her chair, but Aunt Ginny and Aunt Phyllis would serenade the rest of us until they fell over on top of each other and went to sleep. That was our signal that the holiday was over.

"Clean up the dishes, take your bath, and go to bed," Mom would tell me.

Come the morning, everything would be back in its right place. And nobody ever talked about the drunken serenades.

. . .

Everyone comes into this world carrying the baggage of those who came before. You can choose to drag it with you for all eternity, or you can drop it and keep growing.

. . .

TWO

Little Mr. Misfit

ONE MORNING, WHEN I WAS ABOUT FIVE, I WOKE up, looked around, and thought, "I don't belong here."

I don't know whether it was our unusual life at the Shack, or that we were so poor, or that I'd started school and was meeting all sorts of new people for the first time, but in my little mind, I had this idea that I'd been delivered to the wrong planet. I didn't yet have much life experience, but I sensed that there was a world out there beyond Jacksonville Beach and I might fit better in that *other* world.

That was my introduction to a feeling that would be with me for decades.

"The Beach" was very rural and family and church oriented, with little crime and little chance of anyone doing anything too outlandish. No one locked their doors, everyone knew everyone, and everybody's mother was your mother.

This is usually the formula for an idyllic childhood, and in lots of ways, growing up at the Beach was indeed special, even wholesome. But that feeling of otherness stuck around, and as the world started to open up to me, it made me even more curious and daring than I already was.

I was drawn to anything that seemed new or unusual or—best of all—forbidden.

The forbidden world started literally in my backyard. My parents would sometimes talk in hushed tones about "the Browns," the unsavory people who lived a ways out in the woods behind the Shack. We were strictly prohibited from going over to their place, so of course I'd sneak out there all the time just to look around. They lived in a ramshackle shell of what had once probably been a house, with nothing around it except trees and swamp. It was filthy and always smelled like something was rotting. I was around six years old when I started sneaking off and didn't put it together until much later that "the Browns" didn't actually exist; my parents had made them up to keep me from going over there and playing in an abandoned cabin out in the woods. It was the least effective approach imaginable.

The Higgs, however, *were* real people, actually did live in the woods, and their place was definitely a step up from the mythical Browns'. Mrs. Higgs's first name was Claude (she had a twin sister named Maude), and she chewed tobacco. I'm not sure anybody in Mrs. Higgs's family could read or write, but my God, that woman could cook!

Mrs. Higgs was from the backwoods of Georgia and always had a big pot of bacon grease on top of the stove. Whenever she saw me coming, the first thing she said was, "Let me cook something for you." Being the good boy I was, how could I say no? Mrs. Higgs fed me and fed me and fed me, which probably contributed to my weighing nearly three hundred pounds by the time I got to high school.

I was over there so much that, eventually, I had to tell Mom about it. So we worked out a deal. I could go to Mrs. Higgs's after school and help her with her massive garden, and Mrs. Higgs would send me home with armloads of vegetables (tomatoes were her specialty), which we devoured. And everybody was happy!

◆ ◆ ◆

On our road, catty-corner from the Shack, was the home of my friend Sherry, who was about three years younger than me but was my buddy through childhood. Sherry and I used to play Sonny and Cher, and she always let me be Cher. We got our bikes the same year and were always tripping off to fantasy land together. It seemed like neither of us really believed we lived on this dirt road in this tiny beach town. We would get on our bikes and ride around, being whoever we wanted to be.

Whenever I had the chance, I played with Sherry's dolls. The closest I came to having my own was a teddy bear, which I named Suzy, who is still with me. I have a feeling my parents noticed how attached I was to Suzy (and that I'd given her a girl's name) and may have asked themselves some questions about that, but I was young enough at the time that they probably rationalized it away. (I think they found themselves doing that a lot. When I was about fourteen, I stole a bra and girdle from my mother—and kept them for years as I moved around the country. When I got older, I realized that she couldn't have *not* known that they were missing and probably suspected her sissy son of taking them. But we didn't talk about things like that, and she was no doubt more comfortable telling herself some story about it and never mentioning it to anyone.)

I did regular "boy" things, too, like playing with trucks and digging holes, or, once I was allowed to, riding my bike the fourteen blocks to the beach. When we would go visit my father's parents, I would always get in trouble for sneaking around to explore interesting places in their house and on their property—my grandfather

Richard always called me "the varmit" (not "varmint," the correct word for a troublesome wild animal; maybe it was his own variation).

Mr. Mischief

Entering first grade at San Pablo Elementary was a real milestone in getting to know the world beyond the Shack.

I liked school right away because everything there was *organized*. We had cute little desks with a curvy section that connected to the chair, so that you had your own armrest. We each had our own cubbyhole, and there was a tiny bathroom at the back of the room. My teacher, Miss McClellan, had put a little green sign on the door, and before you went into the bathroom, you were supposed to flip it over to the red side so that no one would disturb you, then flip it back to the green side when you came out. (Very civilized.)

Next year was Miss Cathey, who always looked spaced out or stoned. I liked her and thought we got along, but apparently, she didn't know what to do with me because at some point in the year, she approached my mother, who worked at the school, and said, "I need your help. I can't handle him."

Mom looked her coolly up and down and said, "I have him at home. From 9:00 to 3:00, he's all yours."

That year, Miss Cathey would tape my mouth shut with masking tape for talking too much, which, of course, a teacher would get fired for today. That wasn't even as bad as what happened the following year, when Miss Daft washed my mouth out with soap in front of the whole class because I called Suzie an idiot.

I wasn't a bad kid. There was just something inside me that reacted to rules. When I heard the words, "Do not do this," I asked myself, "Well, what would happen if I did?" I wasn't trying to cause problems.

I just knew there had to be more.

In fifth grade, Miss Barrett actually spent some time observing me and realized that I wasn't a troublemaker; I was just bored. She devised a very clever plan. Each classroom had a door that led to the outside, and she created a little garden for me out there. When I finished my work, she would just send me out to the garden. My grades got even better, I was happy, there were no more behavioral problems, and everybody gave thanks.

But the sense of peace, and of finally being understood by a teacher, would be short-lived. By the fifth grade, it was clear to the outside world that I was a "sissy," and the bullying and teasing began. I'd known for years by that point that I wasn't like most boys, but I'd absorbed the lesson that if you can observe the "right" thing to do and just mimic that, you'll be accepted. Now the messages about what was acceptable and what was not were landing in a new and frightening way. My safety was at stake.

My problem-solving, logical mind kicked in: *Okay, I've got to figure out how to not get beat up.* None of us really even knew what it meant to be gay at the time, but I sensed that getting a girlfriend would be the solution to this sissy problem. So I got Deedee Collins to "go steady" with me.

Deedee was a misfit, too. She had failed fifth grade twice and was about a foot taller than all the rest of us. I made her a deal: I would give her my brownie every day and let her wear my watch during school, and in exchange, she would tell people she was my girlfriend—she provided cover, as well as muscle. It was a small price to pay for the social status of having a girlfriend. And we both got something out of it. At least until she decided she didn't want my brownies anymore.

Since my mother was in the school, she had a sense of what was going on and talked to my father about it. Dad would tell me to toughen up and fight back, but I knew that could only lead to more humiliation, not to mention physical danger. All I could do was wait out the year until I could finally be free of that silly school and those silly kids.

Hiding in Plain Sight

I was yearning for a fresh start, but Fletcher Junior High wasn't any better. I found it very frightening to switch classrooms several times a day and brave the hallway where people could beat me up. Junior high also meant physical education with its communal locker rooms. I lived in horror of being in these confined areas with the other boys, especially the older ones, out of sight of the teachers, and never felt safe.

As if it weren't bad enough, by this time I'd started to gain a lot of weight, which made me even more of a target. It was obvious what was causing the weight gain—I regularly stopped at Maryland Fried Chicken on the way home from school for a two-piece box, then still ate Mrs. Higgs's Georgia cooking, and our family dinner. I have no doubt that my overeating was about trying to find some comfort in food at a time when I felt scared and confused and there was no one to talk to about any of it.

By the time I was about thirteen, I had had enough. I thought that maybe, if I wasn't so physically different, I'd have a better chance of blending in and not being noticed. So again, I came up with a plan. It made sense that if I ate only healthy things, I could lose the weight. So no more meals cooked in bacon fat at Mrs. Higgs's house. I would drink juice—nothing else. But since we couldn't afford real juice, I was going to drink what we had instead: Hawaiian Punch. In my misinformed mind, this was how I would get all my vitamins and other healthy ingredients.

What I got instead was a highly acidic "fruit drink," and I drank so much of it over the course of a few months that it burned a hole in my bladder and sent me to the hospital. There was burning and blood when I peed, and the cure was to stick a cystoscope up my penis, into my bladder, take a look around, and cauterize the hole. I was traumatized when I heard what they would have to do and embarrassed because the whole story became about the Hawaiian Punch. So much for not getting noticed. The hospital workers looked at me like I was insane and kept asking what was wrong with me for doing this to myself. To my parents, this was just Thomas being Thomas.

I had the procedure, but I was still fat, so I was going to have to figure out some other way to make myself fit into the cruel puzzle of junior high school.

In the meantime, I would keep to myself, wait for Mom at nursery school in the afternoons, and hang around with Sherry back at home. As I got older, I became even more guarded, constantly assessing situations for safety before I would allow myself into them. It was a terrible, lonely way to live.

The Invention of Church Tom

Ironically, given the reasons I felt as isolated and strange as I did, my social life began to drift toward church. It became one of the places I knew I would be physically safe from bullies. When you're at church, whether you're in Sunday School or on the playground, you have to be on your best behavior.

Growing up, church had been a huge part of my life. I was known to that community as an all-around good boy. (Most of the time. At least until puberty.) My mother was a charter member of the church and taught Sunday School. I attended services with her, went to Sunday School, and later on, became president of the youth group. Once a month, I would even deliver the sermon at Sunday evening service. Everybody assumed that I was going to be a minister.

I had always known I would have to fit into a certain mold to be accepted anywhere, and nowhere was that feeling stronger than at church. Everybody had to dress nicely and behave, but I had the added chore of always checking myself and making sure I was walking a certain way and talking a certain way.

The more time and effort I spent trying to make myself fit, the more I created a shell between the world and who I really was. The outside did not match the inside.

· · ·

"Church Tom" was one of many façades that I was beginning to construct in my life to deal with the imposter syndrome that would follow me for years. Everyone knows about imposter syndrome now, but I certainly didn't have a name for it back then. It can show itself in many ways, and by now, I think I've done them all!

One is in the way we sometimes fudge a bit about who we are or what we have, to create an image that will help us fit in better with a certain group. Another way, which usually happens later in life, is to feel like a fraud who doesn't deserve to be where we are and will be found out, even though we've earned our status and success. Subconsciously, we may feel like we're still fudging.

"Church Tom" wasn't a *complete* fabrication. It wasn't that I didn't enjoy being at church, or didn't have faith, or didn't love others in my congregation. It was that my sense of the world around me was very finely tuned by the time I was in high school, and I knew that the church's definition of who and what was acceptable was pretty narrow.

Thomas, the future minister, was the part I had to play to be safe. And in my preteen and early teen years, that was more important than anything else.

Don't be scared of the voice inside telling you there's more for you in life, that there's more to explore—even if you're not supposed to. Trying to muffle that voice doesn't make it go away. It's going to make itself heard one way or another.

THREE

Sex, Drugs, and Thespianism

A S I STRUGGLED THROUGH JUNIOR HIGH, I DREAMED of getting out of there and moving on, of starting a new life in the wider world of high school, of this big transition to my future. Then I'd have to survive just four more years before I could escape to college somewhere. In the meantime, I just had to keep my head down and not attract too much attention.

When I finally made it to high school, I was still quite heavy, but in the ways that I *could* control, I tried to look like everybody else: Weejuns penny loafers, Gant shirts, pressed chinos. This had been Bubby's look in high school, so I just imitated him. I don't know how my parents could afford to buy those clothes for even one of us. I know Mom always shopped sales, but she must have really stretched every penny.

Life would have been a lot easier if I could fit into Bubby's hand-me-downs—and not just his literal clothes. Both he and my mother had attended the high school I went to, and lots of my teachers had taught my brother, who was very, very smart, just six years before. Some ancient ones had even been around when Mom had gone there, until she had to drop out and go to work. From freshman year onward, the refrain was, "If only you applied yourself the way your brother did..."

· · ·

The boy I was when I entered high school and who I was when I graduated could not have been more different. I started my freshman year with a lot of the same social challenges that I'd had in junior high, but mercifully, by age fifteen or sixteen, some things had begun to shift.

I was still confused about who I was and where I belonged. And consciously or unconsciously, I knew the coping strategies I had relied on—of building up that acceptable image to hide the unacceptable on the inside—would have to change.

I didn't know what the alternative was. I wasn't even sure who *I* was yet. But I knew that a lot of people didn't approve of it.

And I could not imagine hiding for the rest of my life, just to fit into one small part of a vast and exciting world.

· · ·

With high school came a lot more freedom. I was allowed to ride my bike to school and could go back and forth as I pleased—no more nursery school! Academically, we were allowed to choose electives simply because they appealed to us. I liked Latin and took it all four years; there was a logic to the language that engaged my curious brain. It didn't hurt that there was a cute boy named Rick in my Latin class, whom I had a crush on and fantasized about for two years. I also chose Home Economics and Typing, which did have a bit of a stigma attached to them, but I didn't care so much about that. I was one of two boys in my Typing class, and I was the third fastest in the class overall—I think I could do ninety-eight words a minute on those old clackety typewriters.

Of course, PE class was still a huge issue. I was fat and a sissy and sports weren't easy or pleasant for me. And, of course, there was the locker room element, which was even worse now that I had started thinking of boys with romantic interest as well as fear. I had never taken my clothes off in front of anybody, and it was just paralyzing to think about going into a room with a bunch of other boys undressing and having to get undressed in front of them. So between being fat, being bullied, puberty, and all this uncertainty, I would have done anything to get out of PE.

A Lifeline

Luckily, I learned that you could miss PE if you signed up for certain extracurricular activities, like yearbook or *The Sandpiper*, the school newspaper, which I joined. But the one that would change my life was the Thespians.

By tenth grade, I had started making more friends and finding people in this big school who accepted me. My art teacher was a man named Manford Mashenko, who was clearly gay though I didn't consciously know that at the time.

But I did sense that there was something that he and I had in common, some kind of outsider connection that felt like a lifeline, and I took it.

He hung out with another teacher, Nikki Laurert, who taught Humanities, and they were friends with a group of students: Douglas and Lucy, who were juniors, and Bonnie, a senior. Today, Nikki and

Manford would be fired many times over for how close they were to us as students and what we all got up to together. Nikki was a wise woman who inspired us all to think differently. She was part of a little 1960s hippie community out in the woods, and when I was a bit older, I would sometimes skip school to hang out with them and smoke pot.

They were all part of the International Thespian Society, or the Thespians, which I soon joined. And that was when everything changed. I had finally found my people in Douglas, Lucy, and Bonnie. We were all misfits—small-town kids, most of us poor, trying to figure out who we were and leaning on one another in the process. (We would all become so tight that they all waited a year or two before enrolling in college, so that we could all leave town together once I graduated in 1972.)

Theater, and the Thespians themselves, brought a sense of novelty and creativity—not to mention camaraderie and belonging—that was sorely lacking in my life. We had a faculty adviser, Ms. Fouraker, who ran the group, and Mr. Monk was the artistic director, in charge of designing the sets. We'd put on three shows a year, and I started off slowly, helping out backstage or selling tickets. But soon enough, I was performing, and by senior year, I got the lead in a play called *Dinny and the Witches*.

It isn't lost on me that in this time of teenage uncertainty, when I didn't know how to define who I was and had to put up a façade to fit in, I was drawn to getting dressed up and playing other people. It was a kind of freedom I had never experienced before: I could be somebody else on the stage and not have to think so much about who I was off it.

◆ ◆ ◆

Because we were part of the International Thespian Society, we participated in regional or national theater competitions, which meant we would sometimes take overnight trips around the state.

The first time my parents allowed me to go on one of these trips I was absolutely shocked; that level of independence felt like an unimaginable privilege. I was still a good churchgoing boy at the time and at least a year younger than my friends, so I didn't participate in the real fun of the trip: sneaking alcohol into our motel rooms and partying. I became their caretaker instead—something they would need after getting wasted on Boone's Farm and Hop'n Gator, a vile malt liquor/Gatorade concoction produced by the Gatorade corporation. But I'd participate in the shenanigans soon enough.

When my friends first offered me pot, I wasn't very interested. But one day they started talking about something called Orange Sunshine, which sounded so pleasant, like a day at the beach. I was intrigued enough to give it a try. It's pretty unusual for someone's first drug experience to be with acid rather than marijuana, but I, too, was pretty unusual. And its mind-expanding, almost mystical qualities were perfectly in sync with the seeker I was becoming. We all went to the beach, danced around in the sand to Beatles music, and just got lost for hours.

I've never been timid about jumping headlong into new experiences, so I wound up dropping acid five days in a row, which meant that at least three of those days, I was sitting in class while I was tripping. At the time, I had a girlfriend named Gail. She was the first girl I ever kissed. We never had a strong romantic connection (obviously), and I was aware that I was not going down the same path as others who were coupling up, but there was something that we liked about one another, and in high school, you expressed that by "going together." Gail and I both sang in the Chorale and were in Thespians, though she wasn't in our little group. One day, while I was tripping on Orange Sunshine at school, I was sitting behind her in class, admiring her gorgeous long blonde hair, and I decided to braid it. Something about this set the teacher off, because Gail got in trouble.

I was the one braiding her hair, and nothing happened to me, but she almost got suspended. Somehow, it was all her fault.

Pot would eventually enter my life, and it soon became my drug of choice. (I smoked consistently, if not daily, from age sixteen until my mid-forties.) I rarely, if ever, cut class, and my grades were okay in high school, but I did skip lunch occasionally to smoke pot. I'd get in trouble every now and then, but I could usually outsmart whoever was planning to punish me.

One time during my junior year, we had skipped classes to smoke, and I went home that afternoon completely stoned on hash. I was alone in my room when my father came home from work and told me to come out into the yard so he could try out his new camera. He had become very interested in photography around this time and was really into taking close-ups of plants and animals.

"Come here," he said. "I want to take some pictures of your eye."

My whole body immediately went numb, and I started panicking. I tried to walk calmly out into the yard, not wanting to imagine what he might do to me if he found out I was high. Somehow, the reliable, problem-solving part of my brain instinctively kicked in, and I remember thinking, *Okay, I gotta make this work.* So I positioned myself to face the sun so my pupils would shrink, and my eyes would look normal. He took the pictures, and I never heard about it again.

When I was in my thirties, I learned that the coach at the high school had contacted my father, who was also a deputy sheriff at the time, to tell him that I was skipping school, doing drugs, and going down a bad path. My father simply would not believe that his son would ever do such a thing. Not knowing how to confront me about it, I think he came up with the camera plan as a way to look me in the eye, so to speak.

An "Official" Imposter

Most of us turned out to be upstanding citizens as adults, but in high school, we just wanted to have fun. Our exploits were just a way to try to spread our wings and to experiment with things that weren't along the conventional paths our parents had followed.

I started to truly feel like an individual when I got my driver's license at sixteen. The drinking age was eighteen at the time, and as interested as I was in driving, I was even more interested in being able to get into bars with my friends.

In those days, driver's licenses didn't have pictures, and you didn't have to pass any sort of test to replace one. You just had to know your hair color and show proof that you were eighteen. I looked older than I was, so I conceived a brilliant plan to get a driver's license using my brother's identity that said I was his age. I hopped over to the DMV and told them I was Victor LeNoble Jr., here for my driver's license. They told me I needed proof that I'd been born. I said, "I'm standing here!"

That did not suffice, so I took my brave little ass over to the Bureau of Vital Statistics in the big city of Jacksonville and said, "I'm Victor LeNoble Jr., and I need a copy of my birth certificate." No problem. I grabbed the copy of Bubby's birth certificate, scooted back to the DMV, and got the license. I'd been pretending to be a regular young man for so many years, and here, it really paid off!

I was very proud of myself and spent that summer reaping the benefits of my ingenuity and going out to bars with my older friends.

Toward the end of that summer, I was lounging around the house—in my father's chair, no less, because my parents were both away—when the phone rang. I answered it, and the voice on the other end said, "May I speak to Mr. LeNoble?"

"I'm Mr. LeNoble," I said. "May I help you?"

It was the DMV.

"You recently came in for a driver's license, right?"

"Why yes, I did," I said very graciously. "And thank you very much for the wonderful service."

"Well, sir," the voice said. "Your license has been suspended. You came in and got a new license when yours had been suspended, which is fraud. You need to return that license right away. You're not supposed to be driving."

I hung up the phone and immediately thought, "My father knows. I've been caught!" But then I thought it through. I didn't get caught very often. Maybe he didn't know. If Victor LeNoble Jr. was an adult of twenty-two, why would anyone contact his parents? I took the license back as instructed, and nothing happened.

It turns out my brother had lost his license after driving into a ditch one night. Of course, nobody in our house ever talked about anything out in the open, but I poked around and discovered that he had a lazy eye, and they'd taken away his license because of it.

I decided that I'd dodged another bullet, and that the best course of action now was silence. Life went on, and nobody ever discovered that I'd committed fraud. I breathed a sigh of relief. But on my thirtieth birthday, my father announced to me that he'd known all about it all along! (Maybe that's why they hadn't prosecuted me for fraud.) Dad was always doing that, revealing decades later some little thing that he'd been aware of, or appreciated, or noticed.

Seeing the Light

My relationship with the church probably suffered a little after I started hanging out with Douglas, Bonnie, Lucy, and the other high school Thespians. Church Tom remained a good boy for some time after meeting them, but by junior year, I started to have serious doubts that I belonged in that world. My horizons had broadened considerably, and none of what I was doing was consistent with how the people at church saw me or with the teachings of the church.

I was quickly coming to the conclusion that the church and most of what went on there was just bullshit. It didn't seem right that the Methodists thought they were better than the Baptists and the Lutherans, and especially better than the Catholics and the Jews. Or that the Baptists and Lutherans thought they were better than the Methodists. None of it made sense.

I've always felt connected to something that was higher, infinite, and divine—but what I was seeing around me at church had nothing to do with that. Back then, people didn't make much of a distinction between spirituality and religion. I remember feeling a little strange about Jesus, even when I was going to church regularly. It wasn't that I didn't believe His teachings; I just always thought there was more to it.

So, between the raging hormones, the drugs, the broadened horizons, and the dawn of critical thinking, I began moving away from the church.

I did have one priceless experience there when I was around fourteen, which was unlike any other church event I'd ever participated in. I took a sex education class with a troop of Girl Scouts. It wasn't called sex education; it was called something cute like "Reproductive Health" or "Don't Touch Your Penis"—or in the case of the Girl Scouts, "Don't Touch Anybody's Penis." I think I did it expecting to find some validation that I was "normal." Needless to say, I was the only male in the class. I'm not sure why they let me in, other than I seemed to attend every other church function, but there I was.

We were given a textbook at the beginning of the class, and I quickly and slyly riffled through it to look for pictures of male parts. So much for finding out I was "normal." I decided I might as well stay. I certainly was not going to learn anything about this at home.

We did not talk about sex in our family. At all. Ever. Not even when I had my first wet dream a couple of years before my lesson with the Girl Scouts. When I woke up in the middle of the night to discover that there was something coming out of me, I thought I was going to die. I don't know if I connected what had happened to the ways I was starting to feel "not normal" around that age. All I knew was that something had to be terribly wrong with me.

I put a lot of thought into what to do with those underpants. I knew I couldn't put them in with the rest of the washing. In those days, I kept little boxes under my bed to house assorted treasures that I discovered on my wanderings and poking around, so I decided to stash them there until I figured out what to do with them.

Sure enough, it would happen again, and I started to become very interested in these erections I was getting, rather than scared. I would go into the bathroom and look at them and try to figure out what they would do, why they were there, and what it all meant. I had no idea about masturbation at the time, though I soon discovered that if I kept touching this thing, it could open up a whole new world of activity and enjoyment. I also knew that it was dirty, for God's sake, which meant I shouldn't touch it at all! But, of course, since I wasn't supposed to, I was very eager to do it.

Beyond what I learned on my own in the privacy of the bathroom, sex remained a complete mystery for years. As I went through puberty and realized that I wasn't interested in the same things that the other boys were, there was an added layer of confusion on top of it. I knew something was happening, but I'd have to figure it out on my own.

◆ ◆ ◆

There was an area of Jacksonville Beach known as the Boardwalk. Before I was born, it was a real attraction, with all sorts of rides and entertainment. By the time I was a teenager, it had become run-down and seedy, with dive bars, pool halls, and liquor stores. It was "forbidden," so of course I was drawn to it. At age fifteen or sixteen, I had heard somewhere that there was a parking lot at the boardwalk where men would go and cruise. I didn't understand what that meant, but I would ride my bike there sometimes just to observe the scene and satisfy my curiosity. There would be guys driving around or hanging around the lot, some of them in bathing trunks—we were at the beach after all—just checking each other out.

I rode my bike there one day when an older man, probably about fifty, started talking to me. He got me to follow him to his house, which was out behind a bigger house not far from the main road that passed by the boardwalk. I went inside, and as we kept talking, he sat on his couch and motioned for me to sit with him. I just stood there, not sure of what to do. He took off his clothes and was lying naked on his couch, trying to convince me to come over and touch him.

I had never really seen anyone else's naked body out in front of me like that, and I remember feeling just as much curiosity as I did uncertainty about the situation I was in. Every part of it was the exact opposite of the façade that I had been presenting to the world. I was doing something wrong in the world's eyes, but so much about me already felt "wrong." It was very confusing.

Something compelled me to reach my hand out, and I touched him. Then, in a flash, my instincts kicked in, and I was struck with terror.

What was I doing?

What if I got kidnapped?

What if I got killed?

What if I got *caught*?

I burst out of his house, jumped on my bike, and sped toward home, flooded with feelings of fear and shame. I was petrified that someone had seen me leave the man's house. I knew without a doubt that if my father ever found out about what I had done, he would have forced me to take him back there and killed this man. And maybe me.

Of course, this man was a pedophile and should have been in jail. But I had never felt so ashamed. I had done something so foolish and wrong, and I convinced myself that whatever horrible thing could have happened to me that day was my own fault. I told no one, and it would haunt me for decades.

Private Room

It would be years before I would go near the boardwalk again. Thankfully, my first real experiences with sex were under completely different circumstances.

I was at Douglas's house for a sleepover one night, something we'd done countless times before. We were horsing around as usual when our playful wrestling and grappling became more like hugging, and I felt the energy between us completely shift. I don't know who initiated it, but we started kissing, then we followed our curiosity along its natural course.

My reaction could not have been more different from what it had been by the boardwalk. I didn't really know what was happening or what I was doing, just that it was Douglas, and it felt good. And it became our refuge.

We were sixteen and seventeen, we were best friends, and we discovered this secret universe with one another. Once a month—because that's all we could afford—Douglas and I would make a pilgrimage to the Golden Azalea Motor Court, thirty minutes away in St. Augustine. I would tell my parents I was spending the night with him, and he would tell his parents he was spending the night with me, which was technically true. We would bring a six-pack of Hop'n Gator, have sex all night, and drive back in the morning.

I was always prepared with a cover story should my parents ask questions. I knew how his parents were doing, what we had for dinner at his house, what we talked about at the dinner table. But I was still such a good boy in their eyes, I was never questioned. And we never got caught.

Douglas and I never openly talked about what we did together, or even the fact that we were doing anything at all. We kept it completely hidden, as if it weren't even happening. I already had so many things hidden and compartmentalized when it came to sexual feelings that this didn't seem at all strange to me. The Golden Azalea and sex were in one box; our friendship was in another. In a world where I would've had the gay beat out of me if anyone found out I was doing things with another boy, denial was the safest way.

Sexually, I was a total novice, but Douglas was a bit more advanced. I suppose he was bisexual, but really, I think that he just liked sticking it into anything he could stick it into. He'd had little affairs with a girl named Willa Dean and a boy named Lamar, and I would always joke, "You love Willa more" or "You love Lamar more." Amazingly, there were no actual jealous feelings between us.

During the time Douglas and I were sneaking off to the Golden Azalea, he was also having a relationship with our friend Bonnie. I think they might even have told people they were preengaged. Bonnie could never know about us or about the Golden Azalea Motor Court, but our two teenaged male libidos were sometimes too much.

Bonnie lived at the Tahitian Village Apartments, a huge complex with four hundred units and three pools. The three of us were all part-time lifeguards there, and Douglas and I made extra money cleaning out the pools. One of our jobs was to take the filters into the pool room and spray off all the gunk, and I'd sometimes follow him, and we'd get up to more than that.

One day, Bonnie walked in on us. She took one look and said, "I didn't see anything, and I never want to hear anything about this. Nobody will ever discuss this again." And we didn't.

Looking back, it was clear that Douglas and I were in love with one another, but our love was a secret we kept even from ourselves. We wrote poems to each other, and one time I did tell him I thought I loved him. In many ways, ours was a pure childhood romance. But we just didn't know what to do with it.

We carried on our affair for more than a year. At some point, we knew we had to stop having sex. I think we both knew that neither of us would know how to handle it if we were ever found out, and our friendship was too important to jeopardize. We would remain as thick as thieves, the closest of confidants, but we never spoke about it again. It was my first heartbreak, and I would have to endure it alone.

Hello, Tommy!

The summer before my senior year in high school, an odd thing happened. I woke up one morning and decided that I was not going to be fat anymore. By the time I was seventeen, I weighed almost three hundred pounds; I hadn't tried very hard to lose weight after the failure of the Hawaiian Punch diet. But something in my mind made me determined to this time.

This is something I've done all my life. When I make a decision, that's it. It's done.

For the first week, I ate a hard-boiled egg and a salad every day. Then it was just the salad. I must have lost about fifty or sixty pounds in the first two months. It felt great. My clothes got really loose, and everybody noticed and was telling me how great I looked. But all the extreme dieting quickly caught up with me. I woke up one morning and was so weak that I couldn't get out of bed, and I had to come clean to my parents. To them, I'm sure it was just another example of Tom doing something rash and taking it too far.

Still, the weight stayed off. I shifted from my church boy disguise to the cool jeans and belts that reflected the more nonconformist, fun, young styles I was drawn to. I finally started to feel good about the way I was showing myself to the world.

That summer we were part of a countywide production of *Hello, Dolly!* and I starred as Horace Vandergelder. (Given where I'd be just a couple of years later, I probably should've been cast as Dolly!) It ran for three nights at the Jacksonville Civic Auditorium, was a huge, sold-out success, and was one of the highlights of my teenage years. The joys of that summer would propel me through the rest of high school.

◆ ◆ ◆

I had one more year left before graduation, and my daydreams about a world beyond Jacksonville Beach had already been shifting from wishful to within grasp. My friends had already graduated and were getting jobs locally, and we were all saving up so we could leave town together as soon as I finished senior year.

Working was a very big deal in our family. It was like breathing— you just did it. My parents' Depression-era thinking was, "If you can get a job, take the job!" And once you got the job, you never left it, no matter what. Hence Dad working for McCormick for sixty years, and Mom running school cafeterias for twenty-eight.

I'd worked from the time I was about five years old. I got an allowance for doing my chores, I had the typical lemonade stands, and there was the occasional quarter from the tooth fairy. (The tooth fairy wasn't very generous because losing a tooth wasn't considered very hard work.) I used that money to finance hobbies like building fish aquariums and racing slot cars. In high school, I definitely needed more disposable income for extra food and various "in" items—not to mention drugs. Plus, during my sophomore year, my father had promised that if I saved half the money for a car, he would match it. I got busy the next morning on my job applications and have been out earning money ever since.

I'd had the usual boring teenage jobs—grocery bagger, movie theater ticket taker—but going into senior year, I finally had a job that I loved, thanks to Douglas. He had started working full-time in the Admissions Office at University Memorial Hospital in Jacksonville and got me a part-time job there. That was my first foray into the medical world (not as a patient), and I found it fascinating. I got to interact with everyone who came in needing to be admitted, saw all different kinds of people, and got to know a lot of wonderful adults who broadened my world.

One of the great joys of working at the hospital was getting to know Betty Lieb. She was in her late forties, of German descent, and had a voice like Eartha Kitt. I was so intrigued by her gorgeous hair and stylish outfits. She'd had three husbands and divorced them all, but she must have gotten bad settlements because she had to keep working at the hospital to put her daughter, Jenna, through college.

Douglas and I got to know Betty a bit outside work, and I always thought of her as a sort of messenger to me. She was very wise in a grandmotherly way (people in their forties seemed ancient to us!), and I hoped that some of her wisdom would rub off on me when I was around her. She was very beautiful and took care to dress in a way that showcased her beauty. There was nothing provocative or inappropriate about it—you could just tell that she didn't feel the need to hide.

She knew who she was, she valued who she was, and I think she was trying to pass that message on to Douglas and me.

She must have sensed that we were gay and unsure of how we fit in the world. Like our teacher Nikki, she was one of those people who come into your life and open something in you that you might not have discovered on your own. I couldn't have found her at a luckier time.

· · ·

When you've had to hide who
you are, finally feeling seen
can be scary. But connection
is a lifeline, and it can come
from anywhere. If someone
is throwing you a lifeline
out of loneliness, take it!

· · ·

FOUR

Free at Last!

I GRADUATED FROM HIGH SCHOOL ON JUNE 9, 1972, and left town on June 12. With Dad's parting words to "be good," and Mom's wordless tears, I drove the ninety minutes to Gainesville in the car that I'd gone fifty-fifty on with my dad—a 1962 AMC Rambler American named Grace. I couldn't wait to throw my arms around the big, sophisticated, non–Jacksonville Beach world. My grades were good enough to be accepted at the University of Florida, and I enrolled right away for the summer semester because that's what you did to get away from home. Douglas and Lucy had enrolled in Santa Fe Community College nearby and would start in the fall.

I had convinced my father that there was no way I'd be able to share a room with anyone, and somehow, he managed to scrounge up enough money to secure me a private room in the boys' dorm. That's how badly he wanted me to go to school. We never talked about it, but I think on some level he understood why I would be so uncomfortable with a roommate—but that was something he just could not allow into his conscious mind. Neither Dad nor

I knew much about what "gay" meant in the larger world beyond Jacksonville Beach, but I think he sensed intuitively that there was something going on with me and that I really needed a private room for my own safety.

Having my own space was so exciting. I made my dorm room into a sanctuary, organizing and decorating everything just how I wanted it, and no one could tell me different.

And yet...I couldn't stand to be there. My reaction to the dorm after the first week was: *This place is dangerous. I don't fit in here at all.* Even being in a private room didn't block out the fear and confusion of being surrounded by hundreds of strangers. Sure, there were cute boys all around, but it was like being subjected to my high school locker room horror—men, sometimes naked, in close quarters— twenty-four hours a day.

Aside from fearing for my safety, there was no one I had anything in common with. I was not interested in sneaking over to the girls' dorm and pulling the fire alarm or putting too much detergent in the washing machines so the suds would flow down the entire hall- way, which the other boys found hilarious. There were lots of people smoking pot and doing other drugs, but I kept my distance because I was still trying to maintain that outward image that would allow me to hide in plain sight. (I smoked, of course, but I did it alone in my room, in secret, with a towel stuffed into the bottom of the door and tape along the sides.)

Luckily, I managed to find a solution for that first summer semes- ter. I had a friend named Liz who was working on her master's over the summer and living in her brother's house in Gainesville while he was away for summer vacation. Liz was delighted to have me come live with her in this huge house. So, I was officially living in the dorm, but I spent most of my time at Liz's, returning occasionally to keep up appearances. But, come September, I was thrust back in, which felt even more stifling and fraught after such a blissful and peaceful summer. I needed to do something about it.

As hard as they might have been to explain, my reasons for wanting to get out of the dorm had to be valid; I just needed them to make sense to someone. So, I promptly made an appointment at the infirmary and worked my way up to speak to the chief psychiatrist. I presented myself as someone who was fragile and on the edge, and would suffer greatly if I was forced to live in the dorm—which was not all that far from the truth. I pulled out all my thespian skills and puffed on cigarette after cigarette, even though I didn't smoke. It's possible the psychiatrist saw through the act—that he saw me more clearly than even I saw myself—and knew why I felt it would be dangerous for me to live there. I couldn't say for sure. Whatever his reasoning, he sent me off with a letter that I still have today. It read simply, "You have been released from living in the dorm. Signed, Dr. Ball."

Our Found Family

Lucy and Doug were arriving to start their fall semester, and after I left the dorm, the three of us got a two-bedroom, one-bath place in a little two-building apartment complex near their school.

Because we had grown up together, living together was easy. Douglas and I shared a room, and Lucy had her own. We were typical starving students—we partied, occasionally went to class, and just relished being independent, within the security of a very close-knit friend group. It was like entering a new world with a protective little piece of home beside you.

In the safety of this city and the safety of my friends, I finally felt free. We were meeting people and having tremendous fun on our own terms. Here, it was easy to turn off all the chatter in my head about who I was supposed to be and how I fit in. The idea that I'd need a girlfriend as protection, that I'd need to behave as if my true feelings and attractions weren't happening, no longer had a hold on me.

I could finally allow my feelings to be real.

· · ·

I started to be sexually active with men, and Doug continued to be sexually active with everybody. We shared a room, but we never rekindled our physical relationship, though in private moments we would remember it wistfully. (I still joked with him that he loved Lamar more than me.) Our relationship had evolved into something truly unique and special. We relied on each other, we trusted each other, and we knew that our connection would always be strong even as we started to have our own lives and relationships at a pace where we felt comfortable. There was no jealousy—in fact, if one of us didn't like a guy that the other was interested in, that would be a deal-breaker.

All sorts of interesting people came and went during those years—it was like living in a hostel. That may have been why Lucy eventually moved out once Nikki, our teacher friend from home, came out to Gainesville to attend grad school. Lucy and Nikki were in an experimental relationship for a little while and got an apartment together. (Poor Nikki disappeared some years later. It turned out she had been murdered. She had moved back to Jacksonville Beach and was teaching again, and a lot of people in town thought that she'd been killed by an angry, disturbed kid. Her parents halted the investigation when it surfaced that she might be a lesbian, so we never did find out the truth.)

Then Douglas's boyfriend, Marvin Jones, moved in, so they took one bedroom and I took the other. We all used to sing to Doug that he "and Mr. Jones had a thing goin' on." When Marvin moved out, other boyfriends and friends kept on coming through. People would stay for a little or a long time. Some were people we were dating, some were visiting from out of town, some just needed a place to lay their head.

One fateful day a guy named Jimbo showed up from San Francisco, and it turned out he knew my brother, who had moved out there after graduating from Emory. Jimbo had his friend Harry in tow, and everybody in town fell in love with Harry—men, women, drag queens, everybody. Harry was very butch-looking, and I was determined to lure him into my web. To what end I wasn't really sure, but Harry was by far the finest-looking man I'd ever met, and I had to do *something*.

I decided to invite him on a picnic at Devil's Millhopper, now a state park north of town that had a lot of sandy terrain and pine forests and a bowl-shaped cavity 120 feet deep that led down to a miniature rain forest. It was a huge sinkhole, really, and there were a lot of little streams and crevasses and vegetation up and down the sides. You got down it with ropes and slides, and you had to be a little athletic to manage it.

I was trying to be very butch and impress Harry by taking him out to this challenging spot. He was muscular so it was no problem for him, but I fell down and hit my head, and he had to carry me out, which would've been fine if this impromptu "damsel in distress" approach had worked, but alas, Harry and I became friends, and nothing more.

• • •

We were all having a terrific time, but it wasn't all partying—new, deep friendships were being formed. I met Celeste at school—I must have gone to class a few times, I guess—and we immediately became fast friends. She was an English major, very witty and polished, with impeccable taste. Her family lived in Jacksonville, but our paths had never crossed because I lived at the beach and she lived on the west side. She had already been at school a couple of years, so she knew Gainesville well. I was in the process of making new friends and finding my way around town, and Celeste was a big part of that. She loved to dress up and wear wild outfits, and we'd go out to restaurants and clubs and dance all night. We had so much fun.

Celeste and I somehow knew, almost from the moment we met, that we would always have one another's backs. We were like brother and sister, partners in crime, and we'd remain close for the next forty years.

"Nurse" Tom

Living across town from the university was not great for my attendance, and I rarely went to class, but I did take advantage of one huge benefit of being a student: I could work at the university hospital. It was immediately clear that my meager allowance from home wasn't going to be enough to support me in Gainesville, so I got a job as a unit clerk at Shands Teaching Hospital—and from that point forward, I would always be involved with medicine on some level, either as staff or as a patient.

◆ ◆ ◆

As a unit clerk, I did a variety of nonclinical functions and floated around several units: an ambulatory postsurgical, an ICU, and a medical floor. I found it fascinating to watch people get treated and heal and will always remember one inspirational woman who'd had her jaw removed for cancer and displayed an astonishing resilience. I learned so much at Shands and was very good at what I did, which is probably why they tolerated some of my strange behaviors as time went on.

The nurses were very good to me and taught me to do little procedures, which I'm sure was completely illegal. But I was fascinated and a quick learner. I'd wanted to be a doctor when I was younger, but that was not to be. I simply would not have applied myself to all that studying for a variety of reasons (including marijuana), and I had no interest in being as distant and detached as doctors were trained to be back then. I had much more in common with the nurses. One of my favorites was Molly, who wore glasses and looked very studious, but was the marijuana dealer for all the hospital employees. (You had to be selected into a special group in order to be one of her customers, and I qualified very quickly!)

Between my job at University Memorial Hospital in Jacksonville and now Shands, I was becoming very well-acquainted with the medical field and comfortable communicating with staff. I'd already had a number of brushes with hospitals and medical emergencies during my childhood, and there would be more in Gainesville: wisdom teeth, tonsil removal, gallstones…

I learned not to fear what was happening and to be an active rather than a passive patient when it came to my treatment: asking questions, seeking other opinions, and advocating for myself when I was in pain.

I'm grateful for everything those injuries and ailments taught me, because I, and every member of my immediate family, would be confronted with health crises for the rest of my life.

Paradise at The Melody Club

I settled into a harmonious little life in Gainesville, exploring the town with Celeste and working at Shands. Then, one night, a whole new life opened up to me.

Douglas and I went out to The Melody Club, a bar on the outskirts of town, located in a strip mall with a dry cleaner and a Minute Market. There was no sign, just a drab wooden storefront with no windows. I was not expecting very much, and was maybe a bit apprehensive, but we walked in, and it was an immediate sensory overload of lights, music, smoke, and a sea of all different sorts of people. I had discovered my first gay bar.

The first thing I noticed was a big room off to the right with a stage at the far end. To the left was the bar, but I lost interest in that once I saw what was happening on the stage. A goddess was lip-syncing a rendition of "Maybe" by The Three Degrees. She was wearing a custom gown, had her brown hair in a bob, and wore dramatic eye makeup that seemed to magnetize the crowd to her. She was pure glamour, even as she acted out the melodrama of the song, falling on the floor and begging, *begging* her lover to come back to her.

I said out loud, to no one in particular, that this woman was gorgeous.

"You know, that's a boy," said a person next to me.

I was floored. There was no way this creature was not a woman through and through. But I soon learned that "Miss E." was indeed a man. He was actually six feet, seven inches tall, which should've given it away, but my perspective must've been distorted seeing him up on stage. Somehow it all made sense in this fantasy land we'd stumbled upon.

The Melody Club was the only gay bar in town, so it was for everyone. At the time, gays and lesbians didn't frequent one another's bars unless they were invited, and beyond that, the bars often catered to one type of patron: There were leather bars, drag bars, bars with a more closeted, straight-passing clientele, and more. But here, everybody was together. It was Gainesville's gay life all in one place.

I'd never been around anything like this, and I was immediately drawn to the freedom. I'd gotten my first taste of it once I moved into the apartment with Doug and Lucy, and this felt like its apex. It was 1972; most people did not feel free enough to be gay out in the world, and the idea of "coming out" to the people in one's life wasn't done often. But in this protective cocoon, you could be among people like you and just *live*.

I'm not the only one, I thought.

I'd never felt such *relief*.

And being who I was, I jumped in with both feet.

* * *

The discovery of The Melody Club led me and Doug to seek out other places like it outside of Gainesville, just to go explore. We'd drive all the way down to Orlando—nearly two hours—which was a big deal. We'd plan what we were going to wear, get ready at home with whoever else was coming, and build up the excitement for the night. Both at home and on the road, I had some one-night stands, but not all that many and usually with the help of a drug. The sex was mostly trial and error, but it was fun.

In short order, The Melody Club became an extension of my life. I was there almost every night; I got to know the leather guys, and the drag queens, and the straight-laced, successful-looking guys who thought they were better than everybody else. Sure, there were cliques, but I was new on the scene, very young, and very cute, so I had no problem mixing in with everybody and my confidence soared. Everybody took care of me. They all realized I was too young to be in the bar—I was still only seventeen!—so whenever the bar would get raided (not a rare thing in those days), the drag queens would take me backstage and hide me amid all the gowns.

I remember shivering and shaking, waiting for the cops to go away while engulfed by all those dresses. It was a calamity of odors—sweat, hairspray, stale alcohol, and cigarette smoke. (God knows none of the drag queens could afford dry cleaning.) As scared as I was—maybe even because of how scared I was, with all the adrenalin coursing through my body—those moments hiding out backstage lit a spark in me.

I soon started gravitating toward the drag queens. They did two shows a night, Wednesday through Sunday, and I attended as often as I could. Totie Martell (born Emory DuBois in Atlanta) managed the queens at the club and put together all the drag shows. He weighed about five hundred pounds and would, himself, impersonate the comedienne Totie Fields. Another queen named Penny Holiday was just fabulous—she did Diana Ross numbers. Penny had a group called Young, Gifted, and Black with LaShay and Laverne, and together they would do The Supremes. Diana had a full-time job working at a dry cleaner and performed at the club at night. She was probably the only one who'd dry-clean her dresses, by slipping them in with whatever else they were sending out—it paid to get in good with Diana. There was a lesbian named Kathy who frequented the club and who later got a job working at the Minute Market next door to the club. All the queens would routinely steal their hose from the market, and once Kathy started working there, all bets were off.

The one who stood out from all the rest was Anne Marie.

One night, the club was hosting the first-ever Miss Central Florida pageant, and Totie had invited about twenty-five drag queens from all over Florida and Georgia to compete alongside The Melody Club locals. They all paraded around on runways looking stunning and performed their songs, none more fantastically than Anne Marie.

To do "Champagne Taste" by Eartha Kitt, she wore a fitted white sequined gown under a white floor-length hooded cape, bordered in white and pink feathers, that completely covered her head. At a certain moment in the song, she dramatically flipped her head back so the hood dropped, and eventually the whole cape fell to the ground. Her features were delicate and beautiful, and her blonde hair, made of three separate wigs expertly and tastefully woven together, was perfect. Anne Marie was not the best lip-syncer of the night, but the moment she dropped that cape, the title was hers.

After she was announced as the winner and was receiving her congratulations, I saw my chance. I approached the stage in all my cuteness, and like the perfect Southern gentleman, said, "Congratulations! You *must* let me be your escort for the night. Miss Central Florida should have an escort!"

Of course, she said yes, and I carried her cape for the rest of the evening.

Back then, gay bars always had an end-of-the-night anthem. (The most famous one is "Last Dance" by Donna Summer, which would come out in 1978.) At this time, it was "United We Stand" by Brotherhood of Man. The song played at the end of the night, and C.L., the owner of the club, would come on the loudspeaker and say, "Hunnies, it's hotel motel time!" which meant the bar was closing. C.L. would have after-parties at his house, by invitation only, and it was a big deal if you got to go. I had been invited a couple of times, and on this night, he asked me to come and bring Miss Central Florida.

The parties were outrageous. C.L. himself was a sleazy man, very trashy, with hair dyed so black it couldn't possibly have been real. He was always surrounding himself with young guys and hustlers. But he loved the queens and threw great parties. They weren't parties I would go to today, but back then, we were in our own little world, hidden away, it was remarkably easy to get swept up by the energy of the night.

Jimmy: The Man Behind the Feather Coat

Anne Marie turned out to be Jimmy, my first real relationship.

Jimmy was about five foot nine with curly blonde hair. He was from Chatsworth, Georgia, where his father owned a chain of car dealerships. He had an ex-wife named Sharon, a son named Shannon, and a house full of furniture somewhere. Nobody in Georgia knew anything about Anne Marie (though some may have suspected because Jimmy was a hairdresser). He had moved to Atlanta, was doing drag there, and had had the misfortune of being arrested for it in character as Anne Marie.

Totie had invited him down for the Miss Central Florida pageant and wound up renting him a room in his house, which was on a nearby street almost back-to-back with the bar. The night we met, he tried to get me to go back to Totie's with him. But I was actually quite shy when I wasn't being a chivalrous Southern gentleman and never slept around unless I was drunk or high—so I approached this liaison with some caution.

Jimmy had a fondness for me and kept trying. I was still trying to go to school at this point, so I would usually say that I had to go back home for classes the next day. Finally, after a few months, Jimmy convinced me to come to his room. It was very small, with no furniture other than a wall-to-wall, king-size bed. For the next year and a half, Jimmy and I would never miss spending the night together. I wasn't crazy about that room, or about Totie Martell, so we moved into my apartment with Douglas not long after getting together.

Everything changed when I met Jimmy. I truly fell in love and became very active sexually. I gave off a very confident and extroverted impression at the time, and I think people who met me expected that I was very promiscuous, which wasn't the case. I could be a big flirt and loved to do that, but the actual follow-up was relatively rare. A lot of people also assumed that because I was Anne Marie's escort and carried her dresses, I was the "man." That wasn't the case either. Jimmy was very much a boy when out of drag, which is interesting since he would, in fact, transition to being a woman sometime in the late 1990s.

*It was interesting to me that even in this new and free
world, people made all sorts of assumptions and had a lot
of expectations about who you were supposed to be.*

With Jimmy, it was total trust and connection, an uninhibited kind of intimacy that was amazing to me at the time and would be very painful when it ended. After Jimmy, I would meet people and get drunk, and at the end of the evening, I might experiment—but I wouldn't find that sort of trusting love again for another thirty years.

By the time Jimmy and I moved into the apartment, Douglas was head over heels in love with a man named Beau from Colombia, South America, with whom he traveled a lot. (Beau was rich. Finally, someone who had some money!) Celeste moved in briefly and then moved out. People kept coming and going through that revolving door.

After a while, Jimmy and I started to have problems. His solution was to rent another house for the two of us, without discussing it with me first. I was supposed to be thrilled that we would have our own place, but I didn't like anything about the arrangement, most of all that I'd been treated like a piece of furniture to pack up for the move. I refused to move at first, but I wanted to stay together, so I relented.

◆ ◆ ◆

The house that Jimmy rented for us became known as the Green House, for the obvious reason that it was green. He and I had the master bedroom and bath. His best friend, a drag queen named Jackie Fontaine, lived with her boyfriend in the other bedroom. The two of them fought all the time. By "fight," I mean that they shattered windows, broke the jalousies, smashed the glass in the shower stall, and beat the hell out of each other. The police would come around, cart them off, piece them back together, and the next day they would return all lovey-dovey. A few weeks later, they'd start all over again.

The Green House did not fix our relationship as Jimmy had hoped it would, and I sat in the bedroom a lot of the time, in anguish and weeping, listening to Diana Ross sing "Touch Me in the Morning" over and over. Jackie Fontaine of the broken jalousies did not help my relationship with Jimmy. She was jealous of anybody Jimmy dated and usually managed to break up those relationships.

I was in tremendous pain and had no idea what was happening or what would become of me. I was still practically a child and felt like I was losing myself in the emotions of my first serious relationship, the chaos of Jimmy's life, and this house full of people coming and going.

Jimmy and I went back and forth, breaking up and getting back together, for about six terrible months. At some point very near the end, we went to Daytona together so he could compete in a pageant. We fought every inch of the way and managed to make it to a bar in Daytona Beach after the pageant.

I looked very stylish that night in my checkerboard blue and white matching pants and shirt. When I walked in, every queen in the bar was all over me. Jimmy turned to me and, based on a lie Jackie told him, accused me of engaging in nefarious acts with Penny Holiday from The Melody Club, whom we'd taken to calling Nickel Vacation. At that moment, an older man (who must've only been about thirty-five, but I was so very young) locked eyes with me from across the room. It was clear that he was going to have me, no matter what. At that same moment, I locked eyes with a queen called Alexandria, and she returned the sentiment.

It was all too much, and I stomped out. I had already had one Rusty Nail too many and was very drunk and very disgusted. I had slid my car keys down the bar to Douglas, who knew that I meant for him to take the car, go away, and leave me alone.

Soon after, once I'd finally stopped drinking and was beginning to see things a bit more clearly, I realized that I didn't have my car, that

I was an hour and a half from home in Daytona Beach, that Douglas was nowhere to be found, that Alexandria the drag queen was after me, and that this older guy was next to me telling me all about his motor home.

I decided that the best option was to convince the older man that if he drove me to Gainesville, we would have sex once we got there—but that right now, I was a little tired and needed to rest up for our big liaison.

He agreed, and I hopped in the motor home. As we got closer and closer to Gainesville, I started thinking, "I don't want to have sex with this guy. I'm wearing platform shoes. My feet hurt. I can't run too fast or too far. What am I going to do when we get home?"

I told him to park on a desolate street, and the instant the motor home stopped, I shoved open the door and bolted off toward the Green House, four blocks away. (I'm so sorry, mister—but really, it would not have been fun.)

When I got home, Jimmy was in bed, but everybody else was awake, and nobody was speaking to me. They had been up all night, alternating between worried and furious. I jumped into the shower, got into bed, went to sleep, and didn't have another Rusty Nail for months.

* * *

That episode did not help my relationship with Jimmy, which was already in tatters. Still, we clung to it. We loved one another deeply, and the sex was wonderful. We had a huge level of trust between us and could be intimate with one another in a way that we could never be with anyone else.

But we had a lot working against our relationship. There was Jackie, who had also broken up Jimmy and his wife, Sharon. There was the age difference. Jimmy was much older than I was and a father, and I think he may have unintentionally taken on the role of big brother with me. Being as young as I was, I had no idea how to deal with any of this. And somewhere along the line, our trust was broken. That trust was the basis of our relationship, and it was really hard to keep going without it.

So, after six months of listening to "Touch Me in the Morning," crying and crying because my relationship was over, and swearing I'd never, ever love again, Douglas brought home some very interesting news that lifted my mood: The Melody Club was having a talent show.

Feeling seen by another is validating and such an important part of coming into your own identity. But you have to be able to hold on to who you are. If a relationship is all-consuming or codependent, you run the risk of only seeing yourself as a reflection of your partner.

FIVE

Rita Dayworth:
A Star Is Born

I WAS WITH DOUGLAS AND OUR GOOD FRIEND CLIFF when Douglas shared the news about The Melody Club talent show. We had met Cliff at the club and would often go over to the cute little apartment he shared with his boyfriend, Steve, and their two cats, Stiff and Cleve. They had a lovely, "real" relationship, and I remember marveling at their life and thinking, *I want* that!

I believe we were drunk when the three of us decided that we would sign up for the show. Douglas and I had done theater, so we would have jumped at the chance to get on stage even if we were sober. Cliff needed more convincing, but he was game. Douglas and I decided we would do a double act. And, thespians that we were, we were going to go all out.

When I told Jimmy about our plans, he was not very happy about it at all. Our relationship was very rocky, but we were still together, and there was a certain image we were presenting to the world:

Jimmy was Anne Marie and I carried his dresses. I was the "man" in the couple (even though it wasn't that way in private), and this just wasn't done. There wasn't enough room in the relationship for two drag queens. As much as it upset him, it was only for one night, so he went along with it. When the time came, he even helped us all do our hair, as he was quite an accomplished hairdresser.

Douglas was six feet, three inches tall and very handsome but not very pretty, though he did have nice high cheekbones. Poor Cliff was a gorgeous man but did not make for an attractive woman. He had a big forehead and big eyebrows and was very built up and muscular. The halter dress he was wearing did nothing for him. He kept trying to back out, but we wouldn't let him.

I was a stunning brunette without a name, in a high-end thrift store ensemble. When Totie saw me at a rehearsal, she pronounced me, "Rita Dayworth, everybody's day girl." And a star was born!

I was the only one of us who had the honor of being named by a drag mother, probably because I was with Jimmy and already well known to Totie. Douglas named himself Sally Summers, and Cliff was Clitortia.

On the night of the show, Douglas and I did Barbra Streisand's "One Less Bell to Answer/A House Is Not a Home." She'd recorded a performance of this song for a TV special, which had her on both sides of the screen, accompanying herself in this sad story of lost love. Doug and I were the two Barbras singing to each other, and it was perfection. Our history of performing together and our deep personal connection made us so in sync and dramatic, we brought the house down. We got tips! We got encores! We got everything!

Cliff went on stage and bombed, and would beg us for the rest of his life to never bring it up again. Douglas had fun, but he always had fun.

For me, that night was another awakening, another opportunity to relish the freedom of getting up on stage and becoming another person—this time with no script to follow but what I wanted to express.

• • •

For weeks afterward, people would come up and tell me what a terrific show I'd put on, and I thought to myself: *I want to do this.*

I was going to have to make a decision about whether to follow this dream or to push it away and try to appease Jimmy. As would happen to me over and over in life, I just knew I could do this and be great at it, and I wasn't going to let anything hold me back. So I approached Totie about performing again; by the time I got back up on stage as Rita a few weeks later, Jimmy and I were finally broken up, and I was moving out.

Rita Takes the Lead

I threw myself into being Rita with no hesitation. It was as if I'd been doing it all my life. In a sense, I suppose I did have an entire lifetime's worth of bottled-up emotions, energy, and creativity that I could finally let out and be applauded (and paid, however little) for. We did two shows every night, Wednesday through Saturday, and I usually made $35 to $40 for the week, plus tips.

The apartment I moved into after leaving Jimmy's was definitely not worthy of a future star like Rita. It wasn't worthy of anybody. I grew up in a shack, and even I thought this place was a dump. And—God knows how—I wound up living there with Jackie Fontaine, who was also working at The Melody Club. But it was away from Jimmy, and it was all I could afford.

To get ready, Jackie would sit on one side of the room, and I would sit on the other. We would put on our makeup and get in drag, both of us with our bottles of Boone's Farm wine on our dressing tables. She only drank pink (pink was her color), and I was usually so drunk by the time I was done putting on my face, I didn't even remember what color I had.

I often wore my own hair, in a Gibson Girl do with tendrils hanging down. I'd watched Jimmy do hair for so long it had become second nature to me. My overall look was much more natural than the drag queens who wore a lot of makeup. I'd done makeup in the theater, and I had a cute, boyish face—and if you're a cute boy, you can usually make yourself into a fairly cute girl with little makeup. You just have to handle the angular jawline with a little shading.

Rita's star rose quickly at the club, and she was learning all sorts of new things. One of them was that if you mixed a little alcohol with a Seconal, or maybe a Tuinal, you could walk out, fall into somebody's arms, and get a ride home.

Over time, I developed my signature songs and stage moves. If I wanted to stir the place up, I might do "Respect" by Aretha Franklin, climb up on a very tiny, shaky bar table, do a little dance, and take a taste of everybody's drink as I jumped from table to table. By the time I'd worked my way around the room, things were really going, and I was high enough for my next number.

The stage at the club had a big steel beam right in front of it. If you were tall enough, you could jump up a little bit, grab it, and swing out over the crowd! That swing became a big part of my act. One night, I was wearing a cute little gold and garnet ring on my pinky, and the ring got caught on this metal rod just enough to make me lose my grip. I had to let go very quickly, lost my balance, and went flying feetfirst into the audience, landing on my back and slamming my head on the concrete floor!

The music stopped. There was dead silence. I thought to myself, "This probably isn't good—but I'm a thespian!" I jumped up, got the music going, and finished the number. I could've given myself a full concussion, all because I wanted to wear my little gold and garnet ring.

* * *

As life became more and more about Rita and The Melody Club, the University of Florida was receding further and further from my mind. I attended classes just enough to not get kicked out and be able to keep my hospital job and its steady income. My daily routine consisted mainly of working at Shands, doing two shows a night and dancing on tables, going out afterward, and getting drunk out of my mind, usually winding up at Krystal Hamburgers eating square sliders with steamed onion pieces before finally realizing that I just needed to go home and crash.

Those were wonderful, carefree days, but waking up in my horrible apartment was becoming a bit too depressing. It was time to elevate a bit and to be a higher-class drag queen.

* * *

I soon found a new house and Douglas moved in, too, along with a whole cast of old and new characters. We were as poor as ever, living hand to mouth. That's where Mercedes came in.

Mercedes weighed close to three hundred pounds, and we called her Bahama Mama. She was a striking woman with long, extraordinarily beautiful, thick blonde hair, and she came from a wealthy family in Coral Gables. Her parents would have cut her off if she'd ever stopped going to school, so she was the only one of us who attended classes regularly. After going to school all day, Mercedes worked the night shift at the Krispy Kreme doughnut shop. She would come home at four in the morning smelling like sugar, wake everybody up with free donuts, then shower and collapse.

Mercedes was brilliant. She started out as a straight A student—but then, like the rest of us, she started smoking pot and living in a way that would have made her parents' hair stand on end. (At some point, Mercedes's family found out she lived with gay roommates and disowned her. There was a lot of drama for a time, but they reconciled eventually.)

We were all doing odd jobs and strange things to keep ourselves afloat. Sometimes we would go to the grocery store on a mission to find food for dinner, never intending to pay for it. We actually stole food. Mercedes once put a four-pound package of meat down her pants. It didn't even show because she was so heavy. Nobody realized it was there until the blood started oozing out and running down her legs. That day, we left the store even more quickly than usual.

We rationalized that we weren't stealing big things like cars or taking things directly from real people, but it was theft all the same. I'm not particularly proud of that time in my life. I've forgiven myself and released it, but I was certainly not the person I am today.

So much for elevating!

Rita Rises

The challenges of the real world—school, money, relationships, not to mention the persistent question of who "Tom" was—made the world of Rita an all-the-more-alluring escape. It was a lot easier to spend two hours getting my face on and dealing with the pantyhose, bras, and physical contortions of drag than to go back to all the mental gymnastics and effort required to be "normal" in the world outside my close group of friends.

*When I was Rita, I didn't have to try so hard
to be all the things Tom wasn't.*

* * *

At the same time, people's perceptions of me within the world of The Melody Club were changing. Once I stopped being Tom and fully committed to doing drag, I didn't associate as much with the other cliques like the leather guys and the businessmen. To paraphrase RuPaul, they were all busy doing their own forms of drag and did what they needed to do to maintain the image they'd built for themselves.

The lesbians, however, loved the drag queens. The big, tough ones that we used to call "bull dykes"—a phrase that is now very politically incorrect—would often latch onto us. They were extremely nurturing, despite appearances.

What we especially loved about these women was that they would always start the tipping each night at the club. They'd come up to us in the middle of a number and give us dollar bills or fives, then everyone would feel more comfortable following suit. Sometimes they would give us dollar after dollar after dollar. The audience would get all involved in cheering them on, and we might wind up with enough money for Boone's Farm, gas, pantyhose, eyelashes, and maybe even a new pair of Springolators.

* * *

Those of us who worked at the bar were part of our own little clique, and every clique had its own dramas, of course. Even for the queens (maybe especially for the queens), it wasn't all total freedom and individual expression—there were rules and customs in the drag world that Rita had to learn and observe, and different types of slip-ups to watch out for. We could never "take" someone else's song, and as a white girl, Rita was not supposed to do songs by Black artists. She did do a lot of Black female vocalists, though, and "Midnight Train to Georgia" and "The Best Thing That Ever Happened to Me" would become her signature numbers; for some reason, they fit her character. (I would go around the room singing "The Best Thing That Ever Happened to Me" to each person, collecting dollar bill after dollar bill. Maybe some five-dollar bills, if Kathy, Doris, and Joyce were in the room.)

But the Black drag queens didn't appreciate Rita doing this. Especially Sheila, a large, Black queen who carried a gun she named Roscoe. Sheila hadn't liked me when I got together with Jimmy, though she eventually came to accept me as his boyfriend. But she *really* hated me when I became Rita. She thought I was stealing "her" songs. I did do a lot of Gladys Knight, Patti LaBelle, and Aretha Franklin, because they were great skip-and-jump numbers. But I wasn't willing to risk getting shot to do them if Sheila was around. She brought Roscoe and several other guns to the show each night and was always waving them around and threatening people. It scared the hell out of me.

But Sheila also had her kind moments, like when she tried to teach me how to steal bolts of fabric: You just walked into the fabric store and put whatever bolt struck your fancy under your arm. Then you walked out. If anybody tried to stop you, you just turned around and said, "What are you looking at?" She assured me that they would stop in their tracks, terrified, and that you could just keep on going. Of course, unlike Sheila, I would not have been toting a gun, and I knew my presence did not have the same impact as hers had. I just couldn't do it. I still carried guilt from stealing the meat.

* * *

More and more, I would get ready for shows at the club, which was becoming a second home. Backstage, we each had our own station where we kept our little cases and makeup. We brought in our dresses, which we didn't dare leave backstage unattended. I had dresses made, knew just where to find wonderful fabric for specialty numbers, and always added a little dramatic flair. There was only one bathroom backstage, which was really quite a dire situation if you think about what we had to do to prepare ourselves.

Getting into drag takes at least two hours. You spread a towel over whatever tacky table was handy and set up your makeup mirror with the little screw-in lights. Then you laid out all your tools and makeup. Right next to that, of course, was your bottle of Boone's Farm and your glass filled with ice—because that was the only way you were going to get the Boone's Farm down. (After one or two glasses, you no longer needed the ice.)

You had to get the eyeliner and eyelashes on before you'd had too much Boone's Farm, because that required the use of tweezers. And for Rita—for most people, but especially for her—the eyes were what got everybody going. So you couldn't get too tipsy before that was all in place. But by the time you got to the bar for the show, you were feeling pretty loose.

The first show usually had the smaller crowd, which was good for getting warmed up and really into character. People always wanted to come backstage between the shows to see us, but we didn't like that much because the lighting was too bright and not nearly as flattering as the stage lighting. Instead, we liked to sneak out to the Minute Market next door for snacks and pantyhose, or go smoke a joint out back, or maybe enjoy a little Seconal.

Rita was particularly fond of Seconal. On it, she could still dance and do things, but she was very, very relaxed. It was quite easy to feel like a woman in that state—at times, a flawless woman. Her attitude was, "Here I am, looking like this. Who are you to question me?"

◆ ◆ ◆

In the beginning, Rita was very cautious about where she went and with whom. This was the South after all. Though in Florida at that time, drag was legal—minus the breasts. You could be out in the world as a man dressed as a woman as long as you did not have breasts.

One night when I was driving home from the bar, a car started following me. I knew that if I went home, the people in that car were going to hurt me, so I decided that the best strategy was to drive directly to the police station. I drove there, ran out of the car, stopped in my tracks in the doorway, and thought, *Hold on a moment*...I pulled out my tits and held them in my hands, so I would be in compliance with the law, and then announced, "There's somebody following me. Please help!"

They let me hide out, and I wondered if those cops were the same ones I'd hidden from amid the gowns backstage at The Melody Club.

· · ·

As Rita's celebrity grew, she became more daring. Perhaps that was also the influence of Tom—after all, I'd managed to get away with a lot of things in life. I did get caught one night at the club, however. I had been shopping in an elegant little boutique that afternoon and saw the most beautiful shawl that went perfectly with a dress I'd just had made. I thought, "Who's going to stop me?" So, I took it and wore it in the show that night. Everybody loved it, and I got all sorts of compliments.

At the end of the evening, after my last number, a woman walked up and gave me a five-dollar bill. She told me she owned the boutique and said, "Make sure I get the shawl back by the end of the night, or I'll have the police come get it." Then she turned on her heel and walked off. I gave her the shawl and apologized. I knew it was wrong. But it really did make the number.

Worlds Colliding

I had so much energy back then and thought nothing of working all day at Shands and all night at The Melody Club. I was always racing around at the hospital and would literally time myself to see how long it took me, or how many steps it took me, to get from the floor to the lab or from the lab to radiology. One day, I was racing down the stairwell from the third floor to the first-floor lab, slipped, and fell.

Since I worked in the hospital, there was a lot of effort made to get me special care. They liked me, but I'm sure it had something to do with liability as well. I panicked as they took an X-ray. I had a show to do that night! But I had fractured my foot and had no choice but to pull out of the show. My foot was set in a bulky plaster cast from my knee to my toes.

"You want me to wear this for *how* long?" I asked the doctor.

"Four weeks to start, and then we'll see. Probably six," he said.

Drag queens do not wear casts.

The cast seemed to get heavier with each passing day. After a few days, it really started to itch. I put coat hangers down there to scratch it, and baby powder, and God knows what else. The whole thing was really troubling, and I began to obsess about how poorly I was sleeping and how I couldn't do anything I wanted to do with this cast on. Pretty soon, I had managed to cut the cast off.

The next day, I went to work and everybody squealed, "Oh, you got your cast off!" They were all very happy for me—until the doctor walked by and I ended up back in the cast room, getting another one. Then it happened again. I just wasn't willing for Rita to perform with a cast on, and I wasn't willing to forego that many performances. The result was that my foot was not getting better. Finally, the doctor said, "Look, this isn't about whether or not you like it. If you don't wear this cast, you're not going to be able to walk."

That night at The Melody Club, Rita came out in a frilly pink eyelet number and did "Inseparable" by Natalie Cole, massaging and looking down lovingly at the cast while she sang.

It was an instant hit, and I did that number for at least four more weeks. That was the kind of dimension Rita had and how creatively she could think. Anything to keep the show going! Her approach was either "I'm going to come out and do a skip-and-jump number for you," or "I'm going to come out and walk all over your tables and drink your drinks," or "I'm simply going to stand here and look gorgeous, and you will love every minute of it." All three worked.

· · ·

Rita and Shands collided over another issue: my eyebrows. Rita simply could not have Tom's eyebrows, so in the early days, Tom had no eyebrows at all.

That was a bit disconcerting for the people at Shands. My long, curly hair, combined with no eyebrows, created quite a look. People would approach the counter where I worked and say, "Ma'am, can I...?" I would look up and they would be shocked to see that I was a man. The nurses, who were used to me and liked me, would just say to them, "Don't worry, we're as confused as you are."

After I'd been written up several times for "not being presentable" thanks to my long hair and lack of eyebrows, I finally let them grow out. But I bleached them, and when I went to work at Shands, I would simply apply mascara on them. By the end of my shift, the mascara would be streaking all over my eyes and face, but at least I'd made the effort. (I could've really used waterproof mascara back then.) I was a real oddball to them, and I'm sure I was being talked about. But I was also terrific at my job, and patients loved me.

Before Rita, I would visit my parents quite often, but that became harder once performing took over my schedule and my appearance started to shift to being more drag-friendly. Once I was doing Rita four nights a week, my visits slowed down considerably. I remember visiting them on a day that was particularly hot and humid. Everyone was out of sorts, and my parents complained about my long hair, so I put it up in a ponytail. At some point, I caught myself wiping sweat off my face and suddenly panicked, thinking about what my eyebrow mascara must look like in the heat. I made a beeline for the mirror and saw that all the mascara was gone and that I had been walking around with albino eyebrows. My first thought was, "Why has nobody noticed that I have no eyebrows? Why am I going through this, anyway, if nobody's going to notice?" Still, I rushed to my room and put the eyebrows back on before I got caught. No sense in giving my father a heart attack.

The Pull of the Drag Circuit

By 1974, I'd stopped going to classes at the university and was about to be kicked out of school when I decided to withdraw. I gave my parents some sort of excuse and convinced them that it made more sense financially for me to attend Santa Fe Community College with Douglas and Lucy. So, I enrolled and attended classes there, just barely. Instead, I was broadening my horizons by traveling on the drag show circuit and competing in pageants all over Florida.

Rita became a celebrity in the South and traveled around like other circuit stars, big names like Gilda Golden and Charlie Brown (who would later open her own cabaret in Atlanta and go on to raise more money for AIDS than anyone in the Southeast). There was a whole group of us known as the Dollies, girls who traveled between Atlanta, Miami Beach, Jacksonville, Daytona, and points beyond either to be in shows, get into drag and do fun stuff, or just hang out and tease the boys.

One of the Dollies was named Toby Randall. She convinced C.L. to hire her for a week as a visiting drag queen at The Melody Club. Nobody knew much about her, but she impressed C.L. because she had put together a giant portfolio. What we *had* heard about Toby was that we'd better watch out for our dresses, jewelry, and makeup, because Toby took things.

I had just gotten a luxurious new yellow feather boa to go with a beautiful gray gown that was made for me by Gina Lee, a drag queen who wore shoes with heels made of clear plastic with live goldfish swimming in them. After the weekend that Toby Randall spent with us, my feather boa was missing. We all suspected where it was.

Dollies all over Florida were in touch with one another, so we knew that Toby Randall was on her way to Orlando. We got on the horn to some the Dollies down there, Roxanne Russell and Lori DelMar, and told them to watch their dresses because Toby Randall was on her way! I also told them that I was coming down because I just knew Toby was going to wear my yellow feather boa in the show, and I wanted to be in the audience when she did it.

I may have had a quaalude while I was getting ready to go to that show in Orlando, just to get in the mood, and all the Dollies greeted me warmly when I arrived. I had made a point of not going back-stage because I didn't want Toby Randall to know that I was there. Roxanne and I had a secret plan.

Toby came out and did her number, and of course, she was wear-ing my yellow feather boa. I just sat there and watched and clapped along with everybody else, but Roxanne approached Toby and asked if she could borrow the boa. Toby said, "Well, of course you can, I'd be delighted. I always lend my stuff."

When Roxanne did her number wearing the feather boa, I came forward and tipped her. She took off the yellow feather boa and put it around my neck, and I walked off. We never heard from, or about, Toby Randall again.

Double Vision

Miss Rita was known for teasing people but would never do anything in drag. People have no idea how much makeup is involved and how messy the whole thing can get.

I learned this the hard way one night when a queen named Peaches LaRue and I jumped in my little Rambler American and drove from Gainesville to Jacksonville to do a show at a bar called My Little Dude. Since Jacksonville was a big metropolitan area compared to Jacksonville Beach, I was not terrified of running into my mother, my father, or any of their friends—especially at My Little Dude, which was a lesbian bar that presented drag shows. I found it interesting that a lesbian bar would do drag shows and that it would be named My Little Dude.

In those days, the shows at My Little Dude attracted some rough trade. These guys typically had long hair and a bad-boy thing that Rita really liked. That night, a guy named Randy kept tipping me. He was hot, I was drunk, and when he said the magic words—"Would you like to come out and smoke a joint?"—I was game.

We snuck out to the Rambler American between my numbers, smoked a joint, and Randy started rubbing on things. I said, apparently not too convincingly, "You need to stop that."

Now, when you're in full drag, your penis is tucked way away and not easily accessed, usually held in place with tape. Nor is it ever meant to get erect while it's back there, because that could have awkward consequences. Still, something about Randy was getting me very excited. I realized that I had an erection, and that I was sitting there in drag, and that this *did not work*. But Randy was so hot, and I was so overwhelmed with him and smoking this joint, that I suddenly realized that I'd had the equivalent of a wet dream while I was awake.

I remember having this wonderful feeling and, at the same time, hearing this horrible noise. It was a crunching sound that really didn't seem at all healthy. My next thought was, "How in the world am I going to do my number?"

But the show had to go on! We finished the joint, and I rushed back into the bar. I didn't have any time to go to the bathroom and clean myself up. I had on a low-cut red sequined gown that was slit up to the hips on both sides, and my only consolation was that, if what I thought had just happened in my outfit had actually happened, it probably wouldn't show through the three layers of pantyhose I was wearing.

I tore into my famous number, "I've Got the Music in Me" by Kiki Dee. The whole time I was on stage, I was thinking, "I have my own cum in my underwear. I'm dressed as a woman, and I'm in a lesbian bar called My Little Dude." I don't know if those surreal thoughts sparked something new in me, but I had never kicked higher.

The number ended and I brought down the house, but I had another show to do. I debated whether to go through all that I would have to go through to undo myself, clean up, and get myself back together. I definitely didn't have the requisite two hours—and the tough part can either be easy or hard, no pun intended. This problem didn't usually come up because even though you might drink a lot, you train yourself to have a camel bladder and never have to pee. (Even today, I can go for lengths of time that are totally unhealthy and probably inhuman, and that only drag queens can manage.)

I simply could not face the thought of undoing and redoing myself. I figured, "I'm just going to do the second show like this, and deal with all of it later. Anyway, it's probably dry by now, and I'll be home in a few hours. And it came from me, so it can't hurt me. Right?" A very different reaction than the one I'd had the first time this happened to me in the middle of the night at the Shack.

· · ·

Along with the exploration and discovery that drove me during these years, there was a big dose of confusion because there were really two different people involved: Tom and Rita were completely separate personalities. I am neither qualified nor inclined to analyze that in much depth, but it made things interesting.

When people see a drag queen, they sometimes think "woman" and make all sorts of assumptions about roles, preferences, and attitudes. Many of my fellow Dollies did go on to become women. Gainesville was a refuge for a lot of people in the South who were confused about their gender, exploring, or didn't really know yet what direction they wanted to go. It was a safe place to express themselves, where you could try things out a bit before you took any big steps. Lots of friends would eventually take those steps, some in questionable ways, getting implants and silicone face injections from completely unregulated, back-alley sources.

When people saw me as Tom, they made a whole different set of assumptions, none of which were accurate either. Things were even more muddled because many people of all persuasions were attracted to Rita. Some were hot for her, some simply wanted to be seen with a celebrity, and others just wanted to borrow her dresses. As confusing as all of this was to me, it was probably even more so to the people around me.

When it came to sex in those days, the bottom line was that I was simply scared to death. I was very shy and very fearful, which further compounded the confusion because that was quite unlike my normal personality in other areas of life. Nobody at Shands, for instance, would have thought I was shy or fearful. I can appear very extroverted and social, to the point that some people assume I've been in a relationship most of my life. Other people think I'm rather aloof, or above it all, because they've caught me in a moment of shyness or just observing what's going on around me. Throw drugs or alcohol into the equation, and a whole different version of Tom will emerge.

Whatever the situation, I just tried to explore and learn what I could from the fascinating people I came across and keep putting one foot in front of the other.

· · ·

There came a time, though, when I stopped being able to compartmentalize and felt Tom getting swallowed up by Rita. I would sleep all day because I'd been out all night, and when I did go out, it was more often as Rita than Tom. Even if I wasn't in full drag or went to the bar as myself on an off night, people would still call me Rita. At a certain point, Douglas was the only one calling me Tommy.

When I started doing drag, it was not an either/or situation for me. I liked being Tom, *and* I liked being Rita. It was very much about theater and illusion. Rita acted, moved, and spoke very differently than Tom, and they were both equally *me*. The transformation of getting ready was always a thrill—the makeup, putting on the lipstick as the last step, then looking in the mirror and still seeing myself. But once I put the wig on—*bam!* It was like magic.

Rita emerged from me the very first time she took to the stage. She would become more polished and more beautiful over the years, but she was always who she was. And there was always Tom. But for a brief sliver of time, I nearly crossed over into this abyss where I couldn't tell who was who.

◆ ◆ ◆

Since we'd lived together in our first apartment in Gainesville, and after her brief relationship with Nikki, Lucy met a man named Leeland. They got engaged, and Doug and I were invited to their wedding in southern Georgia. Around that time, I had started questioning whether I should take my life in a different direction and start taking female hormones.

My hair was very long in those days, and I decided that for Lucy and Leeland's wedding, I would put a soft perm in it. It was nice curly hair, but I thought it might be even better with the perm. I must have been smoking dope that day, because somehow, I got sidetracked and left the chemicals in my hair too long. Now, this was not the most expensive perm on the shelf to begin with—it was probably the Boone's Farm of home perms—and after a few extra minutes of exposure, my hair had become an Afro.

At the last minute, it also dawned on me that I didn't have any boy's clothes suitable for a wedding. All I had were gowns and dresses, work clothes for the hospital, and a few pairs of black women's slacks. And we had to get in the car right away, because it was a three-hour drive to the wedding and we were going to be late.

To address the hair crisis, I figured that the only solution was to put castor oil in it. I thought that would make it lay down nicely, but instead it just looked like I had an Afro with castor oil in it. I also decided that the only way I could get into these girl slacks was to wear pantyhose underneath them to "slim" myself down a bit. I borrowed a shirt and a jacket from Douglas. To complete the look, I carefully applied mascara to my bleached-out eyebrows.

None of it was optimal, but I figured I could sell it. I would be a boy at the wedding, but I could access Rita's panache and my own thespian skills to pull it off. (Again, I'm pretty certain there were some drugs involved in all of those decisions.)

It was July, and the heat in southern Georgia was unbearable. I made it through the day, but I was, without doubt, the strangest-looking person at the wedding, in my women's slacks with pantyhose underneath, castor oil in my Afro hair, and mascara on my eyebrows. I'm sure her guests whispered among themselves about me, but Lucy didn't care, and that's all that mattered.

Sadly, the only solution for my hair was to cut it.

Tom or Rita?

In the beginning, I think Rita was a way for me to continue expressing myself and exploring my passion for theater in a place where it was physically and emotionally safe to do so. There might be cattiness from other drag queens, comments like "Where'd you get *that* fabric?" delivered with a sneer, but there was no judgment for being a drag queen. There was a sexual element to it, obviously, but Rita was mostly about my general searching and exploring.

I finally had an outlet for everything I had bottled up over so many years of trying to make all those other personas "fit."

Rita was also about acceptance, attention, and accolades. She got a lot of all three, and I loved it. She had a following and was in great demand. When she got to a certain level of fame, nobody even tried to duplicate her numbers. Everybody wanted to know about her gowns and wondered what she'd be doing for her next show. A lot of people just fell at her feet.

During the year and a half that Rita was around professionally, she attracted many kinds of attention. There were tough guys, regular gay guys, straight guys, lesbians, people who were just curious, people too drunk to have an opinion, and everything in between.

There was also the wide range of ideas about who and what I was, and what I did with whom.

For whatever reasons, as Tom, I didn't have a healthy amount of self-respect, self-worth, or self-knowledge at that time in my life—and I didn't yet have the tools to address those issues. Rita became, in part, a way to stroke my ego, or her ego, or someone's ego—which is ironic because being a drag queen is a very low-paid, tip-driven profession.

She had a strong personality, and it was a different personality from Tom's. She could be out there and explore things in a way that he would have been too shy to do. Let's put it this way: Rita never would have been in the closet!

Having two identities came in handy (dubiously) during those years. Because of Rita, I could avoid dealing with many things that were going on in Tom's life. I was supposed to be a student, but I didn't go to school. I wasn't out to anyone beyond the drag world. If my parents had had any idea about most of the things I was doing, they would have fainted dead away. I had a lot of double lives going on.

It was a lot simpler and more comfortable just to be Rita and to make up things for Rita to wear and do.

At times, Rita may have usurped a little too much of Tom— but I believe that we do what we need to do and can learn lessons and gain wisdom from just about anything.

Rita's world also contained a lot of sadness. Many of the people who gravitated there were effeminate boys who had been thrown out of their families, or beaten, or ostracized. There were a lot of horror stories. We also met a lot of guys who were obviously gay but who were trying desperately not to be. Somehow, they thought that coming into the drag world would prove that they were straight. But inevitably, they were gay—and in those days, the choices they faced were very difficult. I don't know how Rita might have helped with those choices and transitions, but I hope she did.

Still others came around in the midst of becoming women. A lot of them were doing hormones and injecting silicone, and I don't mean medical-grade silicone. There was a guy named Michael, who ended up in jail many years later, who was shooting up all the Dollies and laying silicone injections along their cheekbones. One queen, Michelle, actually castrated himself when he was drunk one night.

I think our twenties are a time when a lot of us aren't really in touch with who we are and maybe not even interested in thinking too much about that—but my case was extreme. Not everybody becomes a drag queen for distraction, or does an enormous amount of drugs, at the same time they are working at a hospital and nominally enrolled in college.

I put myself in situations that I would not go near today. Or if I did go near them, it would be to help someone. It was not always safe to be a drag queen. For the most part, you passed as a woman. But if you didn't, it could be dangerous. A lot of the Dollies walked around with straight razors in their purses. I carried a can of hairspray, because I figured that'd stop anybody. If nothing else, the hairspray would glue their eyelashes together. (Thank you, Aqua Net.)

But the longer I lived like that, the harder it became to deny that my life was not moving in the direction I wanted.

My perspective began to shift dramatically in the mid-1970s. I looked at my life, and at the lives of the people around me, and that old feeling arose in me again, the one I remembered from being a little kid running around the Shack: *There is something else out there for me.*

In 1976, I decided it was time to broaden my horizons. Douglas was living in Miami by then, so I jumped into my car and headed south.

It was also time to say goodbye to Rita. For now.

. . .

No one is just one thing. We all have facets to our personality and identity, and we're not honoring ourselves if we insist on sticking rigidly to one aspect of who we are. Every side of us needs space and attention to grow and thrive in the sunlight.

. . .

SIX

The Rebirth of Tom

MY MOVE TO MIAMI IN 1976 WAS TO BE THE REBIRTH of Tom. Rita had been put on the shelf, literally: She was packed in a box and stored in a closet, and there was no plan to bring her out. Of course, her spirit was always in me, but I meant for her to stay hidden; outside, I was going to be a boy.

When I got to town, I stayed with two crazy sisters, Sarah and Sandra, and lived on their little couch. I enrolled in the University of Miami but never set foot in the place. By then, enrolling in the local college seemed to be the protocol; the attendance and studying aspects weren't really a priority at the time.

I managed to grow enough eyebrows, or to get them dark enough, that I was able to finagle a job at Jackson Memorial Hospital in Miami. Not only that, but I stepped up. I became the patient unit manager for three intensive care units: the medical, surgical, and neonatal ICUs. This meant that I was responsible for everything from staffing to supplies—all but the literal practicing of medicine. Even though I didn't work directly with patients, I got to see the entire spectrum of experiences—from people coding to watching cutting-edge surgeries—which would help me better handle what was to come in my own life years later.

After a couple of weeks on Sarah and Sandra's couch, I got my own little apartment. It was behind the home of a little old lady whom I would help out from time to time. Little did she know what a treasure she had in me, a person who had years of experience in caring for old ladies!

First, it was Nana, my old roommate, with whom I was so close all through my childhood. I was quite interested in those messages she got from the electric fan and often talked with her about them. "Well, what are you hearing today, Nana?" I would ask, and she would go on and on. At various points, she refused to eat or accept drinks from anyone who wasn't me.

After we moved out of the Shack when I was twelve to the house two doors down, we moved Dad's mom into the Shack so we—mostly I—could take care of her. She was bedridden, and I remember coming home from school when I was about thirteen and cleaning her. Both of my parents were at work, so there was nobody else to do it. Although I loved her very much, there were times when that was the last thing I wanted to do. Still, we were very close, and I would spend time with her on weekends over at the Shack, talking and talking, and drinking root beer floats.

I've always been good company to little old ladies.

· · ·

Naturally, I could not have only one job, so in addition to working at Jackson, I started waiting tables at Bachelors III, a high-end gay supper club and bar, which I almost burned down one night. We flambéed ducks at the table in a big, dramatic presentation. This particular evening, the handle came off my saucepan and the ducks, the flames, and the saucepan went flying into the air and landed on a dead, very dry eucalyptus tree that was the center of our décor. It had been there since the beginning of time, and we were always afraid it would spontaneously burst into flames one day, even without having flambéed duck thrown at it. I scurried over, scooped everything up and put out the fire, and made it all part of the show.

When I'd saved a little money, I moved out of my little old lady friend's apartment and into a wonderful place on Salzedo in Coral Gables. It was in a beautiful coral-pink building, Spanish style with white trim, and very private. It was a tiny one-bedroom, but I had a Coral Gables address and a four-poster wooden bed. After growing up in a shack on a dirt road, that meant something. I loved living there, until we had a huge infestation of white sugar ants and I had to move out. Two steps forward, one step back.

Dating in Miami

Douglas was here in Miami, living in a wonderful apartment with Michael Hardwick, who would later become well known for *Bowers v. Hardwick*, a hugely important Supreme Court case in the battle for gay rights. Years after he and Douglas were together, Michael was living in Atlanta when the police busted into his apartment one night, arrested him and his partner, and charged Michael with engaging in sodomy. The case made it all the way up to the Supreme Court, and in 1986, they ruled to uphold a Georgia law criminalizing anal sex between consenting adults. It wouldn't be overturned until 2003.

I went out to parties and bars with Douglas and Michael and met a lot of new people. In those days, Miami, Fort Lauderdale, and a few other areas were just hopping and popping with gay bars. But these were also the Anita Bryant years, when the aging beauty queen and orange juice spokesperson began her crusade against gays and started popularizing the hateful rhetoric that persists in Florida today. You were fine as long as you were in a gay bar—but outside of that world, some people were accepting and some were very actively not. (At least we managed to ruin Anita's career by boycotting orange juice and getting her kicked off the Florida Citrus Commission.)

I learned a lot about myself in Miami. I was working hard at the hospital, but since I was salaried and not hourly, I couldn't work overtime, and there were only so many tables to be waited at Bachelors III. I didn't have ten drag shows a week taking up all that time and attention, so I had the chance to think about what I wanted to do and be and generally to come into myself.

That happens to everyone in their twenties, I think, but it was really my first time out in the world alone as Tom, without Rita, and in many ways, I was living as a completely opposite person.

Rita went away so Tom could step out and grow.

· · ·

That was an "anything goes" time in the gay community. People went to the baths or the back rooms of bars, and most people were quite promiscuous. On a typical evening, I would get off work at the hospital, wait tables, and have a couple of drinks. Then I might go to the baths and have either very casual sex or no sex at all because I was even more selective than I had been in Gainesville. It was more a time of figuring out what I liked, what I didn't like, and who I liked to do it with. The kind of "normal" relationship in which you dated, got to know one another, and then grew into something more never really happened for me. Sparks might fly at first but they usually sputtered out quickly, and I rarely got past the first few dates. It didn't take much to scare me off. I might go into his bathroom and see that he was a pig, or that he really wasn't gay because everything he owned was orange and green.

I had never thought of myself as being particularly attractive, but a lot of people started noticing me in Miami. At first, I was attracted to men who were not necessarily butch but who looked a bit more on the straight side. I think that particular attraction may have been something left over from Rita, who always loved the manly bad boys. I also think that when I got more comfortable with someone, no matter how hard I tried to suppress it, my feminine side would show up—and that was not what most guys had expected. They often assumed that I was this big butch number, but that was not the case, and I had it in my head that if I were to be "found out," they'd be very disappointed.

Between that and the aftermath of the My Little Dude situation, I would have a lot of anxiety surrounding sex for years to come.

It was another situation in which I might be seen as an imposter.

What happened in the car with Randy in Jacksonville may have done some damage—probably physically and certainly psychologically. The "crunch" I heard in the middle of it all scared me, and for a while there was, let's just say, some difficulty. I talked to a urologist

once about these problems. He was an old guy and just said, "Put up with it. You're fine. It's all in your head." I believe he thought I was lucky to get it up at all.

Rita did make a single appearance in Miami at Bachelors III. Pride celebrations were starting to take place in several big cities during the 1970s. Miami had a few of its own, and Bachelors III had decided to put on a big splashy party one year.

I was telling Douglas and Cliff about this party, and being two of Rita's biggest fans, they convinced me that she had to be resurrected for the occasion. "Nobody's going to know who you are!" they told me.

As much as she represented the opposite of who I was trying to be at the time, Rita was, of course, delighted to make an appearance, even if just for one night. I wore a fabulous gray gown, made for me by LaShay, who was part of Young, Gifted, and Black from The Melody Club. It was all open on the top and lined with silk. I did my hair up in clusters and curls, and I had big, noisy earrings. (A drag tip: Always have earrings that make noise. If you feel like someone doesn't think you're pretty, all you have to do is shake your head, listen to those earrings, and you *feel* pretty!)

I had to bleach my eyebrows again, of course, but came up with a new solution for the next morning at the hospital. I dyed them, rather than putting on mascara. It was a great fix for those occasions when you had to wake up and be your regular self the next day.

Where the Boys Are

After a year in Miami and countless repetitive shifts at the hospital and the restaurant, followed by some bar or another, I was getting antsy. My future wasn't in that city. I had a fascinating, wonderful career at Jackson Memorial Hospital, but I also realized that being a unit clerk was a dead-end street. I could work for thirty years, never make a nickel, and end up with cirrhosis of the liver or confined to a padded room—or else doing drag shows in the hospital cafeteria.

I had a sense that nothing good would come of staying there indefinitely, and I paid attention to it.

Cliff and Douglas had moved yet again, this time to Fort Lauderdale. They called to let me know there was a job waiting for me if I wanted it, so I quit all my jobs in Miami, packed up, and skipped away into the night.

◆ ◆ ◆

My job was tending the pool bar at the Marlin Beach Hotel, which had been made famous by the 1960 film *Where The Boys Are*. I got the job because Cliff had been adopted by Bill Hovan, the hotel owner. I knew Cliff well enough to know that they weren't doing anything very sexual, but I was confused about what Cliff *was* doing. He went up to Fort Lauderdale this skinny little guy—but by the time I got there, he was all beefed up and managing the hotel. Everybody called Cliff a hustler, but that wasn't true. He hustled but not in that way.

The Marlin Beach was *the* premier international gay hotel, with a clientele from all around the world. They drew people like Sylvester, and Grace Jones came in on a motorcycle one night. There was really nothing like it in the world. At the pool bar, we served very upscale and mostly straight-looking gay guys. Again, I was living and working in a very male environment, truly "where the *boys* are," just as Connie Francis said. The Marlin Beach was above having drag shows, or so they thought. A top, very famous drag queen could come in as a patron, but she would never come in to perform. The clients were interested

mostly in themselves and maybe in one another— if it was a tea dance on Sunday afternoon and everybody was drunk and crazy. That was the role they were playing: beautiful, successful men looking for other beautiful, successful men.

Life in Fort Lauderdale was a party. We were all making lots of money and having lots of fun. I would go home from a four- or five-hour shift with $400 to $500 in my pocket from tips. At the tea dances, people would line up twelve deep at the bar. I always had a nice place to live because money was no issue. I could go to the beach every day, had a great tan, and grew my hair really long. We went to the Copa after work to see the drag shows, and then partied all night.

I always got special treatment when I went out because I was the pool bar bartender at the Marlin Beach. Bartenders were minor celebrities, and the gay rags gave all of us fun nicknames. Everybody wanted us to know who they were so we'd make sure they got a drink—and you never knew who might wind up managing the hotel someday.

Reality Wrecks the Party

One night, I got a call. Douglas had been in an accident.

He was on the road back to Miami when a drunk driver in a station wagon hit his car head-on. Wearing seat belts only became mandatory in 1984, and Douglas wasn't wearing one, so he went right into the steering wheel, smashing his face. A child in the other car was killed, and Douglas was rushed immediately to intensive care. They said his condition was critical, and he would need surgery to rebuild his face. Did I have any pictures I could bring in?

I rushed over and told them I was his brother so I wouldn't get hassled. I'd worked in hospitals long enough to know that's how you got access to someone. They took me to his bed. I remember looking at him, turning to the nurse, and starting to say, "This isn't him." But just as I started to say the words, I noticed his hand and realized this *was* Douglas. I'm sure I sobbed a bit because I could hardly recognize this person I knew so well, but then I gathered myself so I could help him.

His face was crushed, his clavicle was broken, and one of his legs needed to be pinned. There were many other injuries as well, but the primary issue was his face. Douglas was a very, very handsome man.

He was tall, thin, and angular, and had an air about him, a presence, and a way of looking at you with one eyebrow raised that was just stunning. He was also a terrific actor and loved the spotlight, so we all expected that he would one day become a model or an actor. But this crash had injured him so badly, they needed pictures to see what he had looked like.

When the doctor found out 1 wasn't Douglas's real brother, he tried to ban me from the hospital. By that time, 1 had contacted his family to let them know what had happened. His mother, Eleanor, called the doctor and said, "You let him in. He's far more of a brother to him than any of his brothers. 1 want him with my son."

They did the surgery, and 1 brought Douglas home with me. His jaw was wired shut so he couldn't talk, but he didn't want to communicate at all. His dream had been taken away. He would never look the way he had looked before, and he was very angry.

He couldn't eat, so 1 tried to whip up tasty meals in the blender. One time, he spat his food out at me. 1 said, "Look, you son of a bitch, if you're going to spit out what 1 give you, you'll starve to death, and you're pretty skinny already."

Douglas would require multiple surgeries and have a lot of scars. He was in for a very long mental and emotional recovery, and 1 don't think he was ever really the same.

On the Road Again

Cliff, meanwhile, continued his relationship with Bill Hovan. They got along fine, until they didn't. Cliff would get fed up with Bill from time to time, and leave. When that happened, everybody in Cliff's sphere got cut off from everything at the Marlin Beach Hotel.

One day, 1 arrived at work and the doorman, who was also the head of security and supposedly a friend of mine, blocked my way.

"I can't let you go in there," he said. I figured that Cliff and Bill had had a fight, but I persisted and kept trying to get past him. He kept blocking my way and saying, "I can't let you in."

I said, "I work here. I was here yesterday!"

All he would say was, "Today, you can't come in."

I had been fired, ostracized, and forbidden access to the hotel, just because Cliff was my friend. Where would I go? What would I do?

Cliff and I met up and conspired. Our attitude, we decided, should be, "Fuck Bill Hovan!" If he was going to cut us off from everything in Fort Lauderdale, we didn't need to be there. We made a plan to travel across the country in a Jeep with Cliff's dog, a schnauzer named Sophie, and camp out wherever we pleased. Cliff brought with him a whole bunch of flyers and other materials promoting the Marlin Beach Hotel (even though neither of us was allowed into the hotel at that point), and this would make us celebrities at any gay bar in the country.

We set off on our big adventure and eventually did make it all the way out to San Francisco. We stayed at an awful hotel in the Tenderloin, went to the Trocadero, and partied a lot until one night, Cliff got a phone call. That's how it always happened. Bill called to apologize and no doubt added, "I'll buy you this or that."

Cliff was persuaded and told me he needed to go home by plane. I agreed to drive the Jeep back to Fort Lauderdale from San Francisco, but I told him that Sophie would not be coming along for the ride. So Sophie went back with Cliff, I stayed in San Francisco and partied a little bit more—until I got the crabs from the mattress in the awful hotel I was staying in. And I didn't even have sex with anyone! I left the city feeling defeated. On the way back east, I visited some places I hadn't seen, but mostly I just drove and thought about my life. I was at loose ends and didn't know where to go next.

I delivered the Jeep back to Cliff. He and Bill had made up, but I still wasn't allowed back into the Marlin Beach, not that I was particularly interested in going there.

The arrangement between Cliff and me when we were traveling was that we would use my credit cards and Cliff would pay me back. That didn't happen, and I wound up carrying a debt that seemed absolutely insurmountable to me, especially now that my lucrative bartending job was a thing of the past. Cliff never did pay me back, even though he was in a position to do so, and I had to file for bankruptcy. That drove a wedge between Cliff and me that wasn't healed until years later. I'm an extremely loyal person, but something happens when trust is broken.

There was always work waiting tables, so I was soon taking shifts at a big, high-end tourist restaurant and a nondescript little neighborhood spot. But I was going nowhere. I didn't know what the answer was at that point, but I knew it wasn't to be found in either of these jobs.

I looked at myself and didn't like the man I was becoming. I wasn't being challenged, and my frustration was bringing out a negative mindset that I just didn't recognize in myself.

I needed to get more serious about life and about work. So, in August of 1978, I hopped in my faded-in-the-Florida-sun lime green Gran Torino (the Rambler American hadn't done well in Fort Lauderdale either) and headed for Atlanta. I needed to come up in the world.

High Times in Atlanta

One of my first job interviews in Atlanta was at Sonny's Saloon, a wild gay bar known for its crazy promotions. They had *Breakfast at Tiffany's* events, drink specials every half hour, and parties for every imaginable holiday—so people were always sloshing around doing strange things.

Sonny's Saloon had old, weathered wood on the outside and was very nicely done on the inside. The walls were all wood and the place was furnished with antiques, set up to look like a long, skinny Western saloon, with round tables and a big, long bar.

The owner was, yes, Sonny. He had another Sonny's Saloon in Detroit and fancied himself quite the entrepreneur. His plan was to create a huge chain of Sonny's Saloons that would become the McDonald's of the gay bar world.

I was hired to manage the bar and a woman named Pola, who would go on to become one of my closest friends, was hired as the bookkeeper. She had just moved to Atlanta from San Francisco, with her friend Jean, after a divorce. A woman named Sandy was the manager, but she left soon after Pola and I arrived. She was much too professional to put up with all the nonsense that went on there, and I don't think she had a lot of faith in Sonny's big plans.

Sonny hightailed it back to Detroit after hiring us, and Pola and I were left in charge. We made Sonny's Saloon so successful that we became local celebrities. We were asked to judge various contests around town and were even written up in the gay rag. They made up names for each of us around the bar's Western theme. I was Matt Dillon from *Gunsmoke*. Pola was Lillie Langtry from *The Westerner*. Sonny was Black Bart, the gentleman outlaw.

It wasn't perfect, but Sonny's reinvigorated me. I was in charge of something successful; it was fast-paced and always changing, and boredom was never an option.

Plus, it brought Pola and me together. On nights we weren't working, we often ate at Jerusacks, where they let you bring your own bottle of wine. We'd sit there and eat oysters and drink until we were just sloshed—and then we'd go looking for boys. Never mind which kind of boys. They just had to be cute. We'd sort all that out later. We would just find them and love them up, get them over to the house, and whoever they wound up with was whoever they wound up with.

Pola was, and still is, very beautiful, and she always looked amazing. She's of Polish descent and has long, lush brown hair that she used to curl, crimp, or put up on top of her head. Everyone always turned to look at her when she walked into a room. She made a lot of her own clothes in those days, so she had things that nobody else had. Even when she wore clothes off the rack, she did something creative with them. She might have a dress with a low scooped neckline, and wear it backward so that she was all covered up in front, but this scoop went all the way down the back so you could see her incredible figure. We called that one her "sleaze dress," and she wore it with a pair of red spiked heels. We would go out to clubs and just dance, dance, dance all night long. Back then, gay boys would've called her a "fag hag" (such a terrible term), but we were truly kindred spirits, both experiencing freedom and joy together.

Atlanta was a continuation of life as a boy and not a drag queen, so naturally the type of person I attracted reflected that. But I was no clearer on what I wanted than when I decided to put Rita on the attic shelf in Miami. (She remained there after I left. I often wonder who found that box and what they must've thought. I still miss those dresses!)

There was more freedom, more craziness, and more exploration in Atlanta. There were casual, anonymous encounters and lots of drugs, but I did as much watching and wondering as I did participating.

*I was still trying to figure out where I belonged—both in the
gay community and in the outside world. In some ways, it was
a new version of the feeling I'd first experienced at age five
in the Shack: There must be something more out there!*

Looking for the Gay Holy Grail

I think my sexual confusion was as much about being in my twenties
as it was about being gay. When we're young, we get pulled in by
shiny objects—people we find attractive but who may not be the best
partners. I would dart from one person or experience to the next: Let
me try this, let me try that, let me try the other thing. In some ways,
it was like drugs—finding out what drug produced what kind of high,
which ones I liked and which ones I didn't.

I would sometimes look at other people's situations and want
what they had—whether they were in relationships or just hot and
sleeping around. But when I took a closer look, it was never as rosy
and glorious as it had seemed.

I sometimes felt like I was swimming through deep seaweed,
looking for some Holy Grail of relationships; if I could just define
what it was, then I could set my sights on how to reach it.

*In those years, I was very far from understanding that, really, there
is no such thing as the ideal relationship. We can just go ahead and
do whatever is comfortable for us. Everything else be damned!*

* * *

At the time, I was living at an apartment that Sonny kept at the
Darlington, a tall brick building near Piedmont Hospital. It was a
cute little studio with a bathroom, a fantastic view, and more roaches
than you could count, let alone get rid of. Sonny was happy to let me

live there because he deducted the rent from my salary—and since the bar was doing so well, he didn't have to be in Atlanta much. With this wonderful little apartment, I could walk to work. And I was never lonely. Pola lived with me until she and her friend Jean could find their own place.

Meanwhile, we continued to build up our clientele, bringing a sense of occasion and creativity to everything we did. One night, we staged a Spring Fling for which Pola made special tablecloths and put cut camellias all over the walls. We came up with more crazy theme parties, charmed everybody in town, and created an amazing atmosphere at the bar. It became quite a phenomenon.

Sonny started honestly believing that his Saloons were about to become a household name in the gay world. There were only two locations, but he had delusions of grandeur and was spending money hand over fist on things like "corporate learning" and "staff development." He was spending so much money that we could hardly make payroll. Pola and I soon realized that he was grinding this place into the ground—so we might as well just have fun.

Teetering on the Edge

Sonny's Saloon always had a "Christmas in July" theme, because nothing says "North Pole" like summertime in Georgia. Every inch of the bar was decorated with lights and garlands in red and green, and one night I thought it would be a great idea to dress up as Santa Claus. Pola would be my elf. We had a wonderful time getting ready, and I had purchased some fantastic three-inch-long green and red eyelashes. We had been drinking Stoli all afternoon, and when I went to put on these lashes, I realized that I'd forgotten my eyelash glue. We were down to the wire, and there was no time to go home. The show must go on, so I grabbed some Krazy Glue and we had a great evening as Santa and his elf.

We closed the bar, and Pola said she had to go home. I should have gone home, too, but instead said to myself, "Why don't I go over to Bulldogs?"

I was still driving my Gran Torino, otherwise known as the Quaalude Car. There was only one fender on that car that wasn't smashed up—because if you drove around in a quaalude car, things just jumped out in front of you and you had to dodge them, or not.

Bulldogs and Backstreet were two gay bars next door to one another. Both faced Peachtree Street in front and Piedmont Avenue in back. Backstreet had a driveway from the parking lot out to Piedmont—but at Bulldogs, the parking lot was up a level with a big ledge facing Piedmont, so you had to drive back out the front way.

I guess I had a good time at Bulldogs, because when I got out to the car, I thought I was at Backstreet. I headed out what I presumed was the driveway out to Piedmont, but instead the car got stuck up on the ledge at Bulldogs, fifteen feet above the ground. I was sitting at the wheel, dressed and made up as Santa Claus with my three-inch red and green eyelashes, very high, as the car teetered back and forth. I didn't know whether I would crash down onto Piedmont or slam back into the parking lot.

A crowd began to gather, and someone called the police. When they arrived, I opened the door, which was a big mistake, and shouted out what seemed like the most appropriate thing to say: "Merry Christmas!"

The police were not as amused as I was. They hauled my car away and hauled me off to jail. I was allowed to make one phone call, to George, my assistant manager at Sonny's Saloon, whom I had hired because he was even better looking than Clark Gable. At this point, I was coming back to myself a little bit. Part of me felt like I was watching these events from the sidelines, but I soon realized that I needed to pull it together—quickly.

I looked around and saw that I was in a holding cell. One of my fellow inmates was actually handcuffed to the bench where he was sitting, and his condition wasn't good. The other guy looked up at me and said, "I already killed somebody tonight."

There was a little hole in the door, and I realized that everybody on the other side was staring in at me. I still had on my Santa Claus costume and my red and green eyelashes—and I vaguely remembered that I had put on those eyelashes with Krazy Glue. I decided steps must be taken. I took off my Santa Claus suit and folded it nicely, so that I was just wearing jeans and a T-shirt—and three-inch-long red and green eyelashes.

I took a deep breath. I grabbed those eyelashes and pulled as hard as I could. I understood intuitively that the noise I really wanted to make could get me in a lot of trouble with my two roommates—so I clenched my butt cheeks and just made a little muffled sound. The show must go on!

I looked up, and who did I see but George, come to get me out. He told me he'd already called a lawyer, who showed up almost immediately. I told him what I'd done, and he told me he could fix it, but, "The only reason you're going to get out of this is because you're going to give me enough money to *get* you out of this. And because nobody will believe it! But Tom, *you can never do this again!*"

That was our Christmas in July. I vowed to be good, but it didn't last forever.

◆ ◆ ◆

Back at work, Pola and I started making a fuss because Sonny was spending so much money on useless programs, we didn't have enough to pay the staff. Sonny decided it was time for him to come back to Atlanta and "straighten me out." I decided that if he was coming to town, I was leaving—getting out of Dodge, to continue the Western metaphor. I was happy to part ways, even if it meant that I had to move out of the Darlington apartment—the roaches were bad company. This was not why I had moved to Atlanta.

· · ·

There were always other restaurant and bar jobs to be had, but working nights and going out after hours was not going to get me to where I wanted to be financially.

> *If I was serious about reinventing myself,*
> *I was going to need a more traditional job.*

(And, subconsciously, I probably knew that I should find an environment that didn't include crazy chefs, crazy hours, and maybe quite so many drugs.)

Progress isn't always going
to be linear—be prepared
for stumbles along the way
and even some push and pull
between different things you
might want in the moment. And
if you feel you've lost your way,
always keep growing, and you
will come back to yourself.

SEVEN

Stepping Up in the World

THE WORLD OF MEDICINE CONTINUED TO FASCI-nate me, so I applied to work at the Psychiatric Institute of Atlanta, a private, thirty-bed psychiatric hospital. This was an opportunity to experience different areas that were rapidly advancing during the late '70s.

My first job at the PIA was patient unit manager. I also worked there as a mental health associate through a temporary agency, which allowed me to take on more shifts and make a little more money. Very quickly, they also offered me the job of managing the clinical lab. I knew nothing about managing a lab and felt those imposter feelings creep up, surrounded as I was by a staff who was licensed and very experienced.

But I knew I was a quick and confident learner, so I jumped at the lab manager job—and the much higher salary that came with it.

Between the temp role and the lab job, I saw all sides of the place and even got to interact with patients. Like a sponge, I absorbed it all—and not just the technical information. I watched how people were treated, what effect that had on them, and how well and quickly they healed.

I was serving people on a deep level, and it just lit me up inside.

This was a time when people were trying to determine whether depression was biologically or chemically induced, and whether it was the result of external factors or genetics. PIA was doing cutting-edge research in this area that I got to participate in, working with all kinds of patients, from catatonic old men and women to people who had been horribly traumatized. I saw the worst of the worst of what people can do to one another—one poor young woman had been abused by her father and brother using broom handles—and what it took to heal those invisible traumas.

It was tremendously sad, but I never turned away from the horror.

*I seemed to be able to talk to and connect with the
patients, and that made me feel good in turn.*

And there were lighter moments, too. One patient, Marjorie, kept coming over to where I sat and striking up conversations—so inevitably we became friends, even though that was against the rules. She was always working on getting a pass so she could go outside and take a walk or sit in the sun, and she was constantly in and out of PIA. No sooner would we release her than she'd be back again.

Finally, I said to her, "Girl, what's going on with you? You come in here and you're all depressed. We get you all fixed up and you go back, and next thing you know, you're back here again. What's going on with you?"

"Oh, it's that husband of mine!" she said.

I kept wondering how she could afford to stay with us so much. One day, I looked at her and said, "I'm not supposed to say this, but do you realize that for what you're paying to stay here and only get outside in the sunshine when you can get a pass, you could be at the Ritz every day getting room service? Did that ever cross your mind?"

Well, a bunch of doctors came in the next day, asking me what had happened to Marjorie. She had told them that she was cured, that she was getting a divorce, and that she wouldn't be back. I thought, "Damn, maybe this is a calling!"

PIA was a great experience for me. I could work a lot of shifts because I was technically an employee of a temp service, and PIA didn't have to pay overtime. And I felt good about what I was doing there. I decided then and there, shaking my fist at God like Scarlett O'Hara, "I'll never wait tables again."

Heal Thyself

I was beginning to have a more sophisticated view about medicine and health, and I started to consider my own approach to health and how I was treating my body and mind.

I stopped drinking and doing drugs while working at PIA. At the bars and restaurants, as long as you showed up on time for your shifts or to go on stage and you could pull it together even when you were hungover, you'd be fine. And no one would look at you funny if you needed some assistance from half a quaalude to get through the night. That obviously wasn't going to happen at PIA—and nor would I have wanted it to. All around me were examples of where that kind of behavior could lead.

*I took the job, and myself, seriously and was happy
to focus on who I was in the daylight.*

Some of that focus was taking place literally. During my time at
the PIA, I weighed about 150 pounds—but in my mind, I weighed
about 200. At the time, I had semi-reconciled (temporarily) with
Cliff, who had broken up with Bill Hovan (again), and moved with
some guy named Jorge to Asheville, North Carolina. They had
opened a health food store, and Cliff had immersed himself in learning all about supplements, exercise, and health. After a visit to North
Carolina, I started taking some of these supplements and generally
paying more attention to nutrition. It wasn't rocket science that what
you put into your body affected how you felt and that you could help
your body if you put the right things into it! That prompted me to
think about my lifelong preoccupation with weight.

Working at the PIA helped me see things I hadn't seen before. I
realized that, for me, there was a psychological component to weight.
I'd spent so much of my childhood and adolescence feeling like
I didn't fit in where I was, that I didn't belong, and that everybody
around me could tell. Naturally, in my head, this was all tied up with
my appearance and my weight, and unconsciously, I was so fearful
that I would gain it back, stick out like a sore thumb, and once again
be cast out. Even when I got down below 150, I still felt fat. If you've
ever been fat, I'm not sure that feeling ever truly leaves you. Even
today, those thoughts aren't completely gone. My weight fluctuates
very little, but occasionally I still feel heavy—even when other people
are telling me I look too thin.

One night during the PIA years, Pola and I went out and, in the
course of the evening, had our picture taken. She had on a beautiful
denim outfit that she had made, and I had on jeans and a sweater.
When the pictures came back, I could not believe my eyes. I looked

like a stick. I had no hips, no butt, no anything. That was the first time I realized that something was amiss with how I saw my body and how unhealthy it was to have subjected it to stunts like the Hawaiian Punch diet and my one-egg-a-day routine. My determination was activated again, and that was also the time my weight started to get stable.

Surrogate Drag Queen

I had left Rita behind in an attic in Miami. She had made her one appearance down in Florida with the Gibson Girl tendrils but had not been seen since then.

I had, of course, gravitated to some of the Atlanta drag bars: Charlie Brown's showcase at Backstreet, the Sweet Gum Head, and finally, Illusions, which is where I met Vikki Lawrence, who actually resembled Vicki Lawrence!

Vikki and I had the kind of relationship that was becoming a pattern with me. We got to know one another, started hanging out, became close and intense—but quite frankly, we weren't sexually compatible, although we had some fun trying. We could have spent a lot of time together and had a very loving relationship, but we were both looking for the same type of partner and certainly weren't finding it in each other. Still, Vikki and I had a great time together.

I'd been at the PIA for a couple of years when they decided to have a huge Christmas party with several other hospitals at the Hyatt Regency. It was a beautiful hotel with multiple floors open to a huge atrium. I planned to take Vikki as my date and shared this idea with two of my doctor friends. One was married; the other was gay. (He wasn't out, because people did not officially come out much at that time, but everybody knew about him and his boyfriend, though his boyfriend didn't attend the party with him.) These two doctors were simply horrified that I would consider such a thing, but I just wanted to see what would happen. I wasn't trying to hide the fact that I was gay, and Vikki was stunning as a woman. What could they do to me?

Vikki was delighted. She was a celebrity in town, and everybody knew her, so she had no problem at all being "exposed." Now, mind you, Vikki could pass as a woman any day. The only thing you might question about Vikki was her hands—if she had no nails on, they looked a little suspect. I should also mention that Vikki was bitchy, in a very fabulous way. She had been Miss Florida and Miss A Lot of Other Things. She was a star, and she knew it.

I drove to pick her up in my newish blue Caprice Classic. She was wearing a very smart copper bugle bead pantsuit with a top, flowing pants, and a little see-through something over it. She looked stunning, except that her waist-length hair was all up in curlers! I asked her if she was going to take them out, and she said, "No, it's raining, so you're going to drive up to the Hyatt and let me out, then go park the car. By the time you get back, I'll be ready for you."

I decided to let her control her entrance the way she wanted, let her get out, then parked. She waited for me underneath an awning, where she took out her curlers. When I got back, she was shaking her long hair loose.

"Are you ready?" I asked.

"I'm ready," she said.

As we walked into the atrium, she slipped off her jacket and carried it over her shoulder with one finger. She glided on ahead of me, and I trailed behind, taking in all the heads that were turning to watch our entrance. We were *it*.

When we got in, one of the doctors pulled me aside and said, "I never thought you'd have the balls!"

Funny choice of words.

Second Time's a Charm?

In early 1982, I got a strange call. Cliff and Bill Hovan were, once more, back together—and they were on their way to Saint Thomas to oversee the building of their new house down there. They wanted me to come down to Fort Lauderdale for four months, live in their current house, keep an eye on some redecorating they were having done while they were away, and manage the Marlin Beach Hotel. My official title would be assistant general manager. They said they couldn't get rid of the general manager, but that he wouldn't get in my way.

I already had a job—two jobs in one, in fact—but my salary at PIA had hit a ceiling, despite my attempts to lobby for a raise. I was still trying to dig myself out of the financial hole Cliff himself had left me in so I should have known better, but I saw this as a chance to live in a gorgeous house, make a lot of money, and manage a marquee gay hotel on the beach. So I loaded all my belongings into a U-Haul and moved to Fort Lauderdale once again.

Their house was on ritzy Middle River Drive, and it was beautiful. I was to have a little corner bedroom and bathroom to myself while the renovation was happening over on the other side of the house. There was a wonderful pool in the backyard, and everything was lovely—except that I was once again connected to Bill Hovan. Once Bill and Cliff left, quiet descended except for the construction noise on the other side of the house and the cleaning noises of an overzealous maid from Bolivia who didn't speak any English. I didn't speak any Spanish, so our communication was minimal.

That summer, I happened to attend the Miss Florida Pageant at the Fontainebleau Hotel in Miami because I knew many of the queens who were competing. I wanted to be noticed, so I wore a white tux and top hat and had a glorious tan. I looked stunning!

One of the queens competing was Dana Manchester, whom I'd met and hit it off with years earlier. Dana looked like a really cute girl in drag and a really, really cute boy out of drag. John (Dana's boy name) was a theater kid who had trained at Juilliard and probably could have been a very successful actor had he not preferred being Dana Manchester.

Well, who should win the contest but Dana! She wore a fantastic Bob Mackie gown—copper bugle beads, again!—and was just gorgeous. I was quite enamored and did exactly what I had done with Anne Marie/Jimmy. I became the debonair Southern gentleman and said, "I must be your escort for the evening." She had no other escort and called me her white knight in shining armor. We looked amazing together, one thing led to another, and she came back to Cliff and Bill's house with me.

Nothing much came of it, other than that wonderful night at the pageant. The same thing happened with Dana as happened with most of my other drag queen relationships. They thought they were getting a big butch top, so it never really worked. What I wanted, honestly, was just to wear their dresses! Still, Dana Manchester and I enjoyed one another's company and had a lot of fun until we figured all that out.

Meanwhile, I actually did go to work at the hotel. I remembered how much I used to make as a bartender and decided to supplement my assistant general manager income by working a couple of shifts at the pool bar. Just to get the inside scoop on what was going on at the hotel, of course.

I also had a little apartment at the hotel where I stayed sometimes. It was right by a tiny satellite bar where the employees often went after work. They would have a drink and gossip about the day—and had no idea that I could hear every word they said. I knew who was doing what, and who was stealing what, in every corner of the hotel. Suddenly, people were getting fired left and right, and they couldn't figure out how all this compromising information had reached management.

Cliff had once told me that not every penny the Marlin Beach Hotel took in was being reported to the IRS—and I saw that first-hand when I got access to some of the financial information as assistant general manager. It became very clear to me that the pool bar had never, since its inception, even been on the books.

That was where the money for the new house in Saint Thomas had come from—I was earning it for Bill at the pool bar. Several people knew what was going on and enjoyed lifetime job security as a result. In fact, everybody seemed to be making a percentage off this operation.

There was a lot of action at the Marlin Beach that summer. Still, I was disillusioned and very disgruntled by the thought of Bill Hovan living the high life while I worked extra shifts at the pool bar. I needed some distraction.

The hotel was still *the* place to go, but it had deteriorated a lot since its heyday. Everything was broken, and God knows what you might catch in some of those rooms. I was pondering all this one day, and my gaze drifted up to the upper deck above the pool bar where all the tea dances were held. It was covered, so it was nice and shady in the late afternoon, and ran the whole length of the building.

I called John, the superintendent in charge of keeping the building together. He could fix anything—if you could find him. I finally tracked him down and asked him if he could do some light construction work on the upper deck.

"Why?" he asked. I told him it wasn't his job to know why. He immediately called Saint Thomas, and they called me. I told them I had a brilliant idea. They should just stay in Saint Thomas, I said, and trust me to handle it. For some reason, they did.

My vision was to turn the upper deck above the pool bar into a stage. On Sunday evenings, after the tea dances, *we would put on drag shows*. I would bring in the big names: Dina Jacobs, Rachel Wells, Vikki Lawrence, and all the other titleholders.

It had never been done at the Marlin Beach. Drag shows were over at the Copa, for God's sake. We didn't do that kind of stuff! It was a scandal! But I just kept planning and plotting.

I hyped up the event for weeks, and by the Fourth of July, the stage was ready. It jutted out over the pool, so it would be the center of attention. Not only that, but it would take place in the daytime, when we normally did tea dances. Between the holiday and the revolutionary act of staging a drag show on the sacred ground of the Marlin, the place was more packed than I had ever seen it before.

The crowd—and the staff—were everything from thrilled to horrified. I walked around in my Marlin Beach T-shirt and little shorts, tanned and long-haired, looking hot and very pleased with myself.

The show began with Rachel Wells, dressed as a flight attendant, coming out to do a hot '70s number. Dina Jacobs came out and did "Sweet Dreams (Are Made of This)" by Eurythmics.

Then Vikki came out in a crystal coffin to "Dreams" by Grace Slick. She did her number, then got back into that crystal coffin, still visible to the crowd. I draped a black silk sheet over it, spun it around, and when I whipped off that silk sheet, she was gone. The crowd went absolutely wild. (She did the same act for the Miss Florida Pageant— only that time, the sheet was whipped off to reveal a cougar in the coffin, wearing the same necklace she'd worn for the number. Vikki was absolutely sensational.)

The show was hugely successful and became the talk of the town. Vikki was a big hit and wound up moving to Fort Lauderdale and working at the Copa. (I also introduced her to a bartender at the Marlin named David, with whom she was much more compatible than she had been with me.)

The shows happened every week, and their fantastic, scandalous success gave the Marlin Beach the shot in the arm it needed. I had become a bit of a celebrity in town, and the new face of the Marlin.

And without even meaning to, I had started to chip away at the walls that I had put up to separate these sides of my personality. Like I had done by taking Vikki to the Hyatt.

· · ·

The Marlin was doing very well, we were partying all the time, and we started having dress-up nights. I found some wonderful droplet earrings with all different colors of green: fern, sage, forest, Kelly, you name it. They were like little crystal balls, and they made a lot of noise. I used to wear them in the office when I was counting the money, and I would shake those crystal balls to get me through the boredom of it.

There was a lot of cocaine around the hotel that summer, but I had avoided the epidemic until one night when I was counting the money and jingling my earrings. I looked around and thought, "Wow! I'm counting very fast, and these people are counting even faster! Let's just see what they're on!"

One day, I was coming down from the upper deck, walking through the restaurant and thinking about what I might have for dinner after a little stroll on the beach, when who should I spot walking into the hotel but Cliff. Normally, this would have been fine. Normally, we would have had an embrace. Normally, a lot of things would've happened.

Instead, I just walked right past him, out the door to the beach, and yelled over my shoulder, "Good to see ya. You should have called first." I had come into my own over the past four months, gotten the goods on Bill Hovan, and no longer felt compelled to be nice to Bill or Cliff. Bill Hovan was a crook, and Cliff still hadn't paid back the money from our trip to San Francisco—even though he and Bill were apparently rolling in it. He hadn't even bothered to let me know they were coming back. I was hurt and angry, and so full of myself that I didn't feel like hiding it anymore. Nothing about Bill or Cliff felt good, especially since Cliff and I had once been very close friends.

Cliff shouted after me, "Tommy! Tommy! Tommy, come here! Come here." I just kept walking.

· · ·

On the outside, my life looked pretty good at that point. I had a great title, but I had started spending a lot of money on cocaine. I had a good job, but the Marlin Beach was getting stranger by the day, and now Bill was back. Bill, who hated me and was embezzling money.

I see now that the theme for my life in those days was probably a lack of respect. Lack of respect for myself. Lack of respect for money. Lack of respect for the gift of life. Lack of respect for everything. I had moved around, trying to figure out who I was, and opened my eyes and arms to as much of the world as I could.

And I had started being more willing to allow different sides of my life and personality to overlap. But I was being careless with all of it, and that was not at all who I wanted to be in the world, nor the impact I wanted to have.

Not only was I going nowhere, but I must've had some guardian angels looking out for me to keep me from being totally swallowed up by the lifestyle. After eight months, the summer was finally over. The Marlin Beach Hotel was over. My party was over, and I headed back to Atlanta.

Reset on Roxboro Road

I was at loose ends when I moved back to Atlanta. I didn't have a job, I didn't know where my life was heading, and I wasn't sure what the course correction should be.

I had a hard time finding work but finally landed a position as patient unit manager of three ICUs at Henry Egleston Hospital for Children, which was part of Emory University. I started getting paychecks, although when I saw the first one, I was kind of shocked and thought, "This won't even buy a good pair of eyelashes!" Still, I had a steady job where people respected me, and I could work a lot of overtime and keep getting on my feet financially.

I moved with Pola into a two-bedroom apartment on Roxboro Road, with a block of little old ladies all around us. Pola and I had both calmed down a bit since the Sonny's Saloon days, and she was working as a bookkeeper for a chain of theaters. We had always been close, but our relationship deepened and grew into a new phase, just like we were.

My parents came to visit a few times, and of course, they thought that Pola and I had set up house together as a romantic couple. They loved Pola, and I let them think that so they wouldn't be worrying or wondering what I might be doing. It was a great way to hide.

◆ ◆ ◆

Mom and Dad had kept their own secret from me around that time. Maybe not so much a secret as something they just "didn't want to worry me about." At some point a year or so earlier, Dad had been diagnosed with prostate cancer. He had had pains in his back and thought he might have injured himself at work or gotten a kidney infection, so he went to see Dr. Piroman, the same urologist who had performed my bloody cystoscope procedure following the Hawaiian Punch diet all those years ago.

Dr. Piroman not only found the prostate cancer immediately but also discovered that it was quite advanced. He called my mother into the room on the spot and told them, "You need surgery to remove your prostate. You have a fifty-fifty chance of living through the surgery, but without it, you're going to die. You will never control your urine again, and you will never have sex again. I'm going to leave you two alone for fifteen minutes, and then I'll be back to hear your decision."

I wasn't there, and I didn't learn about all of this until much later, so I don't know how that was for them, but I suspect they were struck dumb by the news. They decided on the operation, of course, but before it could take place, they put my father on massive doses of female hormones to shrink his prostate. He grew breasts, and his fingernails fell off. His gray hair turned black again, he got extremely constipated, and he had horrible hot flashes. Later on, he would tell me that the worst part was that it robbed him of his masculinity.

Dad took time off from work, and the McCormick family made sure that he had the best care possible at the McKeever Clinic. He had a radical prostatectomy and was in the hospital for fourteen days. Back then, they cut you open and took out everything except the bare minimum you needed to function.

My father coped with it all very well, but I'm sure he was in enormous pain because he was allergic to morphine and Demerol. He discovered while he was in the Navy that these drugs made him crazy—and that somehow this condition was hereditary, so none of his children should ever even try to take them. (I don't know if that was true, but we had been instructed never to take them, and we didn't.)

Dad had a Foley catheter put in, and he coped well with that, too. He was such a model patient that they asked him to come in and talk with newer patients about it. One of these patients was a little bonkers and always screamed when he saw my father, "Dr. Foley!

Dr. Foley!" Dad called him an old Georgia hick, which I thought was funny because my father was an old Florida cracker.

During the day, Dad had an external catheter with a bag strapped to his leg. At night, he had a different catheter with a leg bag. There were many explosions of the leg bag and many leaks, which led to my parents not staying with me when they visited and taking along all kinds of supplies, metal trays, and contraptions with them when they went anywhere. Sometimes Dad would design and build a new leg bag or some other paraphernalia that worked better for him. I don't know whether those contraptions were actually any better, but they gave him some sense of control over his situation, which was no small thing. He would have to deal with the bags for the rest of his life. But of course, he went back to work as soon as he could.

. . .

If you're feeling stuck or lost and unsure about who you're meant to be, take a step away from focusing on "you" and look outward to others. Just as important as "Who do I want to be?" is "What impact do I want to have?" Making deep connections with people and helping those who need it is not only a way to do good but a way to get in touch with yourself again from a place of compassion.

. . .

EIGHT

Enter the Business Suit

I WAS BACK TO COBBLING TOGETHER MULTIPLE INCOMES to earn enough money to get by. I could always go back to waiting tables, but by this point, I knew that wasn't going to be the thing that pushed me forward to where I wanted to be in life.

So, in 1984, I answered a want ad for a part-time customer service rep at MCI. Until the year before, the Bell companies had had a monopoly on the whole telecommunications industry; MCI was one of the new phone companies that came in when the monopoly was broken, ushering in the era of competitive long-distance telephone service. (MCI was purchased by WorldCom in 1998 and, ultimately, bought by Verizon.) The company was growing fast and hiring like crazy.

Dressed in a suit, I entered the MCI offices at the Ashford Green building for my interview. There were phone books stacked on tables, against the walls, everywhere. They were using the phone books to market to people, calling them up to ask if they wanted to buy their long-distance services. I met with a woman named Cindy Davis and a man named Allen Floyd, who would be my bosses. I don't think they hired me in the room, but it wasn't long after. They desperately needed positions filled. This was a new company trying to get itself together, and chaos reigned.

Fortunately, I am really, really good with chaos. I knew exactly zero about telecommunications, but I'd already proven to myself that I was a quick, eager learner, and I wasn't scared of new things.

Looking back now, I can see that I've always been good at observing people and situations, and unafraid to say what I think or take action when it's necessary. Maybe that came from always feeling a little on the outside—new things didn't intimidate me.

I had a knack for being present, assessing what needed to happen in order to get a good outcome, and jumping in to make that thing happen. Plus, I was (and remain) nothing if not adaptable. Just ask Rita...

All that experience waiting tables and working in hospitals served me well, too.

Whether I was serving food, pouring drinks, or putting in IVs, I knew how to communicate with people, even when they were at their worst, and help them get what they needed.

I didn't think of myself specifically in this way at the time—I wanted the customer service job because it paid well, and it felt like taking a big step forward toward stability and the kind of future I envisioned for myself. What I didn't know was that I'd found a role that seemed built for me, and it would set me on a truly unexpected rise in the business world.

· · ·

I worked at Egleston Hospital during the day, then would do a four-hour shift at MCI in the evenings. I reached back for everything

I'd learned as a patient unit coordinator (the person responsible for managing chaos on any hospital unit), for everything Rita had learned about negotiating and managing the people around her, and into my polite Southern roots that I knew would serve me well in customer service—and then I dipped into the combination of smarts and wiliness (the varmit!) that had kept me afloat since childhood, and I stepped up.

That began my meteoric rise at MCI. I was a master at handling all the crazies and the angry people calling in about problems with their phone service, and other people in the office loved working with me. After about three weeks, my supervisors begged me to quit Egleston and come on board full-time. At first, I somehow managed to do both—a full-time role at MCI with daily shifts at Egleston. When the topic of promoting me to supervisor came up, they told me I had to pick one, so I did. Not only was the pay at MCI much better, but the work itself was more challenging and engaged parts of my brain that felt good to exercise.

Scooting up the Corporate Ladder

As supervisor, I was working directly under Allen Floyd and was managing a group of about fourteen or fifteen customer service reps who were doing the job I had just been doing. Because MCI promoted from within, it felt like a true meritocracy. I sat at a desk out among the people I was supervising, taking calls and coaching them as they handled service calls. They gave me a long, long phone cord so I could get up and walk around as I talked to customers and trainees. I felt like the king of the world, or maybe the queen of the world because it reminded me a little of Rita being on stage!

As the manager of my little group, I did performance reviews and quality control, and then had a weekly meeting with Allen to update him on how everything was running. There were multiple supervisors at my level under Allen, and while there was a sense of healthy competition between us, it really did feel like we were all on the same side, all part of a new type of technology and service that was growing and changing how people used the telephone.

· · ·

My life at MCI was wonderful, complex, and fast-moving. Not only was it a fantastic, generous company, but I sensed that this job would be a turning point in my life—and it was.

Once I was promoted to supervisor, the version of me that I was showing the world changed.

I had to get up in the morning and be presentable, and my old habit of popping a quaalude during a shift was no longer an option (though I still smoked pot at home). I wore a suit and tie to work, or at least a sports coat. I was respected and acknowledged—and paid well! The reaction I got from the people above me, and those on the team I supervised, was not unlike the positive reaction and admiration I'd felt as Rita. These were obviously two very different things on the surface, but both gave me a focused outlet for all my energy. I could use my brain and creativity to solve problems and engage with people. But now, the work had a future. I really couldn't say that about any of the jobs I'd had prior to that time.

My hours were long, but I loved it. In fact, life became largely about work at that point. Pola and I were still living together on Roxboro Road when I started the job, and it's not like we didn't go out and have fun, or that I didn't have sex, but work was so consuming that everything else felt secondary. And I was glad for it. In fact, putting sex on the back burner actually helped me ease up on a lot of anxiety.

I visited home a bit more often, too. I'd always gone back for holidays, and to help out if someone was having a health issue, but in the Rita days, there was always so much more to hide and to work around, which made it difficult. Not so in the corporate world. No more worrying about growing my eyebrows in! Interestingly, now that I had this job, my parents expected to see me *less*. It was like I was excused from visits because I had a reputable job, and God forbid they disrupt it!

My parents continued to visit, still harboring the fantasy that Pola and I were together, which I did nothing to dispute. She would go with me to MCI functions, and Mom and Dad would see pictures from those events in frames around our apartment. Her brothers visited one time—ages fifteen, sixteen, seventeen, and eighteen—and who knows what they thought. If I had been straight, maybe something else might have developed with Pola, because we truly did finish one another's sentences.

Giving the Bride Away

Alas, in 1985, Pola moved back to the Bay Area. To this day, our friendship is one of the deepest I've had in my life, but once she moved, we obviously didn't get to see one another as often as we wanted. She'd met and fallen in love with a man named David, and they were going to get married at their house on Altura in Oakland. I took a few days off from work and flew out early because I was going to do the flowers and help Pola with the final arrangements.

When I arrived, I dutifully went off to the flower mart and came home with armloads of beautiful flowers and vases that we placed all around the house. I was also going to make bouquets for the bridesmaids, and I spread out all those flowers across the bed in my room.

By that point, I had been promoted to a supervisor position at MCI and decided I would give up marijuana, but David came in the

day before the wedding and tempted me with a joint. I said, "I probably shouldn't do this," but you know by now how that goes. I ended
up taking two of these big flowerpots and twirling them around, and
then twirling myself around and around and around, and collapsed
on my bed in the middle of all the bridesmaids' flowers, looking up
at the ceiling. I was clearly more sensitive and susceptible to this
West Coast pot. My head kept spinning even after I collapsed, and I
thought, "What have I done to myself?"

Of course, I pulled myself together. I would've done anything
for Pola (I still would), and this was not going to be how I showed
up for her wedding day. Pola's father had had a stroke and couldn't
walk, so I had the honor of walking her around the yard and down
a stone staircase, then down the aisle to deliver her to him at the
altar so he could give her away. She looked so beautiful in her white
dress with little feathers in her hair. She got so nervous and rigid at
one point that I thought I might have to pick her up and carry her

down the aisle. It was a beautiful
ceremony, and they lived in that
house for years.

◆ ◆ ◆

Back in Atlanta, my awakening
continued. I look back now and
consider myself so lucky to have
found the MCI job when I did. It
was the perfect time and place
for a person like me to come
in and create opportunities for
myself. I wasn't a college graduate, and I wasn't experienced
in this area of technology per se,

but I knew what my strengths were and that I was determined to do my best at whatever the job at hand was.

If there was something I didn't understand or know how to do, I knew I'd find some alternative solution. I can see now that I had a great deal of trust in myself, even if I didn't realize that at the time.

Those around me at the company were starting to see me as someone who could have a real future there, and I was ready for it.

When the imposter feelings start to creep in, remember: You can't be an imposter of yourself! Everything in *your* past has led you to this point. These new and challenging situations are meant to shake up your complacency about yourself and show you just how much you've changed and grown.

NINE

Bubby

I N THE FALL OF 1985, I WAS AT HOME ONE EVENING, tired after a long day of work, and I got a phone call from Bubby out in San Francisco. This was unusual. We spoke every so often, but it was not a regular thing for him to call me out of the blue if it wasn't around a holiday or birthday.

He told me he had been sick and that the doctor he saw had diagnosed him with bronchitis. He knew I had a lot of experience in hospitals and around patients, and he wanted to know what I thought about it.

As he described his symptoms, my heart sank.

This was early on in the AIDS epidemic—it was still known as ARC at the time—and San Francisco was the epicenter. Somehow, I just knew.

Under any other circumstances, I would never have thought to take time off. It was almost a startup mentality dominating the company at the time: You were given time-off benefits, but you never took them because the work was simply too much and too crazy. But I decided that I would be flying out to San Francisco no matter what they said.

Three days later, his best friend, Jimmy, called me at work to tell me that Bubby had been admitted to Ward 5A at San Francisco General Hospital, which would become very famous as the AIDS ward, and that I'd better come out right away.

I didn't tell Allen Floyd any details, other than my brother was very sick, in the hospital, and I had to fly out to be with him. When you're in those situations, people can tell if you're bullshitting, and he knew I was serious.

"Okay, we'll make it work," he told me. "How long do you think you'll be out?"

I told him I had no idea what I was walking into. That they let me take as long as I needed is one of the many reasons MCI remains one of the best companies I have ever worked for.

Though I'd been working at MCI for about a year, I didn't have the money for a last-minute plane ticket to San Francisco. I didn't want to ask my parents for it because I wanted to assess the situation myself before discussing anything with them. They didn't even know Bubby was gay, and to hit them with the bombshell that not only was he gay but also dying from "gay cancer" would have been too much for them.

So, I called my mother's best friend, Liz, who had been like a second mother to me growing up, and told her I needed to borrow two hundred dollars, but I couldn't tell her why. She gave me the money, no questions asked, and I flew out to San Francisco.

Ward 5A

In 1985, the level of care for those sick with AIDS was absolutely shameful. Patients were isolated, ostracized, and treated as less than human by medical staff who were scared to be in the same room with them, even as they encased themselves in the big plastic suits and respirators you'd see in a cheap sci-fi film. The general public was poorly informed and terrified, but even those who should have known better approached patients in a dehumanizing way that would have sapped anyone of the will to live.

When I first walked into Ward 5A, it felt like a world apart—an amazing cocoon focused entirely on people with AIDS and those who were there to help them. It was ruled by compassion, humanity, and the understanding that, despite the ravages of this still-mysterious illness, the patients deserved to be treated as people.

In one sense, it was like the scene in *Gone with the Wind* after the Battle of Atlanta. Everywhere you looked, people were suffering and dying. You knew that nobody was going to get out of 5A alive. Not one soul was going to get up and walk out of there.

And yet, there was also a tremendous spirit of love in that ward. A gorgeous girl named Rita Rocket flew around in this crazy outfit, singing and passing out brownies, trying to make people happy in the midst of absolute despair. A lot of people like Rita Rocket came to 5A and did their best to lift people's spirits. I remember a poster on the wall that said, "When you think you're at the end of your rope, tie a knot."

Before I went in to see Bubby, I walked around checking things out. I wanted to get the lay of the land, and because I knew they would eventually be there as well, I wanted to see Ward 5A through my parents' eyes; once an observer, always an observer. One of the first things I saw was a rack of pamphlets about AIDS. They talked about dos and don'ts—what little people knew about that back then—and contained words like "gay" and "fisting." I thought, "Hmm, maybe I should take a pamphlet and read it." I wanted to preview everything my parents might be exposed to *before* they saw it. I was pretty sure I did not want my father to read that pamphlet, much less my sweet little Southern mother.

When I was ready to go in, a volunteer from the Shanti Project came to talk to me. This organization's sole purpose was to provide emotional and practical support for people with AIDS and their families. They were a godsend. When you came to visit someone for the first time, a Shanti volunteer took you aside to prepare you for what you were about to see. That was probably a good idea because even though I had plenty of experience with hospitals, and even some with AIDS, I hadn't seen Bubby for a long time.

When I walked into his room, he was propped up in bed. He looked very thin, but he looked like Bubby. When he saw me, he burst into this huge smile. He seemed so happy, and kind of amazed, that I was there. I thought, *Of course I'm here. I'm your family, your brother. I'm your blood.* I didn't say those words, at least not then, but they were in my heart. I went to him, and it was as if all the years and distance just fell away.

As we talked, I got a better picture of his medical situation. He had pneumocystic pneumonia and had had an allergic reaction to the sulfa drug they used to treat it. He, I, and our mother were all allergic to that particular drug. They took him off it, but there was really nothing else to give him.

Nobody said the words, but basically it was just a matter of how long he could continue to breathe. It was horrific to realize, in a very concrete way, that my brother was going to die. I'd known that intellectually, of course, but it was still a shock to my system. I stayed in the hospital with him for ten days. It was the last ten days of his life.

I had him all to myself at the start. He couldn't sleep, so he and I would stay up all night talking and laughing and telling stories. It was just like old times in our little bedroom at the Shack.

It wasn't all smooth sailing. I remember one night, he had to pee and insisted that I leave the room while he used the little hand urinal. I thought, *Bubby, really? We're kind of beyond this.*

He had a lot of trouble letting me help him at first and fought me on just about everything. At one point, he sent the urinal flying across the room. I said, "That's it. We're not doing this anymore. We're not playing this game. If you want somebody else to come help you, then call the nurse. But I'm here, so that's ridiculous."

He finally relented and allowed me to hold the urinal for him while standing outside this little curtain he had surrounded myself with. Of course, I couldn't see what I was doing, so I finally said, "I've had enough," and opened the curtain with a dramatic flourish to help my only brother relieve himself.

As he got sicker, he was more willing to let me help him—but sometimes I felt like I was at the end of my rope. When that happened, I would walk out into the hall and stand staring at that poster, which I understood much better after a day or two than I had when I first arrived: "When you feel like you're at the end of your rope, tie a knot." Somehow, I always managed to tie a knot and jump back in.

After two days, I told him I was going to call Mom and Dad.

"Don't bother," he said. "They won't come here."

He was too sick to engage in some big discussion about it, so we didn't, and I called them anyway.

The Hardest Phone Call I Ever Made

Officially at least, my parents didn't know that either Bubby or I was gay, and they didn't know he was sick. But clearly, it was time to tell them. That was the hardest phone call I ever made. I had to tell them, "I really don't know how to say this, except to say it. Your son is gay, and he's in the hospital dying of AIDS. If you want to say goodbye, you need to come to San Francisco. And you need to come *now*."

They flooded me with questions, to which I replied, "I'm sorry, but I don't know the answer to that. I do know this..." And I repeated the message: "Your son is gay, he's in the hospital dying of AIDS, and you need to come right away if you want to say goodbye to him. I'm so sorry…"

My mother was terribly afraid of flying, but they immediately got on a plane and flew through the night. They had some turbulence, apparently, and she was already traumatized by the news about Bubby and the prospect of getting on an airplane and flying three thousand miles. By the time they landed, she was completely undone.

They arrived at the hospital about 2 a.m. Before I let them in to see Bubby, I took them to a conference room and asked them to sit down. It was new for me to be in charge of a family situation, but there was absolutely no other way to handle this. I proceeded to tell them that there were certain things I would allow them to do while they were on 5A, and other things that I would not allow them to do. My father shot to his feet and said, "You can't talk to us like that!"

I said, "Yes, I can. Please sit down." They sat, and I continued, "You're going to see a lot of things here. You're not to pick up anything and read it. You don't get to take any written material from anybody except me. You don't get to read a pamphlet unless I put it in your hand. Dad, I know how inquisitive you are, but I am in charge here. And if I see anything other than love from either of you, I will ask you to leave. I'm sorry, but that's how it is." Something happened at that moment. They seemed to realize the gravity of the situation, and they became very compliant.

◆ ◆ ◆

We went into Bubby's room, and they ran over to him. My brother cried and said, "I never thought you would come."

My mother said, "What do you mean, you never thought we'd come? You're my son. I love you. I don't care about any of this other stuff. You're my son. You came out of my body."

It was a moment of raw, real, unconditional, God-level love—as if, through all the tears and words and emotions, God was just pulling everybody together. All the conflicts just fell away, along with all the years, and all the shoulda-coulda-wouldas.

> *Each of us saw so clearly that the only important thing was that we loved one another, and that anything else was just a big waste of time.*

It was all a little too much for Mom. She had an attack of high blood pressure, and one of the Shanti volunteers ushered her out and took her somewhere so she could calm down. After a few hours, Mom and Dad finally went back to their motel to get some sleep.

· · ·

My brother had this crazy friend, Jimmy, who made a practice of moving to new cities and becoming a taxi driver so that he could learn all about these places. He was the Tripadvisor of his day. Before my parents arrived, Jimmy and I had puzzled over where we should put them up. He said, "Let's just put them at Beck's Motor Lodge in the Castro."

I thought, "They're already going to be immersed in the gay culture on 5A. Staying at a motel in the Castro should be nothing compared to that. What the hell."

The Castro is a beautiful place, but it was not very beautiful in those days because so many people were walking around either dying or afraid they were going to die. Beck's was at the heart of it all, so my parents were ensconced in the middle of the gay capital of the universe at its most difficult time.

Letting Go

I stayed with my brother in the hospital day and night, all ten days I was there. We probably got to know each other better in those ten days than we had in our whole lives. It was one of the terrible gifts that his illness brought to me.

I also got to know the nurses, of course. One night nurse took especially good care of us. She always made sure we weren't disturbed and that we had drinks, snacks, and whatever else we needed. She was a woman but may have been transitioning to a man. She had a beard, and my father, to his dying day, thought she was a man, so I never told him any different. She was an amazing person and somehow seemed to know exactly who we were and just what to do for us.

Over that week, I often found myself wandering into other rooms and talking with other patients.

I kept wondering what all of this was about. There had to be some meaning beyond all the horrific sadness and suffering.

At the same time, in the midst of it all, I saw beautiful acts of kindness. The juxtaposition of life and death on 5A was shocking and very moving.

My brother's friends started to arrive: his best friend, Janet, from high school and a lot of other people I don't remember. As he was going in and out of consciousness, Bubby was trying to be Julie Cruise Director, managing all the different groups of people gathered around his bed because none of his dear friends knew one another. It certainly should not have been what my poor brother was concerning himself with in his last days of consciousness. It was a little strange for everybody. These people were trying to grieve with one another about someone they all loved, but they didn't know one another. Each one knew different things about Bubby, different parts of his life. I tucked that information away for later.

Late one night, eight or nine days in, when everybody had gone home, the night nurse with the beard caught me in the corridor and asked, "How's your brother?"

"He's not breathing very well," I said. "He doesn't look good, but there's a moment every now and then when he says something."

She looked at me kindly. "I wanted to come find you, because I won't see you again."

"Oh, are you off for a few days?" I asked.

She looked at me and said, "No. Because your brother is going to die."

I stared at her. I thought about slapping her, but then I looked into her eyes and realized that she knew something. I am so grateful for the part of me that has learned to take a moment before I fly off the handle. I didn't always have that.

"I've seen them all," she said. "Your brother is going to die very soon, so I'm not going to see you again—and I've been meaning to tell you something."

"What?" I asked.

"I wanted to say that if I had ever had a brother, I would want him to be just like you. You are amazing." And with that, she turned on her heel and walked away.

I was stunned. I didn't know what to do with what she'd just told me. So I went back to Bubby's room.

My father was standing on one side of the bed, and I stood on the other. Mom's blood pressure was giving her trouble, so she was taking a break down in the cafeteria. Bubby was hardly breathing, like he was drowning, and his eyes were closed. You can sense when a body is shutting down. It's a beautiful, elegant, and amazing process—as it should be. It's a little like a computer shutting down, function by function. We go through all this emotional turmoil over death, but it's actually a very organized and natural event. It may look messy at times, but it's really quite normal and in perfect order.

I remember thinking, "I need to divide my attention between him and my father—and my mother is going to need some attention, too." Strangely, it was very easy to prioritize things. Who needed the most attention at that particular moment?

I crawled into the bed with Bubby and talked to him about things he loved—waterfalls, our grandmother, butterflies. I tried to help him let go. My dad was standing by the bed, chatting away. That felt odd and dissonant, out of harmony. I suddenly realized that Dad was in cheerleader mode. I'd never seen him like that. Usually, he was very grounded and realistic, but his message to Bubby as he faced death was, "Come on. You can do it! You can beat this!"

How confusing it must have been to someone who was dying. I didn't know what to say to him to get him to stop, so I just reached my hand around my brother's head, buried my finger in his ear so he could not hear my father, and tilted his head toward me. And I kept on talking to him about our grandmother and butterflies and the beach, and started telling him, let it go, just let go.

I held Bubby in my arms and watched him take his last breaths. It was not pretty. It looked painful. There was a guttural noise, like a volcano venting or a whale sounding. He opened his eyes for the first time in four days. They were so beautifully blue and utterly clear. As he took his last breath, I felt his life energy sweep out through his head. I literally felt it. Something physical left his body. I don't know exactly what it was, but it was palpable—and I know it happened. My brother was dead.

Parenting My Parents

I cried. My father cried. I knew I had to put my feelings aside at that point and go to my mother. She was good at putting herself aside for others, and this was her time. I went and got her, brought her to Bubby's side. I left them alone with him and stepped outside.

After what felt like an eternity, but was really only a few minutes, I went back in to join my family, just three of us now. We were all in desperate pain. Mom said, "You'll never understand what it's like to be a mother. It's your child." She was right. I understood my grief but not hers. I asked her about it later, and she couldn't tell me much. There were so many God-level things going on in those last few days with Bubby, things that were way beyond my understanding.

· · ·

Finally, it was time to leave the hospital. All three of us headed back to Beck's Motor Lodge. I sent them up to the room and ran across the street to my brother's favorite bakery. I bought a loaf of San Francisco sourdough bread and found a bottle of red wine and a cheap corkscrew.

I walked back to the motel and proceeded to sit in my parents' room, eating sourdough bread and drinking wine. They had never seen me drink before, and they just stared at me. Nobody said anything until the whole bottle was gone. Then my father asked, "Do you do this often?" I said, "No." We talked a bit and started telling stories. Finally, there was nothing to do but laugh. It was yet another experience that was completely beyond anything our family had ever done before.

My mother had an upset stomach, and my father stepped into hero mode. "I'll go get your milk of magnesia," he said. That was probably the worst thing for what ailed her stomach, but she believed it helped. I offered to go, but he insisted. So not only were we at Beck's Motor Lodge in the heart of gay San Francisco, but my father was now headed for the Walgreens at the epicenter of the Castro. Gay ground zero.

He was gone for what seemed like hours. I was a little drunk by then and wondered if I should skip down to Walgreens and rescue him—but instead decided that it would be good for him to have just a taste, just a tiny thimbleful, of what his sons' lives were really like. He wouldn't be seeing a façade or any of the nonsense that we often made up for him. He would be seeing the real thing. Eventually, he returned, no worse for the wear.

"How was it?" my mother asked him.

"You would have been safer out there than me," he said.

We had a laugh over that and decompressed a bit. Then the real stuff kicked in.

Taking Charge

We couldn't find a funeral home at first. Even in San Francisco, there were funeral homes that were refusing to take people who had died of AIDS, and the ones that did were exceptionally busy. Eventually, with the help of the Shanti Project, we found one.

The next step was clearing out my brother's apartment. Boxes were stacked up everywhere. You could see that he had never really unpacked when he'd moved to San Francisco from Hawaii to manage Jaspar's, a very fine restaurant. He must have known, on some level, what was happening with his health.

In the hospital, I'd helped him scratch out a little will in pencil, so I knew there were a few items that we needed to pack up and send to various people. One of the many things I learned about him in our long talks was that he was known among his friends as Mr.

Christmas. He had a huge collection of my grandmother's Christmas decorations, and they were going to his friend Deenie.

As my parents and I walked into Bubby's apartment, I suddenly realized, "Dear Lord, what might we find here?" But there was no time for recon and assessment as I had done at the hospital. I set my mother to work in the kitchen, my father in the bathroom, and I took the bedroom and the living room. We started boxing things up and throwing things out.

At one point, I went to check on my mother and found her gazing out the kitchen window at this skinny little sliver of a view. I nudged her gently out of the trance, reeled her in, and got her back to work.

I worried about what my father might find in the bathroom and yelled over to him, "Whatever you're finding, just put it in the box." At one point, he came wandering out of the bathroom with a small circle of metal in his hand. He held it out and said, "I wonder what this is."

To my horror, I realized that my father was standing before me, holding my brother's cock ring in his hand. Visions of where that cock ring had been flooded my mind, and I do believe I started laughing. I grabbed it out of Dad's hand and told him to get back to work. It would be quite a while before I lost the image of my father, recently returned from the Castro Walgreens, walking out of the bathroom, holding my dead brother's cock ring, and not knowing what it was. It was all a bit surreal, but I just kept telling them to get back to work and, eventually, we finished packing up the apartment.

My brother's friend Leander had been around, on and off, during the whole week. Leander ran a pest control service, Godzilla Pest Control, and it may have been exposure to those toxic chemicals that made him a little strange. He and my mother developed an odd, comically loving connection. She just wanted to take care of someone, and he loved nothing more than being taken care of. Leander was harmless, but sometimes harmless people just need to get out of the way. My attitude was: If you can't do something to help, you probably need to move on.

Leander had flitted in and out during the packing process and wound up going with us in the rental car to the UPS. We were to send some packages to my place, others to my parents' house, and the one with all the Christmas paraphernalia to Deenie.

Dad and I got all the packages inside the UPS and left Mom in the car with Leander. The place was packed. We waited in a long line, and when we finally reached the desk, somehow the labels weren't right, and the UPS people started to hassle us. I was worried about my poor sweet mother sitting out in the car all alone with Leander and could only imagine what he was saying to her. Probably their version of the cock ring incident. I had no faith whatsoever in Leander's judgment or in his capacity to be appropriate—and we couldn't get the UPS to take our packages.

I lost it. I threw my hands up into the air and screamed as loudly as I could, "Dear God, deliver me! Can't you people help me? My brother just died! Scotty, beam me up!" Then I pulled a Carol Burnett, put the back of my hand to my forehead, and said, "Dear God, I can't go through any more!"

Utter silence fell on the UPS station. Everyone there scurried around and came together to make sure that our boxes got processed immediately *so that we could leave.* My dramatic moment had worked like a charm. I made a mental note.

As Dad and I walked out to the sidewalk, I looked through the car window and saw an expression on my mother's face that I had never seen before. It screamed silently, "Please! Please come help me!"

Evidently, the conversation had ranged far beyond anything my mother had ever experienced in her little Southern lady life and had touched on subjects that were way, way beyond her ken. Leander seemed blissfully unaware that anything was wrong. I asked Mom later what he'd said, and she answered that she really didn't know. I think that was her way of never, ever returning to those subjects.

Our next stop was Jaspar's to collect my brother's last paycheck. They didn't want to give it to me. Who was I, anyway? How did they know I was his brother? And besides, they were in the middle of serving dinner.

I threw my hands up into the air and screamed, "Dear God, my brother has died! He worked here. Your customers loved him! And you won't give me my dead brother's final paycheck?!"

A silence more deafening than the one at the UPS. I suddenly had the check and was on my way. I made another mental note.

The next morning, we stopped at the bank to cash the check and get access to my brother's account so that we could pay the death expenses. No way, said the bank. How did they know who we were, after all? Well, I thought, let's start with the name. His name is LeNoble. My name is LeNoble. My parents' names are LeNoble. Daddy, Mommy, brother.

The bank guy got irritated and made it his mission to get in my way. He had no idea who he was up against. His manager stepped into the fray, and we repeated the LeNoble conversation. I told them I'd give them one more chance. Mother, father, brother, dead brother LeNoble. Give me the money.

"Sir, we're sorry..."

I threw my hands up into the air in the middle of the bank and yelled, "Dear God, please help me! My brother has just died, and you won't give me his money. This is my mother and my father. I am his brother. What are you people doing?" Silence echoed through the bank. We got our checks, deposited the money, and were on our way.

My mother and father were horrified—just embarrassed beyond words. But it worked, and we got what we needed. They never spoke of it again, but it was obvious they were perhaps even more scandalized by the bank incident than they had been watching me drink that whole bottle of red wine.

◆ ◆ ◆

Finally, everything was done. We checked them out of Beck's Motor Lodge, and they boarded a flight back to Florida. I flew back to Atlanta and went back to work.

Bubby was the first of many people I have been blessed to be with as they died. Being part of the AIDS epidemic afforded me that terrible gift at an earlier age than most people experience it.

I will always be grateful that I got to be with Bubby during that time. He was a fine man and very well-liked. Many people who knew him have contacted me and shared little stories or told me sweet things about him that I hadn't known. I am often aware of my brother's presence. We didn't share a lot of time in physical form, but we were connected and I treasure that.

The Family Trip

Bubby died in October. That Thanksgiving, my parents and I took a trip through the backcountry of the Carolinas. At one point, we drove through an area with some very unusual and colorful houses—the South Carolina version of San Francisco's Painted Ladies.

It was a beautiful, sunny day, and I remember one house in particular that was painted eggplant purple. My father made some comment about "faggots" choosing that paint color. I put it aside and thought to myself, "No, that's not true. If gay men had done that house, the shading would have better, and the shrubbery would have been nicer."

I laughed it off, but later, we were driving through a neighborhood with a lot of what were known back then as "grunge people."

They were pierced, wore black, had tattoos, and looked like they might smell bad. They begged or played music for money. My father looked at them like they were the scum of the earth and made some comment about how awful they were. That, combined with his comment about the eggplant house, made me think, "Enough!"

I asked him in a tone that was not very friendly or respectful, "Why do you care?" He turned and gave me a very strange, shocked look. After a pregnant pause, I asked again, *"Really, why do you care? What is this person doing to you? What does this have to do with anything in your life?"*

I couldn't believe his attitude, after all we had just been through with Bubby. It made me realize that we had more work to do and that his thinking had not magically transformed overnight.

Nor had our experience together in San Francisco miraculously turned around my mother's attitudes. I once tried to press her into talking about something that might remind her that she had a gay son, and she said, "Look, don't push so hard. I'm trying to digest this stuff as fast as I can." At that point, she knew for sure that she had one gay son. She may have suspected that she had two gay sons, but she didn't want to entertain that notion until she absolutely had to do so.

Don't ever wait to tell someone

how much you love them.

TEN

Getting to Know
Mom and Dad

THE CHRISTMAS AFTER BUBBY DIED, I VISITED MY parents back in Jacksonville Beach as usual. We'd been speaking on the phone like we always did, but we didn't really broach the subject of Bubby's death during these conversations so I couldn't always tell how they were coping with it. It seemed to me that they had retreated from their usual rhythms of life and isolated themselves a little bit. When I arrived for the holiday, it was like reopening the floodgates of grief.

Once again, I became their rock. I didn't give much thought to being thrust into that quasi-parental role again, as I had been at the hospital. They had both been the rock for so many people at hard times in their lives. I felt it was only right to do what I could to help them through the absolute lowest point of theirs.

I made it my goal to bring joy and life into the house and make Christmas very special. I had always tried to do that in some way, and in the coming years, once I started moving up the ranks at MCI and doing better and better financially, I would be able to do things for them that would have a material impact on their lives—like buying them a new car, or a new tile floor, or a new stove to replace the one they'd been using since 1960. That first year after Bubby, though, whether consciously or unconsciously, what I tried to give them was simple peace of mind amid the tragedy; I wanted to ensure that they knew I was healthy, successful, and that things were moving forward in my life. If they saw one of their boys—little Tommy the "varmit"— doing well, it might lessen the guilt I knew they were feeling about how Bubby died.

At times, I also had the creeping thought that my being home might have made things a little bit harder for them. With me there, they couldn't compartmentalize and deny the reality of the situation. We were the only three people in their world who knew the truth: Bubby was gay, and he died of AIDS in the famous San Francisco AIDS ward. In that Southern way of saving face, my parents had kept the facts from friends and family. People probably put two and two together, but as far as Vic and Mary LeNoble's social circle knew, Vic Jr. died, far too young, because of a kidney problem. (After Mom died, I found a box of genealogical research about the family that a relative had compiled and sent her, going back four generations. It was wonderful to have such a trove of information about the family. But nearly everything in it that related to my brother was a lie.)

Coming to terms with the experience we'd just had was very difficult and slow for them, and they were lucky to have me there as much as I could be.

I was only thirty-one, but I was already proving to be the type of person you want around in a crisis.

I think my experience working in hospitals prepared me to understand death as simply a part of the reality of life. I didn't yet know just how crucial that exposure would be, going into the late '80s.

On the Road Again

When Bubby was still alive, he and my parents had planned a trip to the Grand Tetons in Wyoming for the coming spring, and Mom and Dad were going to cancel it. "Don't cancel it!" I told them. "I'll go with you instead." Of course, they objected with the usual refrain: I was too busy and shouldn't miss more work.

"Don't be silly," I said, taking charge again. "I'll fly out there and meet you. We'll spend a few days together, then you can go on and finish your trip. End of story."

They finally agreed, and that spring, I took a week off work and flew out to meet them in Bozeman, Montana.

The trip was extraordinary. And just what we needed. Again, I was a ball of positive energy and humor, trying to find the fun in everything.

I didn't cut them off from feeling their feelings—I knew firsthand the pain of pushing emotions away and playing happy—nor did I let them get too lost in the grief.

For four days, we drove through the spectacular landscapes of Utah, down to the Grand Canyon, and back up to Montana, marveling at the gorgeous landscape together, laughing, crying, and talking, talking, talking. They were very interested in my work and so proud that I was doing well. We dropped that Southern pretense and finally said a lot of things to one another that I don't think they would have ever been able to share with anyone outside the family. My mother was carrying so much guilt about Bubby's death. She thought she had "made" him gay because of the way she raised him or because of something passed down through her from her family, and she blamed herself for how he died. I did my best to stop her from believing that, to tell her that she was not responsible for any of it, but I don't think anyone could have convinced her.

"You will never understand what it's like to be a mother, to carry a child, have a baby, and then lose him. You will never understand," she used to say.

And she was right.

· · ·

Still, we managed to laugh—a lot. Starting with the car we'd rented. It was a Mercury Merkur, a new two-door coupe that had just come out the previous year. I don't know why anyone thought it would be the right kind of car for the rugged terrain of Montana and Wyoming, but we tooled around in it, my mother awkwardly struggling to squeeze herself in and out of the little cave-like bucket seat in the back, much to the delight of my father. I even joined in on the ribbing, too, telling her it was good exercise.

Not that we didn't have some laughs at Dad's expense. He had been so disgusted by the powdered eggs he ate while in the Navy that he'd refused to eat eggs ever since. But something compelled him to start eating them again while on this trip, and the smells that came out of that man afterward were practically apocalyptic. It became a big joke that when we checked out of our motel rooms, they'd have to board them up forever. Although I suppose the joke was on all of us, not just Dad.

There were many times when Mom chose not to come on a walk or hike, and it was just me and Dad on our own. Seeing him out in this majestic Big Sky country felt right. He'd grown up in the woods and sand dunes of northern Florida, but he was nonetheless in his element here. We spent hours walking, looking up at the billions of stars in the sky, and talking about everything. I'd been so scared of him as a child, and on this trip, I think we both started to see one another differently.

We Are Still Here

As much as this trip was about honoring Bubby and reflecting on our shared past with him—both what we had as a family and what we lacked—I think it helped us all remember that *we were still here.*

We still had a future ahead of us.

This period of my life was one in which "the future" was starting to feel like something that was within my grasp and could look however I wanted it to. I'll never forget the day we visited Old Faithful in Yellowstone National Park. We stayed in a nearby motel as usual, but when I saw the gorgeous mountain lodge overlooking the geyser, all wooden eaves and majestic as the surroundings, I thought to myself, "No more dinky motels. *That's* where I'll be staying next time." Little Tommy in the Shack had known *something* else was out there for him, and it was around this time that I could start to define what that *something* could be and envision how to achieve it.

I was on an actual career path at MCI, and with that came the notion that this one job, rather than a patchwork of two or three, would give me what I needed financially and be a foundation to build my life on. My parents were very interested in and proud of what I was doing at MCI, and I don't doubt that this also helped them work through the loss of Bubby. To keep them from drowning in the grief and regrets about the past, they had important future milestones that they could look forward to.

So, after five days with Mom and Dad in the Merkur, they dropped me off back in Bozeman and continued on to the Grand Tetons. I flew back to Atlanta and went back to work.

Paying It Forward

After the trip, Mom, Dad, and I continued to lean on each other, each in our own way. We were slowly chipping away at some of that posture of saving face, and for that, I was grateful. I was also immensely grateful for the fact that, even at our most rigid and proper, we were actually better off than many other families touched by AIDS at that tragic time. Thousands of less fortunate people had been all but abandoned by their families and by the medical establishment that should have been treating them with care and empathy. I wanted to do something to help, so I became a "buddy" with AID Atlanta.

For most of my life, I've volunteered at one place or another. That may have come from my parents' focus on giving to others or from my early experiences with the Methodist Church, but it has always made me feel good. I wanted to be a "buddy" because I now had firsthand experience of what went on in AIDS wards, and I saw that humanity and compassion were in very short supply. Each of us buddies was assigned to an individual patient, and we simply tried to give them whatever they needed—someone to talk to, to help them handle the tasks of everyday life, or just to sit with them so they wouldn't be alone. Many of them died very quickly. We had none of the drugs that are available today, and there simply wasn't much hope.

I remember my experience with one man in particular, whom I had been visiting during his last days. I walked into his hospital room and found a tray table with his lunch on it, placed halfway between the door and the bed. He could smell the food, but the person who'd delivered it obviously hadn't wanted to get near him and had just pushed it into the room and left it way out of his reach. This man had lost his vision and was so sick that he was shaking. It was also clear that he had not been bathed for a long time. Just as I went over to the bed and introduced myself, a nurse popped her head in, warned me not to get too close to him, and gave me a mask to wear.

I took him into the shower room and got in with him so I could hold him up and help him bathe. I trimmed his toenails and his fingernails and got him all polished up. Then I fed him lunch.

Something came over me at that point. I went out to the nurse's station and raged, "How dare you even call yourself nurses when you treat this man the way you do? This is criminal. If you can't take care of him, then find somebody who can." It was a Sunday sermon that I'm sure those particular nurses will remember all their lives. He didn't live much longer, and I'm glad I did what I could for him in the short time we had together.

There was so much that needed to change, and we had a long way to go.

· · ·

In 1987, I participated in the original AIDS March on Washington along with half a million other people, many of whom were gay. I felt like people must feel when they visit the Castro for the first time: I was finally with people like myself, there were a lot of us, we were free, and we had become a force. It was one of the most powerful things I had ever experienced. I felt like something wonderful was bubbling up inside me.

I remember marching around the capital, holding hands or being arm-in-arm with people, and then, in silence, unfolding the first AIDS quilt on the National Mall. It was as large as a football field and had 1,920 panels, including Bubby's.

The panels were about three feet by six feet. Some were ornate, and others were very plain. Bubby's friend Leander had made his panel. It was quite simple but full of meaning. Leander had fashioned the name "Victor," which is what most people called Bubby, out of fragments of things my brother had given him: little pieces of denim, a handkerchief, or other pieces of clothing. I had the honor of being the one to unfold Bubby's panel, and I did so with love and reverence.

I was also a quilt monitor that year, which meant that I walked around the quilt and made sure people were safe and felt supported. I might hand them tissues, give them a hug, let them collapse into my arms, or just stand there quietly and bear witness to the love they felt for someone who was now gone.

Phoenix Rising

In Atlanta, I threw myself into work the way I threw myself into volunteering. I was motivated by my own Big Plans for my future, but I also understood that work was the perfect distraction from this horrible moment in history. I was on the rise at MCI, and by the end of 1986, I had saved up enough money to start looking for a house of my own. To buy.

My friend, Moriah, was my realtor, and she helped me find a cute little house on Pecan Street in Clarkston, on the perimeter of Atlanta. It was listed for $85,000, had an old pecan tree in the yard, a big back porch, a sunroom, and gardenias and forsythias out by the front steps. And once I was approved for a mortgage and made my offer, it was *mine*.

I didn't care that it had a washing machine that would leak all over the floor or hideous carpeting—I figured out how to avoid a washing machine overflow, and I pulled up all that hideous carpeting to find beautiful wooden floors underneath! Dad came up to make sure all the mechanical and electrical things were working properly, and he and Mom came up again to spend Christmas of 1986 with me in my very own home.

I had made it. And they were so proud.

◆ ◆ ◆

In 1987, I made my first big leap at MCI. I'd earned various promotions and distinctions in the four years since I'd started as a part-time customer service rep, but this was the first time I would be tapped to go work on a special project outside of Atlanta. MCI had grown so fast as a company that they were operating different technological systems in different areas of the country. The Phoenix Project was meant to unite them all, and twenty-six people from all over the country were selected to work on it out of MCI's corporate offices in the Pentagon City outside of Washington, DC. I was the only one from Atlanta selected to go.

I lived out of an Embassy Suites during the week and would fly home on weekends. The project lasted only a couple of months, but I had made a name for myself during my time there. One of the division presidents told my bosses in Atlanta, "We're not letting him go back. You've got to figure out how get along without him, because we need him, and we're just not letting him go." I wound up living at the Embassy Suites for nine months. I got to know the people there so well that when I'd check out and fly home on weekends, they would let me keep my things there for my return on Monday morning.

◆ ◆ ◆

When the Phoenix Project was over, I moved back down to Atlanta and was promoted to a manager position, overseeing what we called the gold and silver teams, which serviced commercial accounts. I was very proud of my new role. Little did I know, I was walking into a hornet's nest.

There was friction in the office from the start. A woman named Kim had overseen both commercial and residential services, but she had been pushed over to residential and a man named Ralph was hired to manage commercial. They fought like cats and dogs, always seething at one another and building walls between various parts of the department. Everyone was having a hard time, especially me because I reported to both Kim and Ralph for various projects.

Ralph had been a high-ranking head of recruitment for the Navy and had just gotten out. He thought our group lacked discipline and needed to be straightened out, so he treated us like we were unruly teenagers who'd been sent to the principal's office. He wasn't sure that women should be in the workplace at all, and he wanted the men to obey his orders without question. We were never going to be that kind of group. Ralph was a good person on some level, but he acted like we were beneath him as people because we were subordinate to him on the org chart. This was not helped by the fact that he smoked cigarettes and walked around the office ashing on everybody's desks.

For all his strictness, Ralph was also constantly changing his mind, so the whole office was usually strung out on a sense of emergency and impending doom. He would come up with a big idea on Friday afternoon and tell us he needed it executed by Monday morning. So we'd work all weekend to get the pieces lined up, only to learn on Monday morning that he'd thought it over, abandoned that plan, and wanted us to go in a totally new direction, no questions asked, as if he were simply reassigning duties as a commanding officer.

Donna, another training manager and a good friend, had the office next to mine. One day, I looked up to see her coming out of Ralph's office in tears. I went into her office and asked, "Why are you crying?"

She said that Ralph had told her to sit on her hands when she talked to him because he didn't like that she waved her hands when she talked and that it distracted him. I consoled her, and then I got her mad. Then *I* got mad. I walked into Ralph's office and kicked the door shut with my foot—perhaps a little more loudly than necessary because it got everyone's attention. He told me I couldn't do that, and I said, "I just did it."

We had a terse talk, and I reported him to HR. They were sympathetic to our complaints and to Donna's in particular. I think that Ralph was genuinely trying to help us by bringing order as he understood it. But his whole approach had no place in customer service; he was in the wrong job, at the wrong time. MCI was much better off leaving us to our own devices and letting us set the culture for our own workplace—one that was based on encouragement and collaboration rather than rigid and autocratic rule. We had already proven that we did good work and got good results.

That was the first of many lessons I would learn about the importance of developing a working dynamic organically. People will give you their best when they are respected for who they are and valued for what they bring to a group.

My team always had the highest scores in sales, service, and satisfaction, and that created opportunities for me. Whatever new project the directors asked me to do, I did very well—and I worked very, very hard. Shortly after I arrived back in Atlanta, I was tapped to return to Washington to create and run a whole new department as a senior manager in charge of Marketing Systems. I wasn't going to drop in on some temporary assignment but grow a team and a center.

So I sold my little house in Clarkston and prepared to return north to take on this next challenge. The movers pulled up to the house and loaded up all my belongings. Then I got in my Caprice Classic, and off I went to Washington.

· · ·

There would be no living in the Embassy Suites for me this time around. I got temporary housing in a beautiful apartment while I looked for a place to live but quickly realized that you couldn't buy in the Washington area what you could buy in Atlanta. I met and befriended a wonderful real estate agent named Jane who would become a very important person in my life. She showed me several places in Alexandria and found me a beautiful high-rise condo with a balcony overlooking the Virginia countryside. I'd been resisting anything in a high-rise, but like anyone who's great at their job, Jane knew what I wanted before I'd even had a chance to articulate it for myself—she was wonderful at customer service in her own right.

So, at age thirty-five, I bought my beautiful home in the sky. I was working for a company that saw something special in me and was now running the only marketing team in IT headquarters. Little five-year-old Tom had come a long way from the Shack.

When everything has shifted around you and nothing seems certain, remember to hold on to yourself. Who you are and who you want to become is not going to change. Even the moments of greatest upheaval will pass. And you will still be here.

ELEVEN

The Day Everything Changed

I HAD BEEN IMMERSED IN THE WORLD OF THE AIDS CRIsis since Bubby's death, but I had not gotten tested myself. On top of all the volunteering, I was traveling constantly for work and always being groomed for the next level of my career. I told myself that I just didn't have the time. And I'm sure there was a bit of denial or avoidance at play as well. When you're in the middle of an epidemic more horrible and scarier than anything you've ever experienced, it's only natural to find it incomprehensible and to want to push it away, pretend it's not real.

Besides, I was always so healthy! I had never taken a sick day at MCI until I suddenly fell very, very ill one day back in Atlanta. For the first time in four years, I told my assistant I wouldn't be in. No one heard from me for three days. When they finally called me, I said, "Leave me alone. That's the only way I'm going to get well." All very uncharacteristic for me.

I finally went back to work, but the next year in Washington, I started thinking about that horrible illness and about some of my risky behaviors. So, four years after Bubby died, I decided to become well-informed about my own health. The time had come to get tested.

Getting Tested

I made an appointment, anonymously, at the Whitman-Walker Clinic and went in for a blood test on October 1, 1989. I returned a week later to meet with a counselor and get my results. My counselor was an older woman, and that was her day to train one of the newbies. She asked if it would be okay if the trainee was present for our meeting, and of course, I said yes. The three of us squeezed into a tiny wood-paneled room with one small, skinny window set very high on the wall.

The counselor went into her script about what this all meant and why we were there, doing everything by the book to teach the trainee. She went on and on, making the room feel more claustrophobic by the minute. Finally, I couldn't stand it anymore and said, "Wait a minute. I'm okay with this person being here, but I'm the patient. I know you need to do all of this stuff, but *I just need the answer.*"

She looked at her trainee, and looked at me, and obviously felt the need to do the right thing—but instead, what came out of her mouth was, "What do you think it is?"

"I think I'm positive," I said, "and if that's the result, I'd just like you to confirm it."

"Yes, you are," she said.

She took a deep breath and wanted everybody to hold hands.

"Thank you," I said. Then I stood up, turned, and headed for the door.

She called after me, "You can't leave, I'm supposed to..."

"Really, I'm fine," I said.

"No, no, no. This isn't how this is supposed to work. This is not what the trainee's supposed to see."

"Everything is going to be fine," I said. "I'm sorry, but I need to leave you now."

And I left.

* * *

I walked down the street feeling like I was on a roller coaster and got into my blue Caprice Classic. I sat there for a long time, just holding onto my body, to keep my mind from drowning in all the roiling feelings.

When I think about that day now, decades later, I do see that holding onto myself was exactly what I was trying to do: I'd come so far and worked so hard to be the one determining who Tom was and how he was going to live. I wasn't about to allow that to change.

If I did indeed have only a little bit of time left on earth, I didn't want to waste it wondering, "Why did this happen to me?" or "If only I had..." or just roll over and be a victim. I chose to give my fight with the virus a purpose, and that purpose was to discover more of myself, more of my connection with the world, and more ways to contribute. I wanted to evolve, not crumble—even though I knew there were going to be times when I would feel like crumbling.

Then I looked up into the rearview mirror at my reflection and spoke to my unwanted guest: "If you want to live with me and cohabitate, then hello. If you plan to take me out, then get ready for the fight of your life."

That began my journey with AIDS.

Now What?

In some ways, my life divides into two sections: pre-HIV and post-HIV. Though, as hard and shocking as it was to hear that I was HIV-positive, I can't say that I was surprised. You can't overstate how much AIDS loomed over life in the late '80s. The shadow it cast was so ugly and awful that we felt the virus was coming for us all, regardless of sexual orientation.

I believe that illness back in Atlanta was when my HIV seroconverted—extreme flu-like symptoms are common when the virus actually takes hold in someone who has been infected. And I think that some small part of me at that time must have understood what was happening but didn't want to acknowledge the possibility.

Of course, knowing I was positive changed everything. Well, almost everything: I got my results on a Sunday and went right back to work the following day.

· · ·

My focus would now be on my work and on fighting the virus. I didn't have much energy left for anything else.

Medically, I knew I had a lot of learning and experimenting ahead of me, but I was not intimidated by this. My background and years of experience in hospitals had given me a view of the healthcare industry that was objective and pragmatic. I didn't have the usual fear or awe of doctors and medicine that can make the natural anxiety over a diagnosis so much worse. All the same, I had never been one for simply turning my body over to the medical establishment; medicine also has its limitations, and I'm convinced it's not the only thing we can use to heal when we get sick. In 1989, there were no clear-cut solutions for HIV, and best practices were still years away from being established.

*I intended to be a full participant in my treatment, and
that would mean trusting my instincts and taking
things into my own hands to some degree.*

I began by reading everything I could find in the gay and main-stream press about doctors who were fighting the disease and who the best one was in DC. Within a few weeks, I had an appointment to see Larry Bruni, a cutting-edge AIDS doctor who I'd been told was willing to step outside the box and try new things for desperate people. That was just what the doctor ordered, so to speak, for those times.

He ran all the initial tests that were available and told me that my immune system was in very poor condition, and I would need to start taking medications immediately to fight off opportunistic infections that could make me very sick in my weakened state.

The only drug available at the time to fight HIV itself was called AZT, which had a long list of side effects—nausea, vomiting, headaches, diarrhea, muscle pain. It often made people feel sicker than the actual virus did, but it was the only treatment we had. So I went on it, and I was determined not to let the side effects get to me.

◆ ◆ ◆

I didn't tell many people about my test results, but of course, I called Pola, Douglas, and Celeste right away.

"Oh shit," Douglas said. "Not you, too..."

"Honey, I'm so sorry," Pola said. "What can I do for you?"

Celeste just cried.

It was going to be a lot harder to tell Jim Graddick the news.

My dating and sex life had slowed down since I'd started working full-time at MCI and was no longer going out constantly. When I did go out, I would still drink and do drugs, and I wasn't shy about pairing off with men I'd meet, but actual penetrative sex wasn't necessarily the result of these trysts. When it came to sexual partners, I actually considered myself to be on the more conservative end of things, compared to other gay men at the time. But Jim and I had had a fully sexual relationship, and I owed it to him to let him know my status. I knew that I was the only man he'd ever had sex with.

Jim and I had met in an Atlanta bar through my friend Gunnar. That night, we'd both had a few martinis, and we went back to his place. He cooked for me, one thing led to another, and we wound up having sex and dating for a short while.

Jim was amazingly smart and creative. He spoke several languages, designed clothes, produced gorgeous weddings, and grew dahlias the size of dinner plates. His day job was as the property manager and sometime organist at a gigantic Lutheran church in a downtown Atlanta neighborhood where you really didn't want to go at night. He had been there forever and lived in a little apartment behind the church, surrounded by the parking lot, so on Sundays those cars were practically in his living room. He also ran a food mission at the church and was passionate about helping people in need.

His little one-bedroom apartment behind the church was a wonderland of antiques. The walls were covered with wonderful paintings. He collected Pickard Limoges and had beautiful carpets and old Victorian armoires, sideboards, and other furniture. Everything had that perfect touch. (All the lighting was on dimmers, a sophisticated invention I had never encountered before.)

Our ritual was that Jim would cook dinner, and then we'd have our little dirty martinis and wind up in the bedroom. We had a wonderful time together, and great sex, but while I had strong feelings for him, he had even stronger feelings for me—feelings that I could not reciprocate. I loved him, but I wasn't in love with him. Fortunately, we'd remained wonderful friends.

When I told him, his main concern was for me and how I was handling the news. He never would have let on if he were worried about what my sickness might mean for him. That's not who Jim was. We talked it over for a while and determined that he should go get tested. I told him where to go and what to expect. He let me know about a week later that he, too, was positive. He was his usual gracious and loving self and tried to absolve me of the guilt I was feeling for having infected him. Jim would eventually die of lung cancer, not AIDS. Until he got cancer, he remained relatively healthy. But I've never stopped carrying that weight.

Telling Jim I had tested positive was one of the most difficult things I've ever had to do. It would be even harder to tell my parents. But I was nowhere near ready to do that yet.

Back to Work

After my diagnosis and the course of drugs Larry Bruni had me on, my health remained strong, and I skated for a while. I devoted all my energy to work and healing—everything else was low priority. I remember asking the universe: "Please, don't let this affect my face!" My thinking was that if my face looked okay, I could continue to work and interact with people and go on with my life.

My star was continuing to rise at MCI. By the fall of 1989, I was a senior manager in DC and started being included in the vice president's meetings. It was evident that I was being exposed to higher-level matters because they saw me heading in that direction. We had a few mergers during those years, and I had made myself indispensable by helping integrate our MCI customer service with the new companies.

One day, I was looking out the window of my office at the Washington skyline and sensed that there was someone behind me.

I turned around and a very continental-looking woman said to me in a thick Italian accent, "I want to know who you are and what you do!"

Diana was a long-term vice president at MCI and was known as the Dragon Lady in some quarters; people either loved her or hated her. Of course, I loved her because, between her heavy Italian accent and her dramatic sense of style, she could've been a very sophisticated drag queen.

We got to know one another very well and got along famously. She was about to open the first dedicated commercial customer service center in Baltimore for the entire Mid-Atlantic Region. I was known for always being on the edge of something new and opening "first" programs at MCI, so one day she said, "Come with me to open this new center!"

I agreed to do just that.

◆ ◆ ◆

The transition happened very quickly. My new office was in Hunt Valley, Maryland, and Jane, my friend and realtor, found me a house in the Mount Vernon district of Baltimore. I was excited about starting my new job with my new mentor and learning everything she had to teach me.

But only a few short months later, I would find *myself* in charge of the commercial customer service center for the Mid-Atlantic Division. Diana was moving up to open another center, and I had been promoted again without even knowing it. This was an extraordinary vote of confidence. But Diana was my mentor, and the whole reason I was in Baltimore. I wanted to work for and learn from her!

I tracked Diana down and said, "You hired me and got me here. I thought I was going to work next to you—and now you're leaving."

"You silly man, don't you get it?" she laughed. "I hired you because I knew you could lead this initiative...without me."

She explained how, when you leave a job, you do your best to give the new person everything you can. And then you walk away. You don't stay around as a crutch. You don't go back in. If they call, you tell them, "I'm sorry, I'm on to my new job. If you have another few questions in the next day or so, give them to me. But it's your job now, so get on with it!"

That was the best advice I ever got.

Just "getting on with it" is usually the best thing to do—in life, in work, in love, in everything. I've forgotten and had to relearn that lesson many times in my life, but it remains true.

So I decided just to get on with it in Baltimore.

The space was still under construction when I got there, and my office was not ready yet. There were no private spaces available yet at all—except a broom closet.

"Well, I've been in closets before in my life," I said, and offered to take it.

Very soon, my gorgeous new office was ready. This center was a showpiece for the company, I was running it, and because we were the closest to the Washington headquarters, people would be coming in from all over the country to see it. I was in heaven!

In January of 1990, I was invited to the annual corporate kick-off meeting at MCI headquarters in Pentagon City. This was to be a "coming out party" of sorts where I would be introduced in front of a crowd of about four thousand employees as the new head of the Mid-Atlantic Region. I decided that if this was to be my big coming out, I was going to make an entrance. Literally.

Rather than get up from a seat in the audience to take my place up on the stage, I waited outside at the back of the auditorium. When my name was called, I burst through the doors and got a prolonged round of applause as I made my way down the aisle toward the stage. The crowd went wild. And everyone was going to remember who I was. (I've never lost my flair for the dramatic. Once a thespian, always a thespian.)

Of course, this did not mean that I'd managed to get over the imposter syndrome I'd always felt. That was still there, though I was learning to cohabitate with it, too.

It surfaced not long after my big moment, during a high-level meeting where I was well aware that I was the most junior person in attendance. At one point during a meeting, the president of the division asked, "Tom, you should know this. How many commercial customers do we have in the Mid-Atlantic Division?"

This man had just signed off on my promotion to run a brand-new commercial customer service center. I stood up and proudly announced a number. You could have heard a pin drop. I looked around and realized that I had said something terribly wrong. A second later, it dawned on me that I had given the number of customers from my *old* division, not my new one—and that I actually had no idea what the real answer was.

Without missing a beat, a colleague named Rick stood up and said, as if everybody should have realized this, "Tom is in the middle of this big change we're making, and he's doing a great job. What he meant to say was..."

He gave the right number, I sank back into my chair, and everyone relaxed—but for the next four days, I sat in my office waiting to be fired. I may have actually started packing my things. But nobody ever came to fire me, and nobody brought up my big mistake. When I did mention it to Rick, he told me that nobody had given it a second thought. They just got on with it. And so did I.

* * *

Our center launched and grew very, very quickly. We continued to expand, eventually taking over other departments and hiring more and more people. Nothing ever stayed put at MCI, and I always managed to remain a little ahead of the game. It seemed like I always had opportunities to get involved in things that weren't usually available to people at my level. That's how I worked. I was always succeeding myself out of a job.

The next thing I knew, less than a year after I'd landed in Baltimore, they wanted me to go back to Atlanta.

Revolt in Atlanta

My return to Atlanta was to be a triumphal march. I was going to be promoted to director level, and I would now be running the center where I started my first part-time job at MCI seven years before. I'd have six hundred people reporting to me, and many of them were people to whom I had reported in the old days.

We were in the process of moving to a new and improved office space, on the top floors of a building with a huge atrium at least thirty stories high. There were beautiful trees in the atrium and a great cafeteria. Customer service was on one side of a walkway over the atrium, and the rest of the center was on the other side—so you could look down into this awesome space as you crossed. Some people didn't like being "shunted aside," but others thought we were across the walkway because we were special.

We finished the move, everybody settled in, and things seemed to be moving forward as smoothly as could be expected. I had no idea what would be coming just around the corner.

A few months into the job, a supervisor named Lynn, who was a good friend and with whom I'd worked back in my part-time days, came to me and told me in strict confidence, "This has nothing to do with you, but there's going to be a walkout on Saturday. People have been meeting at a Black church not far from here to plan it. They want to shut us down."

Lynn was Black, as were most of the employees, and though she never said it in so many words, I got the sense that their grievances had to do with the treatment of Black employees over the past few years at this center.

I thanked Lynn for alerting me to this and assured her that I wouldn't tell anyone that she had been the one to report it to me. I went into my office and sat down to have a conversation with myself about what to do.

I'd worked with so many of the people at this center before, and we knew each other quite well. I was sure that if I approached the group, I could find a way to listen to and address their concerns and not let things escalate to a strike. At the same time, I knew I had a major responsibility as the director of this center to notify corporate HR about something this big and potentially disastrous. Because I had just come from the corporate offices in DC, I knew exactly whom to call. I explained what I'd been told, and a small team of HR people flew down the following day.

I had a bad feeling about how this would go—corporate would come in and take over, and I would have to do whatever they told me to do, even if it undermined all my goodwill and most of my influence at the center. And that is indeed what happened. HR interviewed everyone at the center, in sort of a discovery process, which I was completely removed from. I would get periodic updates and frequent assurances that the grievances were not about me. Still, I felt terrible because this was all happening on my watch, and I was prohibited from taking part in the solution.

The attention that was given to the group and their complaints actually did prevent a walkout, which was a good thing. But I didn't feel good about it. The group's complaints *did* have to do with racism surrounding some people in managerial positions, and those people started getting fired—one of whom was Allen Floyd, who had been my boss at my first MCI job. He fit the good ol' boy stereotype, which was totally accurate in his case—down to his vocal love of guns and, evidently, his racist behavior.

After a few miserable weeks, I was called back up to Washington to meet with corporate HR. They assured me once again that no one had made any complaints about me and I was not responsible for anything, but their recommendation was that I come back to work in corporate, and they bring in a new director to start fresh. They felt that I would be ineffectual after their intervention, and I couldn't disagree. I didn't argue the point that *they* had been the ones to render me ineffectual. As much as I hated it, I knew this would be the best way forward.

I had never faced anything like this before, but by then, I knew that the only way through something difficult was through it. If I could face it, stand in it, and not try to avoid or deny it, then I would be rewarded with lessons. If I had quit or collapsed into self-pity or despair at any point in this process, I would not have been able to take the next step. And if I hadn't taken that next step, I could not have taken the step after that.

· · ·

I would be called upon to use those lessons much sooner than I thought. One day after the whole debacle, while I was still living in Atlanta, I got home from work to find a letter for me with no return address. I opened and read it and froze in horror. Whoever wrote it didn't sign it, and they called me all sorts of terrible names and blamed me for ruining their career and their life.

I was terrified. I was so shaken that I almost called the MCI general counsel, but even though the writer was clearly referring to what had just happened at the center, they were anonymous, and I had no idea what they would be able to do. I put the letter in a drawer and tried to put it out of my mind, hoping that would be the end of it.

Then another letter arrived, and another, each one more vicious than the last. They included details about my life and what I'd supposedly done to this person, and it very quickly became obvious that they were being sent by Allen Floyd. He had been resentful of me ever since I'd returned to Atlanta and become his boss, and after he got fired for being a racist, I became his scapegoat. He blamed me for his firing, called me all sorts of gay slurs, and actually said, "How dare you do this to me? You ruined my life, and I was the one who let you go be with your AIDS-ridden, dying brother." In one of the letters, he wrote, "I know where you live," and because he so often talked about the gun he kept in his pickup truck, I took that to be a serious threat.

I finally took the letters to HR and the general counsel at MCI. They told me there was little they could do, since Allen was no longer an employee and apparently had moved out of state. That made the threat feel less imminent, but it did not take away the fear. I felt like a target.

◆ ◆ ◆

I could not wait to leave Atlanta. Being director of the center where I had started had been a dream job, but I didn't feel safe there. And the sooner I left, the sooner everyone, myself included, could start with a clean slate. Some people probably assumed that I'd done something terrible and was being pushed out. Others were upset to see me go.

Still others simply had no idea what was going on. But I knew in my heart that I had done my best for everyone. Fortunately, everyone who knew me from the old days understood who I was and how I thought about things.

Pushing Through

I brushed off the dust of Atlanta and moved back to Washington, DC. Jane found me a wonderful place on the twenty-second floor of Skyline—a high-rise, naturally—in Falls Church. It was a spacious one-bedroom with a little office area and a huge balcony with lovely views of the Virginia skyline. It had a pool, a gym, underground parking, and an around-the-clock doorman for safety. I had moved three times in four years and just dealt with a horrible ending to my dream job, so I treated myself to a reward—a new navy blue Honda with a spoiler and a gold pack.

But somehow, Allen Floyd had discovered my new address, and the letters kept coming. I endured that man's disgusting insults for a year and a half. Some of them I didn't even open—I just stuck them in a drawer with the rest and made sure to let Pola know where they were, in case anything ever happened to me. Sometime after the last letter, I learned from an old MCI colleague that Allen Floyd had died of a massive heart attack. Had he lived longer, I'm sure he would have continued spewing his vile words my way. I was sad for him, as I would be for anyone who was so clearly disturbed and full of hate. At the same time, I was glad my letter ordeal was finally over. (Years later, I burned them all.)

◆ ◆ ◆

My rise at MCI continued. The job I'd landed back at the corporate headquarters in 1991 was as director of Consumer Markets Customer

Service. I was managing more and more people, at higher levels, and was doing more course management and training.

I had a great team in the DC office and wonderful teams of people out in the field implementing some fantastic programs. The most memorable was the Service Council Summit. We brought supervisors and above from all over the country together with some of the highest-level executives to Denver for a three-day conference, to discuss their most difficult issues and help one another identify their needs and solutions.

I hired a team of outside consultants to organize the summit; we had a big budget, and no detail was overlooked. We got off to a terrific start. The president and other executive board members flew in on the first day to give a talk at our kickoff meeting ... and were stuck in Denver when a blizzard shut everything down.

"We didn't plan for this! What are we going to do with them?!" those in my group said.

By that point, Diana's advice from way back in Baltimore had become my way of working. "We just have to figure it out and get on with it!" was my response.

We incorporated the executives into the sessions and discussions that we had planned for the attendees and treated them like any other participant. People seemed to think that we couldn't possibly treat our biggest bosses like everybody else. But we did. And it was amazing.

Everyone benefited: The higher-ups got to hear and understand the concerns of the people who ran their service centers and interacted directly with customers. When it came time for me to request the resources they needed to address those concerns, the executives already knew who I was and understood our plans to take our services to the next level.

That blizzard was one of the luckiest things that could've happened for my career. It made me known to those in high places at

MCI and allowed them to see me be effective in the role of director—even in the face of an "act of god."

Over the course of that year, I could tell that I was being eyed for even greater things. Given where I had come from and how I had spent my early years, it was inevitable that that nagging voice would butt in every now and then: *How did I get here? Have I really earned it? Will they find out that I don't belong and send me packing?*

But I was getting better and better at managing myself into accepting that level of success. When the doubts crept in, I would ground myself so as not to drown in the thoughts. Yes, I am a boy who grew up in a shack with no bathroom floor. Yes, I am a drag queen who's led a wild life on stage and off. Yes, I am HIV-positive and medically vulnerable.

And yes, I am also a corporate executive, wearing the hell out of this business suit. And I made it here because of, not in spite of, who I am.

There will be times when you will be hit with an absurd number of challenges, one after another. Focus on the knowledge that you *will* be rewarded with valuable lessons on the other side of the storm.

TWELVE

Six Months to Live

I N THE FALL OF 1991, I TURNED THIRTY-SEVEN—ONE year older than Bubby's age when he died. Two years into my diagnosis, I was working just as hard on maintaining my health as I was on succeeding at MCI.

From that very first afternoon, sitting in my car after getting my test results, something crucial began to happen on the level of sheer will. Ever since I was a little boy, my determination had been the strongest part of my personality, and that part of me hadn't changed. *I was determined to be the one in control of how the virus affected my life.* If there was even the slightest chance that I could slow down the disease though nutrition, exercise, and taking care of my mental health, why not try it? (I'd always said I'd try anything once—twice if I wasn't sure.) And if it's worth trying, it's worth doing all the way.

I had let AIDS crash the party, but no way was I going to let it steal the spotlight.

* * *

I was on a variety of drugs—all the while continuing the meteoric rise at MCI. I would get stable on something, but it wouldn't last. We would try something new, but that would make me sick. It was up and down, up and down. I looked forward to the periods of stability, but the thought of the next drug failure was always looming. Then there would be a different cocktail of drugs and different side effects.

It seemed like an endless cycle, but somehow, I managed not to go under. I would not be defeated. I just kept on going, taking whatever drug was next, trying to figure out how to survive this illness.

And there was richness in this experience. I was observing it at the same time I was inside it. I tried never to reject or deny it, but to embrace the chance to deal with it and learn from it. I kept reminding myself that I could focus on the horrific parts of it, or I could find the gifts in it.

More often than not, I felt great. I ate well, slept well, and had the energy to keep up with the pace and travel of my job. The drugs I was on had nasty side effects, but I would push through them and try to carry on as usual, always knowing where the nearest bathroom was located.

But you can't argue with numbers. And AIDS was all about numbers.

I didn't realize how sick I actually was until I went in for a regular visit with Larry Bruni. He did the usual tests and came back with shocking news about my T cells, a certain type of white blood cell essential for a functioning immune system. A low count means you're open to a whole host of opportunistic infections. A healthy adult usually has a T cell count between six hundred and one thousand. My T cell count was 109.

Ever since my first appointment with him, he'd been talking to me about resigning from work, or taking advantage of the health benefits through my job and going on disability to focus on my health. I qualified for it and was making a good salary—certainly enough to live on for however much time I had left. I never took that suggestion seriously; I wasn't going to let the virus change my way of life and who I was becoming. Leaving work felt like giving up.

At this visit, he told me flat out: "With numbers like this, you probably have six months to live. Do you want to die at your desk? Don't you want to do something else with the life you have left?"

This time, the message started to stick. I still had all my energy and didn't look or feel sick, but I was starting to lose weight. I sensed internally that some things were starting to change. And at that time, there was only one way this could go.

· · ·

There was something very painful, and very powerful, about coming face-to-face with my mortality in those early years after my diagnosis; terminal illness brings things into focus very quickly.

It was as if everything I'd ever experienced or learned in life was coalescing and gathering around me—not for me to look back or dwell on, but to help me look forward.

The hardships at the Shack, the illnesses of those around me, my insatiable curiosity, a lifetime of feeling out of place, the death of Bubby—I knew there was great wisdom to be found in those experiences. I knew I could reach out and hold onto that wisdom to use in the fight ahead. I understood that the fight would ask me to look at everything differently, but that my path would be simply to be present, assess what was happening, use all the resources I could muster, and keep putting one foot in front of the other.

Once more, the answer was not to avoid, deny, or try to get around the illness. I learned to stand in the middle of it all with both feet and to continue to make choices.

Coming Out to Mom and Dad

When I made the call to my parents from San Francisco General about Bubby being gay and having AIDS, it would have been the perfect moment to say, "I'm gay, too." But I didn't. It just seemed like too much, for them and for me. When I first learned I was positive, I still wasn't ready. Perhaps it was my way of continuing to take care of them, of shoring them up with the good news of my stability and success and shielding them from bad news they didn't even know was out there. But I couldn't put off telling my parents any longer.

The last time I had seen them was a couple of months earlier, for Mom's retirement party. She had worked as a lunch lady for twenty-eight years, and I can't imagine how she spent all that time on her feet. She was trying to make it to thirty years, but I think one day she finally looked at the difference between her retirement benefits at twenty-eight and thirty years and decided that she'd had enough. "I can't stand on my feet any longer."

The school board put on a big party every year to honor those who were retiring. It was always at the Thunderbird Lodge in Jacksonville, which used to be a stylish restaurant and entertainment venue. Lots of people were invited, and each retiree was recognized with gifts and a little speech. It was a very gracious, generous event. Mom was one of a handful of people retiring that year, but she'd been there so long and was so well-liked, she was really the belle of the ball.

I was, of course, working and traveling all over the country during this time, but I had a plan for this retirement party and enlisted my father as a co-conspirator. I told Mom I couldn't come, and she was very, very disappointed. Dad explained to her that I had to work, that I was traveling and climbing the corporate ladder, and so on. I told her how sorry I was, and as far as Mom was concerned, that was that.

On the day of the party, I secretly flew into town, rented a car, stopped to pick up two dozen red roses, and drove over to the Thunderbird. I had to change into my suit in the Thunderbird parking lot and got caught by the security guard. (I think he let me be because I was getting *into* the suit, not out of it.)

I snuck into the banquet room where the luncheon was being held and hid behind a big column as everything got started. I felt like a character in a spy movie, sneaking from one column to the next around the edge of the room, waiting for the perfect moment to surprise my mother. The only other person who knew I was there was my father. He was in photographer mode, moving around, taking pictures of everything I did.

I waited through presentation after presentation. Mom was up at the head table with the other retirees and the school district bigwigs. She wore a stunning emerald green dress and, of course, had her hair coiffed perfectly. She looked so beautiful, and I was so proud of her. Finally, I couldn't stand it any longer. I snuck around behind her and tapped her on the shoulder. When she saw me, she jumped up and threw her arms around me. She was astonished and kept saying, "I can't believe you're here!"

I gave her the roses, tears started streaming down her face, and we just held onto one another. I sat down next to her at the table, and she was so proud to have me there. Many of those people had known me as a child—through all the craziness—and there I was in a suit, flying in to celebrate her retirement, and showering her with roses.

My dad, of course, captured nearly every moment. Thanks to him, I had photos of the whole sequence—me coming in and hiding, Mom and I embracing, sitting at the table together; if I spread them all out, I could relive the whole event.

I hated that our next time together would be very different.

· · ·

To coach me through the process of telling my parents about my condition, in the fall of 1991, I decided to see a therapist. We determined that I would write my parents a letter laying everything out and send it so they'd receive it before Thanksgiving. By the time I visited them for the holiday, they would have had some time to digest the information, and I could answer all their questions face-to-face. I would come back again at Christmas, which would give us all a second chance to talk and just be together to process the news.

In the letter, I tried to be as straightforward as I could and let them know that I was doing everything humanly possible to stay healthy and stay alive. I assured them that this wasn't going to be the same sort of situation we'd had with Bubby—that we had time and that we would deal with it together.

They were devastated, of course, and extremely concerned. In November 1991, it was all over the news that Freddie Mercury died of pneumonia resulting from AIDS, and Magic Johnson announced that he was HIV-positive. Tragedy felt inescapable. Now, they had a second son who was gay, had full-blown AIDS, and who I'm sure they thought was going to die before their eyes.

Thanksgiving that year was very sad. We didn't see many people, just spent time together and talked a lot. That's when I made Mom and Dad a promise that I was going to outlive them both. That's always been my way, after all: I put a stake in the ground and commit myself with my entire being to whatever I decide I'm going to do.

I said I would be around for years to come. And I'm still here.

Who Am I Without Work?

When I found out I was sick, I knew I would not stop working. It wasn't so much about the money; it was more about losing my identity. I loved being on the fast track and doing things I'd never dreamed I'd have the chance to do. I was discovering a big, wonderful world and learning how to master it. I didn't want to give that up, but by this point in 1991, my body just wasn't going to let me continue.

So I decided to switch jobs. My new job would be to take care of myself.

After writing that letter to my parents, resigning from MCI was one of the hardest things I've ever had to do. When I told my boss, John, that I was sick and could no longer come to work, he received the news in the most compassionate and understanding way I could have hoped for. I've always thought that he must have had a friend or loved one die of AIDS, because he was so much more empathetic than any straight person I had encountered up to that point.

"We're going to take care of you," he said.

I thought I would start on disability right away, but John pulled some administrative strings and kept me on the payroll for a few more months, though I was no longer coming to work. He waited until I hit a certain employment milestone in June 1992 to officially put me on disability, so as to maximize my stock and insurance benefits.

John's generosity spoke to the kind of company that MCI was and embodied one of the many lessons I learned in my eight years with them: *If you do right by people, good people will want to work with you—and they will perform miracles on your behalf.* Because of our relationship and our mutual respect, he made it possible for me to focus on my health: to face the music, do what needed to be done, and keep moving forward.

· · ·

I turned to my new set of priorities right away, and because it was as important for me to help others heal as it was to heal myself, I became a leading member of the HOPE Foundation: Healing Opportunities and Positive Energies. (I came up with the name myself.) We were a buyer's club that worked with nutritional health and experimental HIV treatments—some on the books, some off the books. The group of us who put together the foundation got very close, and I think that network of support was one of many important factors in my healing.

Two men in the group, Bill and Paul, were a couple and both worked for senators. Bill was positive; Paul was negative. That was a common situation. The building they owned and lived in had a vitamin store on the ground floor, where we would do nutritional counseling. We also sold vitamins or gave them to people—and if we got to know you, you might get invited back to take part in some of the experimental treatments we were doing.

Nobody had answers back then, so we tried everything from injecting ourselves with a bovine thymus from Mexico called Thym-Uvocal, to drinking Aquaflora antifungal formula until we glowed in the dark, to rubbing enzymes on ourselves, to bitter lemon enemas, to any combination of these and many other things. We were desperate enough to try anything, no matter how crazy, just to stay alive until something better came along. I will never really know whether any of these treatments was the thing that kept me going. I just know that I am alive today.

The HOPE Foundation was a center for spiritual care as well as cutting-edge treatments. We became like a band of brothers on the front lines of this epidemic, healing one another as we tried to heal ourselves.

That work reinforced for me, once again, how important it is to me to be of service to people, especially those people who have had everything taken away from them—their careers, often their friends and families, their health, and their sense of being in control of their own lives.

HOPE turned out to be a unique resource and became very popular; even those in the mainstream medical community began sending people to us or working with us themselves to administer treatments that were experimental or on the cutting edge. Larry Bruni gave us infusions of IL-2, Interleukin 2, which was usually given only to end-stage renal cancer and kidney cancer patients—if they could get it. Some studies showed that it raised your T cells, so we tried it. We did a series of infusions that were very debilitating and very difficult. Before we even started these infusions, we were given prescriptions for Vicodin and Xanax to help us withstand how painful and stressful they were. I still have a scar on my arm from where the fluid leaked out from the injection site and burned my skin.

We later learned that you could get the same T cell–boosting results with much lower injections over several months. I hope our experiments helped with that discovery in some way, so others didn't have to go through what we did.

The side effects for many of these treatments were horrific—nausea, vomiting, diarrhea, and gas. Because I had become so finely attuned to my body, I learned to intuit when I just had to stick with a treatment until I got through the side effects and when I should stop.

Everything we did had one goal: to stay alive until they found a cure. By 1992, AIDS had become the number one cause of death of men aged twenty-five to forty-four in the United States. Science was simply unable to keep up with the epidemic. I knew my body very well, and I knew that what I was getting was not enough, so I grabbed at anything I could do to bolster my immune system. If somebody had told me it would help to put leeches up my rectum, I probably would have tried it.

Throughout it all, the theme that kept running through my mind was still, "You don't have to die. There's no reason you have to die from this." That's probably one of the reasons I didn't die from it.

Full-Time Job

By the time I went on disability, I had only about nine T cells. The lab work said one thing; my body yearned for something else. AIDS was a wasting disease; it wanted me to lie around, do nothing, not eat, allow my muscles to wither and atrophy. But I knew intuitively that the key to my health was to be active, engaged, and strong.

The Skyline had an amazing fitness center with classes, weights, machines, pools, anything you could imagine. I was not an athlete and, of course, had been terribly locker room–phobic in my youth, but one day I decided just to go down and stick my toe in the pool. I checked out the classes and signed up for one or two. They weren't so bad. Before long, I was doing three high-impact aerobics classes back-to-back each morning, plus swimming and lifting weights. Then I'd jump on my bike, not at the gym but out in the beautiful countryside, and ride to Mount Vernon and back—a round trip of five hours! It was typical of me to go from sticking my toe in the pool and maybe taking a little bike ride around the corner to that kind of intense regimen. Once again, if it's worth doing, then it's worth doing all the way.

This fed me in all kinds of ways. I was in the best shape of my life, and all that exercise made me want to eat, so I was keeping my weight up. All the activity fed my soul as well. I would ride my bike by the Potomac River, watch the sun's light reflect off the water, and just imagine that I was physically breathing it in as an energy source. The light became an elixir that I could take in through my eyes and imagine distributing to every cell in my body. It was so powerful— and empowering. During these bike rides, I would stay present to the beauty and the cycles of nature around me. Both the inner and outer healing took enormous amounts of energy, and being out in nature replenished and fed me as much as the healthy food and supplements.

The Potomac River became my metaphor for God and the universe. I melted into it and let it take me places where I hadn't been before, spiritually. I was becoming one with the whole. That was not the first or the last time I would use nature to heal and strengthen myself, both spiritually and physically. But that period was when the spiritual and the physical really began to come together.

I don't want to paint too rosy a picture. While I was drinking in the sunlight off the Potomac, I was also taking all those experimental drugs, whose side effects were notoriously brutal—so I was often vomiting or on the toilet between aerobics classes. But I looked so amazing that I worried the disability people might come after me and claim I was a fraud.

And yet—I still had practically no T cells. If you looked at my lab work, I should have been dead. It was amazing that these two conditions could occur at the same time, in the same person: being so sick and being in such great shape.

Somehow, they found a way to coexist. I think what tied them together—tied me together—was the spiritual element.

Spirituality would become a huge part of what I would call my Healing Wheel. It came about in a funny way. Jane once took me to see a condo with a dining room light fixture made from this horrible, gigantic wagon wheel. I could not go on, it was so terrible. But oddly, I couldn't get that fixture out of my mind, and the wheel became my central image for healing.

I was at the center of the wheel, and the spokes were everything that was helping me get better. One was my doctor. Another was my acupuncturist. Another was my masseuse. Another was therapy, and another was spiritual. Each spoke represented one aspect of my healing. At certain times, one spoke needed to light up more brightly than the others. Then it would fade back, and another spoke would become more important.

The key was that I was at the center. I was in charge. I would describe this Healing Wheel to doctors, and if it wasn't okay with them to be a spoke, then I knew we wouldn't be a good match.

Looking Inward

I believe I've always had a relationship with the unseen, the spiritual, and the metaphysical, even as a child. I left the church because I felt it didn't approve of me, but I never lost the conviction that there was something greater than us at work and that I could still connect to it in my life.

That yearning toward the spiritual, toward connection,
has remained a part of my life ever since.
I didn't have to step into a church to feel that.

As I started to think more intentionally about my spirituality at this point, and as I confronted the realities of AIDS and the loss that it was inflicting on the world, the need to reconnect to a spiritual community became essential. I explored different approaches during this time. I knew I wasn't going to go back to the Methodist Church. There was a brief flirtation with the Unitarians at the end of my time at MCI, but even that was bigger and more formal than what I was looking for. I wanted something that was based less in Jesus and more expansive.

I was still working when I discovered the Arlington Metaphysical Chapel. This was closer to what I was looking for. It was a small, white, wooden chapel, but it felt all-encompassing. I'd always been interested in the metaphysical, in asking questions about the world beyond what we can sense, and this organization was all about that. Their services were based on spirituality and consciousness rather than formal religion, and all types of people were welcome.

Every year, they held a Sunshine Week, which featured every kind of metaphysical worker imaginable: psychics, tarot readers, mediums and intuitive readers who helped connect you to your angels and guides, and all manner of healers. It was run like a fair, and you had to sign up in advance for a slot with this or that practitioner. I had been so busy traveling that I had forgotten to sign up. When I got back to town, I headed for the Arlington Metaphysical Chapel— totally depleted, desperate for some energy and succor, and looking forward to diving into Sunshine Week. But when I arrived there were no slots left. Everyone was booked solid, and I felt bereft.

I must have looked very blue, because someone came up and whispered that there was one practitioner available. He pointed across the room to a woman sitting by a crystal ball. That was not exactly what I'd had in mind, but I figured what the hell. I was very out of sorts as I dragged myself across the room, imagining myself looking into a crystal ball like Dorothy in *The Wizard of Oz* with some woman who was probably a charlatan. At the very least, it might make for a good story.

Her name was Julia Jackson. She looked to be in her sixties, maybe five feet, two inches tall (if she had heels on), with gray hair up in a bun. I slumped into the pew beside her and very quickly realized that there was a great deal more to this person than met the eye. I felt a very, very strong connection to her and sensed that whatever she was about to do to me with this crystal ball, it would be good, and it would be important.

I think that anybody who met Julia, with or without her crystal ball, would be curious about her because of the way she held herself and the presence she projected. She was serene and almost regal and filled the space more than her five feet, two inches frame would suggest. I just wanted to *talk* with her, about anything. It turned out that she was a very well-known and respected social worker and therapist and was also very involved with the Press Club in Washington. She just happened to be into metaphysical practices that allowed her to stretch into other areas she was personally interested in when it came to helping people.

My reading with Julia Jackson was one of the most profound experiences of my life. It wasn't so much about the crystal ball; it was really just an intense, intimate communication with a uniquely gifted person. The conversation ranged from who I was, to who I might be, to what was going on in my life, to what I was looking for at the church that day. Whatever happened during that hour, I needed more of it.

I began having sessions at Julia's house, a big old family home in Maryland. We would sit in her living room, in two comfortable chairs with a coffee table that looked like it was a stack of books. It was like being in a safe, wonderful cocoon, surrounded by shelves lined with her pottery and other art projects.

We did standard therapy, focusing on several issues, including sex and work. She also helped me communicate with people on the other side, such as my friend Peter, who had died of AIDS before I'd had a chance to say goodbye. Julia helped me see that in the time we had spent together before he passed, I had already let him know how much I cared for him and loved him. She took me on a mental journey where Peter and I sat together on a bench and said our goodbyes. There was no doubt in my mind that Peter was there with me.

Julia and I developed a beautiful, synergistic connection over the course of those years in Washington, DC, that I felt sure would prepare me for events that were to come in my life. We always looked forward to seeing one another, and I don't think either of us ever wanted those sessions to end.

Looking Outward

Though I spent a great deal of time working on my body, mind, and soul, I was by no means a hermit. I would still have visitors from out of town, go out with friends, or visit friends in other cities. I even had the occasional romantic tryst, though I never did anything with anyone that would put them, or myself, at risk. I was never one to hold back on doing things, and that still held true—unless someone else was trying to wheedle me into doing them.

My twentieth high school reunion was scheduled for the spring of 1992, and I had no intention whatsoever of going. I had always hung out with older kids and had been a thespian, not a prom king. I had gone to the reunion for the class a year ahead of me—with Sandy and Lucy and Douglas—and thought it was kind of fun. I'd also gotten to see my parents, which was nice. But I thought there would be absolutely nothing for me back at Duncan U. Fletcher High School with people from my own year. My parents were under strict instructions not to give out my contact information to anyone who came asking for it. *Anyone!*

My mother always had the best intentions, but every now and then, she would call me with some big sob story. Somebody needed, really needed, to get in touch with me—and I would give her permission to tell them where I was. Well, evidently, the reunion committee chair called her up one day and knew just what to say to her. They buttered her up by asking for her professional opinion about how much food to order and begged her for my contact info because they really, really, really wanted me there. They would not leave her alone, so she called me and said, "You need to go to this thing."

One day, I caught a look at myself in the mirror and thought, "Based on how people looked at that other reunion, I just might be the highlight of this party. Plus, most of them probably haven't strayed very far from Jacksonville Beach—and I have."

So I decided to go. I put on a suit and showed up at the Sawgrass, a big, fancy hotel and golf club in Ponte Vedra—and I *did* turn out to be a bit of a celebrity. I was one of the few people who had moved away, and people seemed stunned to see me. One person even said, "I thought you were dead!" I had to explain that no, that was my brother. I was very much alive.

A number of people came up to me to say hello, people who never would have spoken to me when we were in school, and were actually very kind. Some even said they wished they had gotten to know me better back then. That made me feel really good.

Late in the evening, one of the big football stars came sidling over and seemed really interested in talking to me. Finally, I said, "Look, you wouldn't have gotten near me back then. What are you doing?"

He said, "Well, I'm gay, too. I want to talk to you."

How the tables had turned.

· · ·

In the end, it wasn't so bad. I reconnected with a few other people and shared some old stories. Four sets of husbands and wives emerged from our class, and they were all now teachers at the school. There was a lovely memorial table for all the people who had passed, one of whom was Suzie, the little girl I had called an idiot in third grade when the teacher washed my mouth out with soap in front of the class.

As the evening ended, everybody was talking about having a twenty-five-year reunion. That was a little much, so I said, "Talk to me if you can find me."

Looking West

Pola was still living in San Francisco and was due to give birth to her first child in June 1992, seven years after she and David were married. I had plans to go visit three weeks after the baby was born, to help out after everybody else had gone home. I arrived on schedule, but the baby had not!

Pola was still hugely pregnant when I got there. She was so uncomfortable, and I really felt for her. Her doctor finally said that if the baby didn't come by a certain date, she would either have to have a C-section or find a new doctor.

On the appointed day, Pola, David, and I drove over to the hospital. We got all gowned up and were waiting for the ob-gyn to begin when I pulled out my video camera.

"You're going to record it?" Pola asked, horrified.

I said, "Pola, what do you think I'm going to do with the video? Sell it? I'm going to give it to you!"

The ob-gyn said, "It's fine with me, but you need to get permission from the anesthesiologist."

The anesthesiologist marched in, and Pola asked her if we could record the delivery. She clearly wasn't very excited about that prospect, but I said, "Look, I used to work in intensive care. You won't even know I'm here."

She looked at me, then looked at David, and asked, "Who's the father?"

"We don't know," I said slyly. "That's why we're both here."

At that point, the video camera became the least of her worries, and she decided we could do whatever we wanted.

Being present for the birth of Starr was one of the most amazing experiences of my life. I remember her first cry, and showing her to Pola, and watching the two of them almost reaching out into each other. It was an honor to be there as she was welcomed into the world. And I made a silent promise to this baby that I would be around to be a part of her life.

I became a father figure for Starr, especially after Pola and David got divorced during her childhood. I would dress up as the Easter Bunny and Santa Claus, surprise her on my visits, and did everything I could to be in her life. Pola was very much thought of as a part of my family, so my parents became Grandma Mary and Grandpa Vic to Starr, since Pola's mother had died and her father was so badly affected by a stroke. Mom and Dad were delighted that, in my own way, I had managed to give them a grandchild.

Sometime the year after Starr was born, Pola and Starr came out to visit me in Washington. I was still doing well, but it finally felt like things were starting to catch up with me. I was having a course of Interleukin-2 infusions at that time and was feeling so sick as a result that I threw up as we were pushing Starr in her stroller down Pennsylvania Avenue. Something was shifting, and it was going to get harder and harder to keep doing this on my own.

You can't keep someone from crashing your party—but they don't have the right to steal the spotlight. Don't deny that what's happening: get sad, get mad, then remember that you are still in control. And keep making choices.

THIRTEEN

San Francisco!

I LOVED THE LIFE I HAD BUILT IN WASHINGTON. I HAD friends, I had my all-consuming health regimen, I had a good doctor, and I was decently close to my parents. I was still alive more than two years after Larry Bruni had given me six months to live, so I was doing something right. But if I wanted to be where I had the best chance to live, I really needed to be in San Francisco. It was the center of America's gay community and the hub of the AIDS epidemic, where all the research and new treatments were happening. I still looked great and was remaining very active, but my labs continued to be terrible, and I grew concerned that my illness might outpace the resources and experience available to me in this city.

Plus, I wanted to be with my people. Pola and Starr were in the Bay Area, and Douglas's boyfriend, Michael, who had lived in San Francisco before, had moved back and was working on getting Douglas to follow him out there from Denver.

So, in September of 1994, I flew out to look for an apartment. I went around looking at rentals for days and couldn't find anything I liked. The day before I was supposed to fly back to Washington,

I met with an older couple who owned several rental buildings in Twin Peaks. They showed me one apartment on the top floor of a beautiful building on Portola. It had everything I wanted, but I knew I couldn't tolerate the noise from the traffic below.

They showed me another, which didn't work for me, and then told me reluctantly that they had only one more apartment coming available soon. It was just like the Portola place but on a higher floor, so there would be less noise. But the current rental situation had been "a bad thing"—that's all they would say about it.

The tenants had to be out by nine o'clock the following morning, so we gathered there the next day, a few hours before my flight.

Knock, knock. No answer. The tenants had already left, so in we went.

The first thing I noticed was that there were no light fixtures, only bare bulbs, and no switch plate covers. There were beautiful wood beam ceilings, but they had metal hooks protruding from them. I spotted a pool of what I am sure was urine on the hardwood floor. The bedroom had murals of an orgy, with men doing everything imaginable to one another.

I took one look at the bathroom, turned around to the old woman, and said, "Please don't come in here." There were mirrors inside the toilet.

There were beautiful skylights and huge, panoramic windows, but they and the sliding door to the deck had been covered with black paper. Food had been left wherever it landed after being tossed aside. I imagined slices of pizza flying across the room, splatting against the wall, and dropping slowly to the carpet. Half-empty Coke cans littered the living room. You couldn't even tell what color the carpet was.

It was just utter filth, everywhere. I kept yelling to the old lady, "Don't come in here!" She finally came in and saw everything. I thought she was going to have a heart attack. Their beautiful apartment that had been completely trashed.

I excused myself and went out onto the balcony for a minute. It was a very foggy day. The balcony jutted out over the land beneath it, and I felt like I was suspended in the air, among the thick clouds, with no one around me. I couldn't see the view, but I knew the city well enough to know what that view would be on a sunny day. I imagined standing out on that balcony in the sun, taking in all the energy reflecting off of the buildings and the bay, just as I had done by the banks of the Potomac.

I went back inside, looked at this sweet older couple, and said, "I'll take it." The woman's jaw dropped. The man looked at me and said, "*What?*"

"I'm assuming it will all be fixed," I said.

"Yes," he stammered. "And you can pick the new carpet color."

"Okay. Great."

And with that, I was off to the airport, knowing I had a place to live when I moved the next month.

The first time I stood out in the sun on that balcony and could actually see all the way to the bay, the view was even more stunning than my mental picture had been.

My Fortieth Birthday Party

When my brother died, one of the things I noticed was that none of his family or friends knew one another. At a time when he had a lot more serious concerns, he was trying to play Julie Cruise Director, introducing all the people who had come to see him in his final days at the hospital. I realized that I was in much the same position. Most of my friends and family didn't know one another either, and I had no interest in being Julie Cruise Director. None.

The move to San Francisco coincided with my fortieth birthday that October. The doctors were telling me I would not live to see my forty-first birthday, so I put together a party with the people closest to me—both to celebrate and so they could meet one another.

I had sent out "Save the Date" invitations as soon as I knew I would be moving to the Bay Area, so people would have plenty of time to plan. I created a gray scale of my first-grade picture for the invitation that became the theme for this whole event—a three-day sojourn at the Lighthouse Lodge in Pacific Grove near Carmel, about two hours south of San Francisco. It was the perfect way for me to start my new West Coast life, alongside everyone who was special to me.

I invited my parents, Pola and David, Douglas and Michael, and a few other close friends from MCI and DC. People came from all over the country, and I arranged for each person to have a special flower in his or her room that had some meaning for that person, along with a personal welcome note from me.

We had a little meet-and-greet dinner together the first night and breakfast the next morning. The only other scheduled event was the big birthday dinner at Fandango's wine cellar the next night. Other than that, everyone was free to tour around or do whatever they wanted. Some people went on little outings to the beach. Others went shopping in Carmel, to the pier in Monterey, Asilomar, the Monterey Aquarium, or just walked around beautiful Pacific Grove. I spent the day working on little touches and special preparations for the evening.

The dinner at Fandango was wonderful. I'd asked my father to send me a bunch of family pictures, which I hung around the room and used to create a slide show. Everybody made a big deal out of giving me their presents, and the food was absolutely fantastic. Douglas got really drunk and said "fuck" in front of my parents, so I had to take him aside for a moment—but all in all, it was a great success.

The next morning some people were hungover, but it was great fun because everybody was in good spirits. Mom and Dad were so excited to be there, and it was fun to watch them take it all in.

Each person took home a little personalized photo album of the weekend, which I put together specifically for him or her before that final breakfast. This was before digital cameras, so I got all those pictures developed and organized while they were off on their outings or sleeping after the dinner. Each album was different, but each had the picture of me as a kid on the cover, and each included a picture of that person's individual flower inside.

After the breakfast, most people left. Some, including my parents, stayed another day or two to enjoy Pacific Grove and Carmel. I disappeared immediately and got my butt up to San Francisco as fast as I could, because I had to put together my new apartment before my mom and dad arrived to spend time with me before going back to Florida. I slept on the floor in my new apartment that night and met the movers the next morning. By the time my parents got up to the city a day later, everything was finished. I'd even hung all my pictures.

Not only was it a wonderful weekend for all of us but I knew I'd never have to play Julie Cruise Director.

Rita Reemerges in San Francisco

This celebratory spirit carried on through my first month in my new home in San Francisco—so much so that, for the first time in ten years, Rita Dayworth reemerged!

She'd been very well-behaved for a long time, and that Halloween, she made her San Francisco debut. I had very long hair at the time, so I didn't need a wig. I had my hair and makeup done at a salon in Union Square called The Atelier, then got dressed there. When I was

 all done up, I posed in the salon window, reveling in the attention of all the people walking by.

I hit the streets around Union Square in full drag, meeting and greeting tourists and residents alike. Then it was off to the Castro! It was the beginning of a Halloween tradition that would last for years. I became a neighborhood celebrity. I don't know how many people took pictures of me over the years, but it has always tickled me to think that there are images of Rita in the photo albums of people all over the world.

"Body by Romeyn"

After the excitement of the move and my first few weeks in the city, I settled down to business. I was very sick and needed to find a whole new Healing Wheel for myself here in San Francisco.

AIDS doctors were in very high demand in San Francisco, and the wait lists for the best ones were often two or three months long, so I made appointments with several. The first doctor I met with was supposed to be a big shot. I was terribly anemic, and he thought I should have a blood transfusion, but I wanted to try to raise my red blood cell count with a drug called Epogen instead. We went back and forth, and I made another appointment at which we were going to make the final decision.

A few days later, I got to his office for the second appointment and waited. And waited. He was an hour late. We sat down and, after what seemed like only a few minutes, he looked at his watch and said, "Your time's almost up." The metaphor was too much for me, as was his attitude. I crossed him off my list and prayed I would hear from one of the other three doctors whose waiting lists I was on.

Miraculously, I got a call from the office of Dr. Mary Romeyn—somebody had canceled, and I could see her at the end of the week. I was thrilled. I had heard great things about this doctor. She was cutting edge and worked with nutrition and other modalities beyond pharmaceuticals.

Mary's office was way out in the Sunset District. I remember walking in and thinking, "This is a storefront!" It was a nice office but not exactly high-end or downtown. She partnered with a cardiologist, which sounded interesting, and she had a whole lending library full of books in the waiting room. Next to these books, on the ground, was a life-sized ceremonial African statue of a woman dressed in black that lit up, and that I was sure would scare children and small animals. I'm certain there was a story behind it, but many years later, after I got to know Mary better, I did say, "We have to take this out of here. It's frightening people!"

I sat down and looked around. There were chairs and a person behind the counter, but I could sense that the experience of being in this office was going to be more like a clinic than a quiet little doctor's office. That was a good thing. Just then, I heard a woman's voice and sensed immediately that it was Mary Romeyn. I could tell by the way she was talking that she had a presence and was obviously very open. Then I saw her looking at me from the hallway, and something about her face and her voice and her smile reassured me. (I later learned that she was looking at me in such a way because she didn't have her glasses on and had no idea who I was!)

I filled out copious amounts of paperwork in record time, because I was so used to doing it, and was taken to Exam Room 2—which later became known as Tom's Exam Room. I sat down on the table, and something on the wall, something very familiar, immediately caught my eye. It was a photograph that looked like it had been taken from the balcony of my apartment in Twin Peaks, looking out toward the bay. Either that, or I was sicker than I thought and was hallucinating. I decided that this was a good omen and relaxed a little more.

Finally, Dr. Romeyn appeared and introduced herself. I didn't know as many specifics about Mary's history as I do now, but I could sense even then that she must be one of the most giving, generous human spirits on the planet. I later learned that her whole family had been activists, and that she had started med school when she was already the mother of three boys and a grandmother to boot. She has been with me in voice, body, and spirit for most of the crucial moments in my life since that day.

My presenting symptoms were fatigue, anemia, diarrhea, gas, weight loss, a systemic fungal infection, and a bit of Kaposi's sarcoma. Mary convinced me that I was so sick I should be in the hospital—immediately. That wasn't an easy thing to do, since I had tremendous resistance to being in the hospital. (In our years working together, we would go back and forth about hospitalization many times. I came to accept that when she really insisted I do it, I just needed to listen to her.) That day, we compromised. I agreed to go to the hospital—but the next day, after I'd had a chance to go home and gather myself and my things. Somehow, I always managed to negotiate for the next day.

Once I was admitted and they started their tests, I ended up on amphotericin, otherwise known as ampho-terrible, for a systemic fungal infection. The first dose of this drug is always administered in the hospital because some people have a severe reaction to it. I didn't, but it turned out that I had many, many other things wrong with me as well—so many that it was smarter just to stay in the hospital while they did more tests, and everything could be sorted out.

I was a walking target for all sorts of opportunistic infections because my immune system was shot and I had very few T cells. I think the only reason I was alive was that I'd been propping myself up with exercise when I could do it, a lot of vitamins, and God knows what I had injected myself with in Washington that might also be helping.

There was also my will and my intention. I had told the virus that it would have a fight on its hands, and it did.

On a less clinical level, Mary told me that I looked "translucent, at best" and that she could see right through my energy. She said there was just no density to me at all at that point. I didn't like what she saw, but I did like the fact that she was looking at energy and other things beyond what appeared in the lab reports.

As much as I resisted being in the hospital, complained about being bored, and kept asking if I could go home and come back when they were ready to do all these tests instead of waiting, I stayed because I instinctively trusted Mary.

They administered every test imaginable, and Mary and I had a very frank conversation. She told me I was going to die in six months or less if we didn't move quickly. And still there were no guarantees. I had heard this two other times by now, but my body had never been in such a compromised state. She jumped in and literally saved my life. Because she said I needed it, I had the transfusion I'd refused earlier, and we began a regimen of drugs and nutrition.

Mary insisted that I eat everything I could possibly get down to keep my body as strong as possible to fight off the next infection that would try to take me down. Eating and nutrition were the cornerstones of her whole philosophy, and she was very strict about this. She would go on to publish many books and articles on the topic. Even her license plate said EAT, EAT, EAT.

Pills, Pills, and More Pills

The next few years were a time of experimenting with various drugs and treatments, going through the horrible side effects, having them either fail or stabilize me, and just putting one foot in front of the other. I remember filling out a form once to get into a drug study. They listed all the AIDS drugs, and you were supposed to check the ones you had taken. I had taken some of them twice. Was I supposed to make two check marks?

I had very few T cells to begin with, and over these years, they would go up and down based on what I was doing and what drugs I was taking. It was a roller coaster. Something might happen or I'd get sick, and they would drop or I'd lose weight. Then I would build it all back up. There might be a period of stability in which my body healed and bolstered itself—and that's when I could try something new because I was going at it fresh. These "drug holidays," when I would cut back or eliminate the drugs, were illuminating because I got to see where my body really was.

At one point, I was in the hospital for some treatment or other, and they gave me a triple dose of a necessary colonoscopy laxative by mistake. I ended up on the toilet for quite a while, needless to say. I moved the bed stand with all my books and other hospital amusements into the bathroom, repositioned the TV, and just sat on the toilet until it was over.

It went on for so long that I started hallucinating. A huge group of people, most of them deceased, were in the room with me. People like my grandmother and Bubby were saying things like, "Really, it's time to think about leaving. You don't have to go through this anymore. Do you want to come with us or not?" It was very, very real—they were truly standing there—but rather than scare me into thinking I was about to cross over, *they reminded me that I had a say in the matter.*

Putting My Trust in Dr. Mary

Through all of this, my relationship with Mary was getting deeper and more trusting. There was just something about the two of us together that was synergistic and magical. We fought—or rather, tussled—because I never wanted to go into the hospital. She tried to respect that, but sometimes she needed to be tough. She never actually *made* me go, but she would always point out what might happen if I didn't, and somehow, we always worked it out.

I remember one time being very, very, very sick. I called her and said, "I'm lying in bed and I can't get up." My blood pressure and heart rate were normally very low—a "benefit" of my bike riding and my exercise days. I had a normal heart rate of about 50 (normal for an adult is 60–100), but that day it was below 40, and I had bradycardia, which the Mayo Clinic defines simply as "a slower than normal heart rate." There was a class of drugs that had the side effect of lowering your heart rate and blood pressure, and they always gave me trouble because mine were already below normal.

"I'm calling an ambulance," Mary said.

"I won't answer the door," I said.

"Then I'll have them come in," she said.

"They can't. I have to buzz them in."

We went back and forth and finally Mary said, "They'll break down the door." We both started laughing, and she said, "I'm coming over. I'll do four hours. You've got to find somebody else to do the next shift."

That was the kind of doctor she was. A saint.

I had to take drugs up to five times a day, which could be awkward socially. And it seemed like the more need there was to hide all these pills, the more brightly colored and enormous they became! I had pills that were hot pink, or orange, or a rather startling blue. All kinds of strange colors. And they were horse pills, so you couldn't just slip them casually into your mouth and swallow. They were always saying, "Hello! I'm here! Pay attention to me!"

At first, I wondered how I was going to take all these pills when I was out with people. Hold them in my mouth and try to hide them? Take them into the bathroom and wash them down with water from the faucet? After a while, I started noticing that everyone was taking pills. Gay and straight. Sick and well. They took food supplements, diet pills, depression pills, skinny pills, acid reflux pills, blood pressure pills—the whole world had a handful of pills. It was not the end of the world.

Eventually, I would just toss back a handful wherever I happened to be, and if anyone looked startled, I'd just reply: "Gay San Francisco Male."

Trial and Error

Mary slowly pieced me back together, and I became much more functional. I was always on the lookout for ways to contribute, and obviously, I admired her and her work tremendously, so I started volunteering in her office. She was a clinical investigator for the recently founded Andrew Ziegler Foundation for AIDS Information and Testing, and I ended up leading clinical trials on new drugs in her office. In between my ups and downs and reactions and illnesses, I became executive director of the foundation, which had been set up to give people with HIV and AIDS access to care regardless of their ability to pay.

I loved finding a niche in San Francisco where I could not only give back but also be around information and treatments from which I could benefit and stay on the cutting edge myself.

We did clinical trials for Expanded Access Drugs. The idea was to speed up the FDA's process for approving drugs, so that they could go to patients earlier. And if we were the ones doing the trials, then our patients would already have access to them.

Today, you would have to be an RN or MSW to do what I did, but I was very good at it, and we had an amazing team. I learned the drill very quickly, as I had at MCI, and just had a natural talent for setting up systems that made this kind of thing work well. Our community was in a crisis. I was a really smart guy, and Mary was a really smart doctor, and together we were saving lives.

I was still sick enough that I needed to be watched closely, and of course, it was helpful to be working in Mary's office. If I needed to be thrown in the hospital for twenty-four hours, she could do it—or try!

Another benefit of working there was that I was in a unique position to counsel other patients or at least comfort them. I had already been through what a lot of them were facing. I knew all the side effects and could talk them through what was going on and compare it to other drugs. I could also help them be specific about their symptoms, which streamlined their process with Mary and helped them communicate with her in a way that made the most of their treatment (and wouldn't get them kicked out of the trial).

I knew the psychological side as well. I knew what it was like to have the disease wear you down and make you feel like giving up. I felt as if part of my role, apart from managing the clinical trials, was just to get people into a good space to see Mary. Over the years, I watched some of them thrive, and I watched some of them die.

We got to work with children, too, and get both the kids and their families access to better drugs, vitamins, and nutrition. Some of these studies led to the development of the first nutritional standards for children with HIV.

Helping with the clinical trials became part of my new Healing Wheel. I believe that doing that work is one reason I'm alive today. Not only could I access cutting-edge treatments myself, but I could also help other patients approach their situations with less fear and emotional overwhelm, and a more positive, realistic spirit.

Helping them realize they were in control helped me immensely in return.

I also had the benefit of being near Mary—not just as a doctor, but as a friend. She started calling me "Little Brother," and we were always in each other's presence, even when we weren't in the same room.

Building a Support Team

AIDS was life-threatening, certainly, but it was important for me not to focus on the prospect of dying from it.

I made it about learning to look clearly at my situation for what it was, not for what I was afraid it was. I could look at life, and death, and illness as part of the journey. It was about learning what was important in life and strengthening and deepening my connection with the divine.

HIV was also about using all my resources—my ability to think clearly and figure things out, my trust in my own intuition, the wonderful people around me like Mary, and my own will—to keep the virus from interrupting my party. I might spend hours hunched over the toilet on any given day, but I was going to keep moving on and moving forward.

Part of moving forward was putting together my Healing Wheel in San Francisco. I had moved partly to take advantage of all the healing modalities available here, and I didn't want anything to fall through the cracks. I made my way around the healing circuit, meeting various people and getting referred around, and was very careful about the people I chose to work with me. I got plugged in very quickly and, for the most part, have stayed with those people through the years.

I began with my own environment and routines. I would get up early every morning and watch the sunrise. I chanted and meditated and journaled. There were 263 plants in my Twin Peaks apartment because I found them beautiful and healing. I continued riding my bike as I was able and started taking little pilgrimages to some of the beautiful spots around the Bay Area—especially Point Reyes and a gorgeous little Vedanta retreat in Olema in Marin County.

Next, I needed a chiropractor, then a massage therapist. And since I believed that a great part of my healing took place beyond the physical, I needed a regular therapist, but one who would take a similarly open approach to healing. Thankfully, I found Barbara Berkeley, DC—a healer with a huge heart.

A woman named Maureen Redl started out as my therapist, but we quickly became friends instead. At one point, we were both falling asleep in our sessions, which was fine, but it didn't make sense to pay for that—and we really, really enjoyed one another's company.

Maureen was a remarkable woman who had had stage 4 ovarian cancer but was in remission. She led a group called The Healing Path associated with her nonprofit, Voices of Healing, which included three women and me. We would meet every week and do work with auras and other healing techniques. Our little healing group had all sorts of adventures. We met a guy named Phillip Scott, who was a shaman. He claimed to be a Lakota chief and was really quite an amazing man. I'm not sure if he was actually Native American, but two or three times, we paid our ten dollar donation and joined Phillip Scott at his healing circles (called Medicine Wheel, interestingly enough) up on Mount Tamalpais. I took Moriah with me. We would march out to a holy place on the mountain in total silence and find our place on a circle of stones. As the ceremony progressed, we might move, chant, listen to a talk, or offer various issues we wanted to heal or transform.

Maureen found a fantastic tree on Mount Tam, and we started having our own healing circles up there. This tree had been struck by lightning, so one half of it was green and the other half was not. It was a great metaphor for healing, and we used to go up there and talk about death, dying, healing, and anything else that was occupying our thoughts.

The healing circle was one way that I pursued healing beyond the world of blood tests and T cell counts. It helped me work in realms beyond the physical, which is where I think healing really happens.

San Francisco was also the perfect place to search for a larger spiritual community to reconnect with. There was a spiritual teacher, church, or workshop on every corner in those days. I was thrilled to find my people at the Unity Christ Church on Ocean Avenue, a little jewel box of a church with a wonderful feel about it. It had been there since 1918, and back in the 1950s, the Unity movement had counted Maya Angelou among its congregants. The minister, Sharon Connors, spoke to my soul. She gave inspiring, thought-provoking talks and brought in extraordinary guest speakers who embodied the positive, loving, and accepting elements of religion that I was so hungry for.

Everything I heard there reminded me that my life was about connecting with something greater and expressing that connection. That's what brought all the widely divergent elements of my life together—that sense of something higher, of being one with the whole.

Abundance

The through lines of my early days in San Francisco were staying alive, deepening my connection with the divine, exploring the city and its people, and getting to know myself better. Despite being sick, I felt like I was living life in abundance. As much as I was working on my health and well-being, I could not forget how fortunate I was compared to so many others living with AIDS. Thanks to my job and disability benefits, I didn't have to worry about where my next paycheck would be coming from.

Money becomes a strange thing when you're living with a terminal illness. One school of thought is to live like there's no tomorrow: spend everything you've got, max out your credit cards, and don't worry about the bill because you won't be here when it's due. I never subscribed to that way of thinking—it felt messy.

Instead, I took a different approach: I beefed up my life insurance as much as I could, and opted for viatication, which is akin to a reverse mortgage. In 1995, I had a $400,000 policy through MCI. I negotiated with a viatication company and signed it all over to them in exchange for a certain percentage of the face value up front. This was during one of my "You have six months to live" countdowns, and I wanted some ready cash so I could live the good life. There were so many people dying from AIDS at this time that the viatication business was booming.

The terms of these viatications are based in part on your Karnofsky score, a conglomeration of medical information that basically predicts how long you're supposed to live. Based on my medical information in 1995, nobody on earth, except perhaps me and Mary Romeyn, would have predicted that I would still be alive today. I was supposed to die. So I negotiated to get paid $365,000 up front.

I was getting disability payments of $5,000 a month and now had this extra infusion of cash to do with as I pleased. I had enough to pay my rent, to support Mom and Dad when they needed it, to pay for medical treatments, and to simply enjoy life. The viatication company expected to receive my $400,000 in death benefits in the near future, so everyone was happy.

Only...I didn't die. I just didn't.

Because they thought I wouldn't be around much longer, part of my arrangement with them was that they would direct any correspondence to the representative who set it all up for me, so I had no real legal obligation to them whatsoever. My policy has changed hands four or five times since I did it. I have no idea who owns it now, nor do I care. All they care about is that they will get their money when I die, which I assume I will. Someday.

· · ·

With all this money, I decided to buy Mom and Dad a new car for Christmas that year. They had been driving the same Caprice forever and were still taking trips with their friends, so I thought they should have at least one more new car in their lives. I was in Florida that Christmas and visited the dealership there, but everything seemed to be working against me. They didn't have what I wanted on hand, and I wasn't even sure which color my parents would prefer. The dealership was closing, and I had to go home the day after Christmas. So there would be no car.

Then I had an inspiration. I remembered when I was little and the keys to our new house were on the Christmas tree at the Shack—and I decided to do the same thing. I took two blank keys, a red one and a green one, and hung them on the tree.

When we'd finished opening all the presents, I said, "You haven't found them all." After much searching, they discovered the keys on the tree. What did it mean? When I told them I'd bought them a car, they were beside themselves.

Still, there was no car in the driveway, and I was leaving town. I needed co-conspirators to pull this off, so I called my parents' friends, Bryant and Mary Jo. I hadn't been able to surprise my parents with the actual car at Christmas, but that didn't mean I couldn't surprise them at all.

Bryant and Mary Jo often traveled with my parents, and they all loved to go to the Cracker Barrel on their road trips. Bryant organized a trip to the Cracker Barrel for the whole gang. He and Mary Jo somehow fixed it so that when they came out of the restaurant after dinner, a Sandalwood-colored Caprice Classic was waiting for them in the parking lot, with a big red bow on the hood. They took pictures and sent them to me, and I cherished those old photos.

I loved being able to do that for my mom and dad and to have them share in this new life of abundance that I was so thankful for.

Trust is a huge part of transformation: Trust in yourself and your instincts, and trust in the friends and loved ones you invite to share in your journey. You're in control, but there will be times when you need support and someone else to take the lead. They may be able to guide you to a place you wouldn't have reached on your own.

FOURTEEN

A Different Kind
of Doula

I WAS NOW SIX YEARS INTO MY DIAGNOSIS, MAKING THE most of all this time that no one was expecting me to have, and living a pretty enviable life—despite the obvious. It sometimes felt a bit strange to have to confront other, non-life-threatening situations while also dealing with a terminal illness. Couldn't I get a pass on everything else?

One day, Pola's husband, David, and I were riding our bikes out to Tilden Regional Park in the East Bay. It's a gorgeous area filled with wildlife and beautiful wooded trails. We were having a great ride, but we started coming down a very steep hill too fast. Suddenly, my rear tire slipped on wet leaves and started to skid out from under me. The hill was to my left and a deep ravine fell away to the right—in a split second, I decided that it was probably wiser to use my left leg as a pogo stick than to fall off the mountain into this deep ravine. I fell and hurt my hip, and my bike got banged up a bit, so I had to walk down the rest of the way. I was sore, but it didn't seem like a big deal. It could have been so much worse.

After several months, my hip still hurt. I got massages and chiropractic treatments and all the things I usually do, but nothing helped much. Finally, I gave in and had an MRI. The hip is a ball-and-socket joint, and I had torn the protective tissue in the joint when I fell, so the bones were rubbing against one another like sandpaper. I was going to need a hip replacement. To this day, all the doctors I've seen blame the weakness in that hip on the protease inhibitors I took for AIDS because avascular necrosis in the joints was a common side effect. I don't know if that was the case for me; I just know that the accident at Tilden was enough to cause the damage.

Everybody agreed that this hip was only going to get worse, and I should schedule a hip replacement as soon as possible—but almost immediately, I had another priority: my mother.

Mom's Secret Diagnosis

My mother had been getting mammograms and doing breast self-exams long before there was so much publicity about them. (I didn't know this at the time, because we certainly did not talk about her breasts!) One day, she found a hard lump, like a kernel, on the side of her body. She showed it to her ob-gyn. He said it was probably nothing and sent her to a dermatologist, thinking it could be a skin growth rather than something in her breast tissue. The dermatologist was a woman, and as she started to remove the growth, she realized it might be something else, though she didn't share this with my mother at the time. She sent the growth out for a biopsy. The lab results confirmed that it was breast cancer.

But, true to form, my parents didn't tell me about any of it at the time. While I was fighting to keep myself alive, so was Mom. I learned about all of it after she had been treated with radiation and chemotherapy and was preparing to have a mastectomy (which they also told me not to fly out for).

After her diagnosis, she had gone to the Mayo Clinic, and they had treated her like a queen—but I don't think that their one-size-fits-all, Western medicine approach worked very well for her. Though she beat the cancer, I believe she was treated far too aggressively. But Mom was from the generation that believed you simply turned your body over to the doctors and took it back when they were through.

About eight months later, they realized that she had myeloblastic leukemia, cancer of the blood and bone marrow, which can sometimes result from radiation and chemotherapy treatment. I had my own opinions about how we'd gotten here but had learned many years earlier that it was her body, not mine; I could share my thoughts, but she got to make the decisions.

So, we took in this news, and we all did our best not to dwell on things beyond our control.

With the myeloblastic leukemia diagnosis, they gave her six months to live (I'd certainly heard that before), and I wanted to make sure she got as much out of that time as possible. I knew that if I had my hip replaced, I couldn't be there for her—so I put it off and resorted to mind over matter, a lot of Vicodin, and creativity.

I conspired with my father to keep her alive by planning trips and trying to make her life as beautiful as possible. I thought that if she stayed active and engaged, we might keep her around a little longer—and it worked. Those trips picked up her spirits and kept her busy.

I brought Mom and Dad out to San Francisco as much as I could. She had to get transfusions every two weeks, sometimes every week, and Mary Romeyn took care of her when she was with me. Once,

"Dr. Mary," as my mother called her, was helping her get one of her regular transfusions at Saint Francis Hospital, and Mom became extremely anxious. She started babbling nervously, so Mary went and sat down on the floor in front of the couch where Mom was sitting. She said to Mom, very gently but firmly, "I need you to be quiet now and listen to me."

It was the equivalent of telling my mother to "sit down and shut up." My mother did just as she was told, but Dad was flabbergasted. He said, "That's the first time anybody's told her to be quiet."

* * *

The most memorable trip was to Disney World in Florida. Our group included Pola and Starr, who was then five, my parents and me, and Jim Graddick, who also knew my parents. I coordinated the trip, and all of us descended on Orlando.

Starr was our little princess. Everybody bought her toys and clothes and little amusements. It's hard not to feel like a happy child when you're at Disney World, regardless of your age. We had tremendous fun and, of course, spent a lot of money. We were astonished to discover that the little books with all the Disney characters' autographs cost fifty dollars—but we had brought our own autograph books, purchased at Target for five dollars. My mother said, "Thank God we bought those books before we came here."

We walked around, went on rides, and had a fine old time. Mom was in a wheelchair, and I told her, "You may not like being in this wheelchair, but we get to cut in front of everybody in line—so you're staying in it whether you need it or not!"

On the second day of this adventure, I had plans to slip away to see Jimmy, my first love from The Melody Club days. I hadn't seen him in many, many years, but I knew he was living in Orlando, so we planned to meet at Applebee's.

I left the group in good hands, I thought, and drove over to meet Jimmy. I sat there forever, waiting and waiting in a seat where I could see the door. Suddenly, I heard a loud roaring noise—and then watched as a huge white monster pickup truck barreled into the parking lot. Out of it emerged...I wasn't sure who. I knew it was Jimmy, but he had long, long blonde hair and was wearing short shorts, with bruises all over his legs from what I later learned was sclerotherapy to get rid of varicose veins. He looked like he was in some sort of transition (but whatever was going on, it was not a good time to wear those shorts!). The whole thing was confusing to me because when we were together, even though he was a drag queen, he was far from being a woman in the bedroom. I thought I understood his sense of who he was, beneath the gowns and makeup.

We started talking and catching up, which naturally led to a conversation about his transition. My basic message to him was, *"Are you sure?* I was there, I know what happened, and I know you better than almost anyone else. I want you to be happy, but *are you sure?"* We chuckled over the times we had together, and after a while, we went our merry ways. That was the last time I saw Jimmy. He is now living as Anne.

I raced back to Disney World to rejoin my family. When I arrived, it was quite a scene. Jim was over in a corner, white as a ghost because, as I later learned, he'd been puking his guts out from a roller-coaster ride. My mother and father were huddled together on a bench, looking distraught. She was kind of buried into him, and he was trying to hold onto his sunglasses and somehow comfort her at the same time. Pola and Starr looked stunned.

"What's going on?" I asked in alarm.

Well, my mother loved the little trains that go around the whole park on a track. Toot-toot, ride around. They were going to take her on the train—but instead, this whole group somehow wound up on a roller coaster. My mother, who had gotten out of her wheelchair for the ride. Starr, who was five, and not only too young for the roller-coaster but too short. Jim, who was taking God knows what drugs and battling horrendous side effects. Everybody. Pola later told me that the minute she heard those first click, click, click, click noises as they started up the first hill, she realized they had made a terrible, terrible mistake. She imagined that everyone was going to have a heart attack, and then I was going to kill *her*. All she could think of, the whole ride, was my poor mother and how she was about to die on her watch.

I looked around and thought, *Damn, I was only gone two hours.*

Once they were all visibly recovering, I said to Mom, "You know, you look really good! Maybe shaking your blood up was good for you. You have more color than you've had in a while. We should put you back on there!"

"Oh, Thomas!" she replied, in the exasperated but loving tone we always heard when we were giving her a hard time.

The only one who enjoyed the roller-coaster ride was Starr.

Sweet Douglas

Knowing that Mom didn't have much time left was an unexpected blow to me. But by this point in my life, I was rather comfortable with death, not just as an abstract concept but as an imminent event. All my hospital jobs certainly contributed to this, as did my natural ability to handle a crisis:

> *I've always been good at cutting through the noise, focusing on what can be done and not wasting precious resources—time, physical energy, emotional attention—on what can't be helped.*

In the era of AIDS, being good around death was a natural progression.

The death of Bubby had been a baptism by fire, and for the last ten years, I'd been staring down my own mortality, having heard the six-month prognosis no less than three times by this point. Mom was now contending with her own prognosis, and in my work with Mary, we were always trying to find new and creative ways to keep one step ahead of the inevitable. But it didn't make it any easier to deal with when it came for Douglas.

Douglas had tested positive for HIV a few years before his move to San Francisco, when he and Michael were living in Denver. They had been together since about 1980, and I used to visit them a lot. I remember one night in Denver, we all got really, really drunk, and when I passed out on the couch, they proceeded to dress me up in drag and put flowers all over my hair. The whole event was caught on video. I threatened their lives when I found out about the tape, but I'm now glad I have it as a memento.

When Douglas got AIDS, he was so angry. Something was being taken away from him all over again. He'd grieved the loss of a part of himself after the car crash in Florida nearly twenty years before, but he had found Michael since then, and they'd built a wonderful life together. In Denver, Douglas became the director of Food and Beverages at the Denver Athletic Club—a career he was terrific at and identified so strongly with—and had gotten back some of the spark he had lost. He had been a fighter all his life, and he had a lot of pride, so it was extremely difficult to convince him he had to leave all that behind in Denver. But San Francisco was the place to be if you were sick with AIDS, so he finally agreed to join Michael back in the Bay Area. (Interestingly enough, Michael was negative.)

Around the time of Mom's diagnosis, Douglas also started to get really sick. He got all the usual opportunistic infections and could no longer walk. He had Kaposi's sarcoma on his face, so he never left the house because he didn't want to be seen. He took his medicine, sometimes, but continued smoking cigarettes and drinking the equivalent of a fifth of vodka a day. It was so hard to see him that way, but he was not a good patient. He was very angry and mean, and Michael—unfailingly loyal Michael—was near the end of his rope. At one point, he called an organization named Respite, which got him away for a long weekend just to give him some space and a chance to recharge.

When Michael went off to his Respite rest, I said to Doug, "Come on. We're going for a ride."

"I'm not!" he said.

"Yes, you are," I said. "I know what this is about. You're afraid somebody is going to see you—but we're not going anywhere where anybody will see you! We're just going for a ride."

He kept refusing, and we went back and forth about this until finally I said, "I'm going to pick your ass up and carry you out there."

At that point, he changed his tune.

"Fine. But I'm going to walk."

The only walking Douglas had done in quite a while was to the bathroom, with a walker and somebody helping him. But in his mind, he was going to walk.

"Fine," I said. "I'll stand at the base of the stairs, and watch you fall and hit your head. Then we'll take you to the hospital." I was losing my patience and spoke to him as only one of his oldest friends could. "You ornery son of a bitch; you're being mean to everybody. But I don't care. I'm going to carry you and put your ass in the car."

I loaded him in, and we headed out to Stinson Beach and Point Reyes. I'd brought along a couple of bottles of water and was glad to see him drinking so much of it. It was good for him to be out in the world again, and our conversation picked up as we drove. I loved him too much not to direct it toward the inevitable. I think that was the first time anyone had said to him as directly as I did: "Douglas, do you know you're going to die?"

He was very mad at me for saying that, but I let him have his anger reaction. Then he opened up, and we were able to talk about a lot of things we hadn't talked about before in a very honest way. I told him, "You're being a real jerk. You're not helping the people who are trying to help you. Michael's dealing with a lot. Do you want to be remembered as a total asshole?"

I've had some very difficult conversations with people, and some of them have thought I was cruel—but I think I've always known how to hold a loving space in those conversations. It feels like "tough love," but they know I say those things because I care about them. Douglas finally understood that.

We pulled over to the side of the road in Point Reyes, at a beautiful outlook over the water. We walked out to the end of it as best we could and kept talking. That was a precious time. When we got back to Douglas and Michael's Noe Valley apartment, I helped him into his hospital bed. Michael came home from his Respite. Life went on.

Shortly after that day, Douglas told me that he had decided to commit suicide. It was common back then for people who were very sick to ask their doctors, if they'd developed a genuine relationship with them, to help them stockpile drugs for a cocktail. The doctors usually weren't present themselves when you took that cocktail—they had to have plausible deniability because they were risking their license to do this for their patients—but they made sure you had what you needed to end it all. There was so much hopelessness back then, and many doctors just wanted to give people a way to exit with grace and dignity from a world that they thought hated them.

Douglas asked me if I would help him. I believe everyone is entitled to their own opinion when it comes to this issue, and what we say we believe may not be what we wind up doing when we are faced with such a decision. I can't say what I would have done in Douglas's situation, but I was very clear in my response.

"No, Doug. I will not help you commit suicide. I'll be there and hold your hand when you go. I'll support you and love you, but I won't participate in it. Tell me what else you need, and I'll do it." I tried to be as compassionate as I could.

Douglas had picked a date, and he had a plan. He got himself all set up in his hospital bed on the appointed day. When I arrived, the cocktail had already been mixed—a disgusting blend of Xanax and Valium and God knows what else. The idea was that he would just go to sleep and not wake up. It was supposed to be straightforward and effective.

Michael was on one side of his bed, and I was on the other. I held his hand as he drank it down. We talked and reminisced. There were long silences as well, and a lot of not knowing what would happen. I remember thinking, "God, be here." As I had done often in my life, I asked people on the other side to be with us and just tried to amplify that energy and presence.

Douglas got a little high, and we joked around. I started talking about waterfalls and butterflies, as I had with my brother. Then he got a little higher and a little funnier—and all of a sudden, out of nowhere, the doctor showed up. Doctors sometimes planned these unannounced calls just to make sure everything was going well, all the while pretending they weren't there.

"He should really be asleep by now," the doctor said with some concern.

I was still talking about waterfalls and butterflies. Michael was still on the other side of the bed. Douglas was getting higher and loopier—and then suddenly, he went completely white. He sat up and violently spewed out the whole drug concoction, all over us and all over the bed.

The doctor was horrified and said quickly, "I have to leave."

I asked, "What about us?! Are we okay?"

He said, "Just make sure you don't get it in any orifices." Michael and I started cleaning things up. I said something about how strange it was that someone who had taken so many drugs in his life would have such a reaction.

The doctor looked at me on his way out the door.

"He never told me he used to do drugs!"

Apparently, a man with Douglas's drug tolerance was going to need a much, much stronger cocktail if he wanted to be knocked out before his body rejected it.

After we cleaned Douglas up, he simply went to sleep. I can't say whether it was caused by the drugs, but he slipped into a coma and remained in that state for several days. And then he died. I believe he just wanted to go and, drugs or no drugs, that was his time.

＊ ＊ ＊

Michael notified Douglas's family and arranged his Celebration of Life. I didn't attend because I was traveling, which I'm sure seemed off to some people, but anyone who knew me well enough to have an opinion knew by then that I don't do funerals. I preferred to say goodbye in my own way. I want to tell you I love you when you're alive, not when you're gone.

Though, after Douglas died, I had been feeling like things were unfinished. I thought back to Julia Jackson in DC, and the many talks we had about Bubby and everyone else who had passed on, how she helped me see that I had shown my love for them by being there to help them prepare for their journey. Douglas and I had spent that meaningful day together out in Point Reyes, but when he finally died, it felt incomplete.

One day, a few months later, I returned to Point Reyes to process, recharge, and clear my head in the beauty of nature. I drove out to the spot where Douglas and I had sat overlooking the water. I looked down, and there in my car was the bottle of water that Douglas had had with him that afternoon. I walked out toward that beautiful outlook—with water all around and rocks below—and spent some time there talking with Douglas, reminiscing about what we had meant to each other, how fortunate we had been to know one another, and how special our relationship had been and would continue to be.

Then I had a little ceremony. I poured the rest of the water in that plastic bottle over the rocks and gave it back to nature.

· · ·

I stayed in touch with Douglas's family and paid them a visit the next time I was in Florida to see my parents for Thanksgiving. I hadn't driven through his neighborhood in years, and the whole area had since exploded into a big subdivision. I drove up one street and down another, looking for his house, and finally spotted it when I saw Doug's brother and sister standing outside. I hadn't seen them in more than thirty years, but I recognized them immediately. I parked the car and approached them and told them who I was. They screamed and rushed me inside to see the rest of the family.

Everyone was gathered in the kitchen, as they always were. Doug's mother, Eleanor, was cooking and started crying when she saw me. His older sister Pammy couldn't believe I was there. His much younger sister Jennifer only knew me from stories and just kept staring at me. Even his father, who was kind beneath a rough alcoholic exterior, cried when he saw me.

They asked questions about Douglas and told little stories about him, and even the brief time we spent together seemed to anchor them somehow. Babies had been born, and people had died. The family was getting bigger and smaller at the same time, and they needed touchstones to deal with all the change. I think one of those touchstones was our fondness for the time when we were kids together. We were all very poor, but we shared a lot of love and fun.

I had to get back to my parents' so the visit was short, but I felt like I had brought them Thanksgiving that year. They had needed Douglas's presence, and I had brought his spirit back into their house. As I left, I could see him standing there in the driveway, leaning against the car, watching his brothers drink beer.

Goodbye to Mom

In the meantime, Mom had been outliving her prognosis of six months and was starting to feel quite sick. I spoke to her every day. Then, in March of 1997, I got the call I'd been dreading. Mom was dying. I needed to go home—now.

By this point, I knew well what I needed to do when the death of a loved one was looming—for myself, for the person dying, and for those who were still here. I started to think of myself as a "death doula"—macabre to be sure, but it's the type of person everyone wishes they had around when it comes time to say goodbye.

I had learned from my brother's death, and all the other AIDS deaths, that I had to do my own grieving for Mom before I flew to Florida, so I could be strong for everyone else. I drove out to Point Reyes, which had become my place to grieve. I had a Celine Dion CD in my car that had been there for months, but I'd never opened. As I sat there surrounded by the beauty of nature, looking out to the Pacific, I decided to play the Celine Dion CD. The second track was "Because You Loved Me," which I had heard a million times out in the world but had never really thought very much about. That day I heard it differently, and it became the anthem for my relationship with my mother. To paraphrase the song, I am everything I am because she loved me.

I wept and relived my whole life with my dear sweet mother. She had done so well, given the difficult circumstances of her life. She had loved me unconditionally, even though I was very different from the son she might have imagined for herself. Mom was an angel on two feet. With deep faith and a huge heart, she was loved by many. Including me.

* * *

I left for Florida the next day. Just as I had imagined, the house was in total disarray when I arrived. The surprise was that my father was the only other person there. That was strange, because my mother had a huge group of friends, some of whom had known each other for forty-five years, who were very close, and often ran in a pack. They had a pact—when someone got sick, you got your assigned day to go and offer support. If you couldn't make your day, it was your responsibility to trade with someone else. They invoked this pact many times during their decades of friendship.

But no one was there. And the house was a mess. A Southern woman would never allow such a thing to happen, especially one who had a group of friends like Mom did. So I cleaned the house, and she thanked me profusely with the little strength that she had. Until then, I hadn't imagined how important it was to her to have a clean house.

Mom was set up in a hospital bed in the living room, drifting in and out of sleep. The hospice people came around, gave me their little caregiver training, and asked me if I would be okay. Little did they know that I was probably more experienced and better equipped than any nonprofessional medical person in the country to take care of my mother. I didn't want her to be in any pain, so they left fentanyl patches. They would make her a bit loopy, but it was important for us that she be as comfortable as possible.

She called me to her bed, and I crawled in with her. We had some very touching moments, just lying there and talking. At one point, she produced a ring. It was three diamonds—her engagement diamond, her wedding diamond, and her mother's wedding diamond— all redone into one setting. The diamonds weren't meant to go together, but they did. I thought it was stunning, as much for what it meant as for what it was.

She put this ring in my hand and said, "I was going to give this to your wife, but we all know that's not going to happen, so I decided to give it to you." It was one of the few times in her life that she had overtly mentioned my being gay, and we laughed together.

My father's role at my brother's deathbed had been the cheerleader. He picked it up again at Mom's death, until one day she asked me to stop him. I took him into their bedroom and told him, "I'm sorry to tell you this, but your wife is going to die. You need to stop acting like a cheerleader. It's not helping." And for the second time in my life, he cried, just as he had when I asked him to stop being a cheerleader with Bubby.

Eventually, I convinced her that it was time to call her friends. She had apparently already warned them about tears and gave me strict instructions about what to say: "You can come now. As discussed before, there will be no tears or sadness. I am fine. If you're going to cry, don't come." My first call was to Liz, and she put the word out.

The next day, there was a knock at the door. When I opened it, nine women stood there. Some I had seen recently; others, I hadn't seen since I was twelve years old. They all fawned over me. I told them Mom was slipping in and out of consciousness, but they were welcome to come in.

Mom hadn't said anything in hours, but suddenly I heard her voice wafting in from the living room. "Come in, come in. Gather around." They all did as she said.

She called them all around and sat up in the bed as if she were perfectly healthy. I stayed quiet as a mouse at the dining room table in this tiny house, watching and listening to what was going on in the living room. I learned for the first time that my mother was called their "queen" because she had always been their role model.

She looked each one of them in the eye and gave her a special, individual message. They were very loving but very frank. She advised one person to do this, the other person to do that. She told one woman, "You know you're in this relationship you shouldn't be in. What are you doing? Stop it immediately."

Then she told each of them what they had meant to her, and she started crying. But then she remembered that there were to be no tears, not even her own. She said she would see them again and asked them to please leave. They did exactly as she asked and filed out like good soldiers.

After her friends had left, my mother laid back down and went to sleep. I held her, and my precious mother died the next morning in my arms.

Celebration

My family did not have funerals. We all knew that when my mother died, there would not be one. Nor would there be an obituary or even an announcement. There was not going to be anything. That custom came from my father's family, and it was quite unusual for its time.

However, I decided that my mother should have a Celebration of Life. I wanted to do something, and I thought I could get this idea past my father. There were a lot of people who knew and loved my mother, and I understood how important it would be for everyone to have some sort of closure.

We did it in the Methodist church. A blind woman minister showed me around the space, and I was flooded with memories from my childhood. She gave me the hymnal from my childhood days, which felt just as heavy as it did when I was small. I remembered the smell, and being in the choir and the pews, and getting smacked on the leg for not paying attention or falling asleep. Being president of the youth group and going to Sunday School. And, of course, my sex education class with the Girl Scouts.

I placed pictures of Mom all around the chapel and gave a eulogy. I talked about Mom and some of the things she had done in a way that I hoped was fun, humorous, and moving. There was nothing too woo-woo or New Agey, but I tried to focus the energy in the room so that people could grieve and also express their appreciation of Mom and who she had been to them.

I remember her presence there that day and being so grateful for all I had learned from her and how much she had loved me. Overall, the tone was very lighthearted—just what Mom would have wanted—and when it was over, we had lots of food. I think that celebration was a good day for everyone. By the end of it, I was exhausted and just wanted to return to San Francisco for a little break.

· · ·

As I knew it would, her death hit me once I returned home and was relieved of the duty of being strong for everyone else. I was kind to myself and let myself grieve in the knowledge that we had had a meaningful and tender goodbye. I checked in with my father daily afterward; he was in deep grief. I planned my next visit back to Jacksonville Beach just a couple of weeks later.

There was a lot to clear out of the house, and I didn't want to burden my father with the chore, so I called Liz to come over and help. When I was cleaning out Mom's closet, I found the strangest thing.

There was one outfit in a size eight, and the exact same outfit in sizes ten and twelve. Then I found another outfit, also in multiple sizes. Most of them had never been worn. I was baffled, especially since nothing else in the house was particularly well organized.

I asked Liz, "What's with these multiple sizes of one outfit?"

She laughed and said, "Oh, that's an old trick of Southern women. It's how we deal with our weight. We buy the three sizes, and if you gain a little weight, nobody notices, because you've got the same out-fit on." I thought that was a brilliant solution to the age-old problem of yo-yo weight gain.

I arranged for Goodwill to come and pick up boxes full of her clothes and said goodbye to them all. Except for a nightgown. I had found it hanging in her closet and held it up to my face. It smelled like her, and I decided I would take it home with me.

· · ·

In the months following her death, I was very sick and flying back to Florida a lot, both to recharge my batteries and to check on Dad. With Mom now gone, I thought my dad would fall apart and not even be able to find his socks. He was a very strong, independent man, but the two of them had very clear roles. Every day, Mom laid out his underwear and socks, and he made it so that she never had to worry about things like how to turn on the lawn mower.

But Dad did amazingly well. He loved and grieved her, but he didn't go to pieces as I'd expected he might. I think it helped that I went in and reorganized the whole house, then just told him where every-thing was—including his socks. There were hundreds of pairs of socks.

One evening, we were sitting in the living room, and he told me that sometimes he heard Mom's voice in the night.

"I'm a little apprehensive to tell you this, but I talk to your mother," he said.

I looked at him and said, "I couldn't be happier to hear that. Tell me more."

We had a great conversation about how it was perfectly appropriate, even wonderful, that he should talk with her, and I told him I did, too.

◆ ◆ ◆

Since nobody in our family was ever buried, Mom's ashes were delivered one day a few weeks after she died. Dad just put them on the little table between the two chairs where they always sat. Those ashes remained there for months, in the tacky little box from the crematorium with her photo in a frame on top. I pointed out that this might make any visitors a bit uncomfortable, so he put them away in a cabinet beneath the table.

But she was still there with him, in their spot.

Your memories will always be with you, so death is not goodbye. It can be a new beginning or a continuation. I often talk to those no longer here in the physical plane. Give yourself permission to try it.

FIFTEEN

Welcome to the Party

B Y THE TIME EVERYTHING WAS SETTLED AFTER
Mom's death, my hip was in very bad shape. About a year had
passed since I'd injured it on the bike. I was in horrible pain,
and even with my bottle of Vicodin by my side, I couldn't engage in
a lot of the physical activities that I had relied on to keep me healthy
and sane, but the situation with my hip felt like a walk in the park
compared to the medical battle that I'd been waging for almost a
decade. Here was an injury you could point to on a scan, one that
had a clear solution—what a luxury!

Back in San Francisco, I started making appointments and
interviewing doctors—including a celebrity doctor who was widely
acclaimed. He was very late for the appointment and told me that a
new hip would last about twenty-five years—but in my condition, *I*
certainly wasn't going to last twenty-five years, so why even bother
getting it replaced? I wanted to reach out and hit him, or at least clue
him in on the fact that I was still here after three separate six-month
prognoses, but I decided that the better course of action was to leave
his office and never to let him touch my body. It was not uncommon

for doctors to treat people with HIV that way back then. We were going to die anyway, so why waste time and resources on us?

Thankfully, I learned about Dr. William McGann at the San Francisco Orthopedic Group, a genius when it came to hips, and I approached the situation in full control. Once again, I called upon my comfort with medical professionals and was not afraid to ask questions, draw boundaries, and be fully involved in my care.

Talking to My Body

I picked a date for the surgery based on where the stars would be—no Mercury in retrograde for me! Plus, I knew from working in hospitals that you always wanted to have surgery on a Monday or Tuesday because, starting midweek, the doctors were booking times on the golf course. (And you definitely shouldn't get sick in July when all the doctors are on vacation!)

Leading up to the surgery, I made a number of preparations. I watched videos of the actual procedure, so I could talk to my hip and tell it what was going to happen and what I needed it to do. I used my brain, my voice, my thoughts, my prayers, and my will to tell it which muscles would be cut and exactly how it should react and heal. Most of my body's work would be in knitting itself back together after the surgery, at which point I would talk to the new hip in the same way, to help it integrate.

I wanted my body to understand all of this; and in the process of explaining it to my body, my mind also came to understand it better. It is quite a thing to acknowledge that you will be cut open and then put back together even better than you were before. I was confident that this was how it would go.

On top of these mental preparations, I was going to have a physical reminder of my intentions with me as well: a special rock I had picked up during an outing with Maureen Redl's healing group. It had a vein of quartz running through it in the shape of a spine and pelvis, with the pelvis disconnected on one side—perfect for me. I had become very close to the women in this group and asked each of them to put something of themselves into the rock as we passed it around our circle. One put in "motherhood." Another put in "strength." I held it in my hand when I meditated and fed it healing energy of my own.

The morning ritual that I'd been doing for some time around AIDS—watching the sunrise, reading, ringing my bells, and meditating—worked beautifully in support of my new hip. I was meditating a lot back then. One of the tapes I regularly listened to on my Walkman was a recording of sounds from a man in a canoe on a lake at dawn—birds, wildlife, and moving water—which was great for meditation because it was very subtle and quiet.

I made more physical preparations as well. Mary Romeyn put me on a special diet and drug regimen, and I scheduled a session with my massage therapist for the day after surgery to make sure there were no adhesions. My acupuncturist was ready to swing into action as well.

The day of the surgery, I arrived at the hospital, my rock secured to my hand with white surgical tape. It made quite a statement. And, of course, I had my trusty little Walkman so I could listen to the sounds of the lake.

As always when I was going to go under general anesthesia, Mary Romeyn was on the scene, telling me everything was going to be okay. They wheeled me into the surgical suite, and there must have been about twenty people standing around. The doctor strode in, looked at me, and said, "Hello. What's with the hand?" I gave him a challenging look. He shrugged and said, "You're gonna have to talk to the anesthesiologist." That reminded me of when Starr was born, and we had to get permission from the anesthesiologist to attend the birth.

The anesthesiologist came in, stared at me a second, and asked, "What's with the hand?"

I said, "I want to keep this rock with me. It's taped to my hand very securely, so you can just put my hand wherever it's out of the way."

"What is it? A talisman?" he asked.

"Sure," I said. "I just need your permission to have it in my hand."

He kind of squinted his eyes at me and said in an amused tone, "Okay, you can have the rock. Is there anything else?"

"I want to listen to this tape while the surgery is being done," I said.

"You know you're not going to hear anything, right?" he said. "What's on the tape?"

"It's a man in a canoe on a lake at dawn."

I'm not sure what sort of answer he was expecting, but this seemed to satisfy him.

"Okay, anything else?"

"Yes," I said. "Could we have a prayer?"

I led the little operating room group in prayer. By then, none of them seemed at all shocked, even the doctor.

They knocked me out, and the next thing I knew, I was waking up in a recovery room. As I came to, I could already sense that something was very different. On a deep level, the hip pain was gone! I was in a lot of superficial pain from the surgery, of course, but that would subside and could be managed in the meantime. Because I was allergic to so many medications, they had devised a special little pain cocktail for me and gave me a button to push whenever I wanted some of it.

Lying there in bed, I made my recovery the main focus of my thoughts. The insurance company's rule was that I had to spend at least twenty-four hours in a skilled care facility after the surgery, or they wouldn't pay for any of it. To do that, I had to be able to walk up three steps on this wooden contraption. Easy enough. But before I could even get to the skilled care facility, I had to earn my way out of the hospital, and I planned to do so as quickly as possible.

As I lay there plotting, all doped up, a cadre of people in scrubs entered the room. I don't even remember who they were, but they asked me, "How are you doing?"

I tried not to be rude, but what a question—I was in pain! Thank God for my little button.

To my surprise, they wanted me to stand up and walk to the door. Even I wasn't expecting to have to start on my walking journey immediately after surgery. Though I wanted to be out of there as quickly as I could, I told them it felt way too soon to test the hip.

"We need to get you moving as soon as possible," they told me. So I made it to the door and back to the bed, but that was it. I don't remember anything until the next day because just doing that took everything I had. And I may have pressed the button some more.

The next day, they showed up again. Walk to the door and back. I had a friend who was a physical therapist, and he assured me I couldn't hurt my new hip, that this was, in fact, good for me. That gave me courage and inspired me to go farther. Once I made it to the door, I walked a little ways down the hall, then a little farther still.

The bed used in hip replacement recovery is called a Harrison bed. They strap you into it, press a button, and it slowly lifts you into a vertical position. You're basically standing up, strapped to the bed. They undo the straps and help you walk over to the door or wherever you are going. When you get back to the bed, they strap you back in and slowly lower you down from vertical to horizontal.

A couple of days after my surgery, I returned from the walk and got strapped back into the Harrison bed. The physical therapist and a number of other people were hovering around doing their jobs. They started to let the bed down—when suddenly, there was a huge metal crack. The bed slammed down flat onto the floor, all at once. I bounced up and down a couple of times, and everyone in the room looked horrified. I thought, *Dear God, what's happened?* And I reached for my button!

The next thing I knew, the director of Nursing and a hospital administrator were in the room. I'm sure they were terrified that I would sue. By that time, I'd pressed the button enough times that I was laughing and saying, "This is fun. Let's take another walk because I need to get up these three stairs." They switched out the broken bed, and I had never had so many visits from staff to make sure I had everything I needed!

Eventually, I did the three stairs—far ahead of time, I might add. When I got into the skilled care facility and they asked me what my objective was, I said, "To get out tomorrow." I was ready to go home. This institutional recovery felt like a prison sentence.

· · ·

I had the surgery on a Monday and got out of skilled care on Friday of the same week. I didn't like being a convalescent at all, but I did develop some skill at it. I had worked out an elaborate schedule for the month after I got home. I'd learned how to do this from my mother, who had done it for her friends when she got sick. Everybody wanted to help, so I gave each person a day to come visit and bring food. That way, they didn't all arrive at once, and I had a steady stream of people and dishes.

While I was entertaining this parade of visitors, I devised a host of little tricks to get things done and go places without the full use of my hip. God forbid I should stay home! If I wanted to drive my car, I could put a trash bag on the driver's seat, lean back into it, and turn myself around to face the front and reach the pedals. I got to brunch this way the next Saturday, and on Sunday, I went to the Unity Christ Church.

When I walked into church with my cane that day, there was a huge "Aahhhhh!" from the whole congregation. Now I was really motivated. I had a doctor's appointment in about a week, but I was doing so well that I thought, *Why wait?*

I went in early, walked around the office with no cane, and asked him, "What do you think?"

He looked at me and said, "Well, you're young." He refused to give me the satisfaction that my speedy recovery was my own miraculous doing and insisted on trying to make scientific sense of it.

I've never had the slightest problem with that hip. It's completely integrated into my body, and you'd never know it was there. Each time I have it checked, I'm told it's like it was the day they put it in.

I still have my wonderful healing rock, too. It's currently in a water fountain in my foyer, with others from around the world. But I'm not so sure about the Walkman.

Back on My Turf

Before too long, my body, and its nine little T cells, was back in working order. I continued to grieve the loss of Mom and Douglas, but I still felt very close to them, each in their own way. I communicated with them nightly and called on their memories as a part of my overall healing.

By the late 1990s, San Francisco life was settling into a groove. I was taking care of myself and staying at the forefront of research and experimentation thanks to Mary. I was a regular at the Unity Church, reading lots of spiritual books, meditating every day, and studying and falling in love with the practice of qigong. I became an instructor and taught a class every Saturday morning at Castro Yoga. And to balance out all that good behavior, Rita made her appearance on Halloween every year, of course.

By then, Moriah had moved to San Francisco as well, and it was wonderful to have an old friend to share in new things with. She had come out to visit from Miami and decided almost immediately that she wanted to move here. The rental situation in San Francisco was unbelievably tight, but I found her an apartment just down the street from me in Twin Peaks and convinced the landlord—the son of the older couple from whom I was renting—to rent to her without even meeting her.

Everything seemed to be connecting, and life started to get easier. Or maybe I was just starting to feel better and getting stronger. Whatever the reason, San Francisco was becoming *my* city, and for one of the first times in my life, I felt like I belonged.

· · ·

Moriah and I attended services at Unity one Sunday and saw something about an upcoming workshop they'd be hosting called "You and Money." By this point, I had already done every sort of transformational workshop or course one could imagine, so I thought, *Here comes another one*. But this was billed as a chance to understand how you related to money, which actually interested me very much. Money and I had had a complicated relationship. The Great Depression mentality that had shaped Mom and Dad set the tone for my entire childhood. In our family, the quarter the tooth fairy left was like solid gold. As a waiter, bartender, and drag queen, I had learned to survive mainly on tips. Even at MCI, when I was making a great living and climbing the corporate ladder, my humble beginnings made me feel like an eternal misfit, no matter how great I was at my job.

Maria Nemeth, the psychologist and coach conducting the "You and Money" workshop, was having a free hour-long informational talk for anyone who wanted to find out more. So, with equal parts curiosity and skepticism, I decided to check it out and convinced Moriah to join me.

Maria led with a question: "Would it be all right with you if life got easier?"

I chuckled at that because my life was pretty easy. I was on disability and had just viaticated a rather large insurance policy, so I had a very nice lifestyle without having to work. I mean, how much easier could things be? Then I remembered, *Oh yeah, I've got this life-threatening illness that I'm supposed to die from.*

What I did not know at the time was that this talk was what was known in California Consciousness Circuit lingo as a "guest evening" or "enrollment opportunity." It was put on by a cadre of Maria's volunteers who had all been rigorously trained by Werner Erhard, the controversial father of the self-help movement and founder of the infamous est seminars, which would eventually become Landmark Forum. God knows what those women had been through—they were all women—but their specialty was "enrollment." What that meant was getting all of Maria's workshops filled to the brim with eager, paid-in-full participants.

I thought of them as enrollment vultures. They hovered around the edges of the room as Maria spoke. I eyed them warily. I could tell they had me and Moriah in their crosshairs, ready to pick our bones clean. I wouldn't give them the satisfaction.

Moriah and I huddled in the corner after this little talk, reassuring one another that even if we got the full court press from the enrollment vultures, *we could not do this workshop!*

We told one another that things were already going really well for us! Moriah had just scored an apartment in Twin Peaks without even being seen. I had this great setup, even though I was sick. Still, we were both struggling with certain issues in our lives and felt there had to be some greater point to them. But what?

The enrollment vultures seemed to sense this and pointed it out to us. They assured us that we needed help—and they told us in such a loving way that we sort of believed them. Maria's talk was all about transformation, and that sounded a whole lot better than ruin, which was what the enrollment vultures vaguely suggested would happen if we didn't enroll. Good cop, bad cop. In the end, we couldn't fight them. We enrolled!

Before Moriah and I knew what was happening, we had been lovingly but firmly clutched in the velvet-gloved talons of these delightful people who, oddly, all wore whimsical batik outfits.

Breakthroughs

This class was held over four days, for eight hours a day. Moriah and I arrived for the first session with some trepidation and found places in a big circle of folding chairs in the church sanctuary. The enrollment vultures sat at a long table in the back of the room, taking mysterious notes and looking very busy and officious.

As the twenty or so of us took our seats, Maria Nemeth wafted up to the front of the room, trailing batik, and began.

She was tall and slender, with short brown hair and sharp, intelligent eyes. She started by reminding us that we had made a commitment to ourselves and one another and to follow the very strict rules of the workshop. Everything was extremely regimented—we were told what we could and couldn't bring, when we could eat, when we could pee. It felt like we were being inducted into the army. But there was nothing more important than being *on time, sitting in your chair, with your binder underneath it.*

I hated it.

It was my natural habit to be on time for everything, but the fact that this was being drilled into us in such a regimented and draconian way really raised my hackles and triggered my defiant streak.

There was an enormous sense of relief and release when our first break rolled around. A bunch of us stood around talking about what we had all just experienced. Some had the fear of God struck into them. Others thought, "How bad could it be?" Others of us were thinking we could actually leave and get our money back! (In fact, you could get your money back—but you had to go through the enrollment vultures to do it, so that wasn't really an option.)

When we moseyed back from this first break, we were all kind of milling around, talking and laughing, leaning on our chairs, and goofing off—completely oblivious to the fact that we'd promised to come back exactly on time and be sitting silently in our seats, ready to go, with our notebooks open on our laps, at precisely eight o'clock. Eventually, we did find our seats and looked expectantly to Maria at the front of the room.

You would have thought the world had come to an end. Maria looked solemn and pale. The enrollment vultures at the back table cast furtive glances at one another and looked as if they might explode. We had broken our promise! We had no integrity! We had not sat quietly in our chairs! We didn't have our notebooks open on our laps! *We were late!*

I remember thinking, *Dear God, I have to get out of here. I don't know if my nine little T cells can take this from these women.*

Well, after we had been dressed down, it got very quiet, and Maria started "coaching" us about what we could do to fix things. People dissolved into tears, and some looked on the verge of leaving.

Over the course of the first session, there were many times I wanted to quit, get myself thrown out, or simply run out of there screaming, "Keep my money! I'll pay you to let me leave!" A few hours in, I was invited outside by Maria for a talk. She asked me whether I really wanted to be in the course, what I wanted to get out of it, and ultimately, whether I should stay or leave. Something about her directness got through to me, and I thought to myself, *There is something here.* So I decided I was going to put my annoyance aside and just be here. (Later, I would learn that this very confrontational approach had roots in the est practices that had kicked off the entire self-help movement. Maria's was much more gentle, thank God.)

Despite my initial resistance, I soon was able to see that there was method to this madness and that real transformation was going to be possible. Those four days would turn out to be extraordinary.

Maria was a psychologist, but her focus was not going to be on analyzing what was wrong with us (though she could've fooled me after that first break), what had been done to us, and what was holding us back from our goals and dreams.

This was to be all about shifting our attention away from worries and doubts to the best qualities within ourselves and how we could use what we were going through to make a difference.

In that moment, she had put words to the way I had been living ever since I first got my HIV diagnosis: I was not going to let it take the lead. I wasn't going to wallow in my misfortune or misery. I was going to see my situation clearly, realize there was a future for me, and believe that there was always something I could find within myself, in the present moment, to keep moving forward.

That first day, we met a woman named Brenda, who lived near Moriah and me, and we wound up giving her a ride every morning. There was no way I was going to be late. Brenda couldn't decide which shoes to wear so I panicked and finally said, "Princess, just throw all the shoes in the car and decide as we ride, because *we are not going to be late*." She kept a half dozen pairs of shoes in my trunk for the duration of the entire course so we'd be sure to get there on time.

One of the goal-setting exercises we did involved making treasure maps. We decorated big poster boards with beautiful pictures of some dream we had: owning a home, taking a trip, finding a great job, planting a garden—nothing was too small or big. Then we spelled out our intentions and actions with letters from magazines. All of this, of course, had to be performed within strict time limits and overseen by the enrollment vultures—who, admittedly, were beginning to feel more like encouraging songbirds who did want to see us succeed.

Imagine a big room with about ten large tables, three or four participants to a table, with stacks of magazines all around them, and all thirty or forty people trying to find just the right pictures and letters from these magazines, on a deadline, with their hands all sticky with glue. And at their feet, under the tables, also covered with glue, about a foot of discarded magazine scraps.

It was bedlam, but the enrollment vultures pointed out that not only was this a great way to start putting your dreams into physical reality (a very sticky and frustrating physical reality), but it was also an opportunity to exercise focus within chaos.

Unity Christ Church had a tile floor, and since everything from the magazines had to be cut out just so, there were infinitesimal scraps of paper everywhere. They stuck to the tiles since, like everyone and everything else in the room, they were covered with glue. And you guessed it: We could not go home until every scrap had been removed from the floor.

But like so many other things we did, it was worth it. We went home with these beautiful treasure maps. My big goal, post-hip replacement, was doing the AIDS Ride—a seven-day bike ride from San Francisco to LA. Some people created beautiful gardens, or volunteered for causes they had always loved, or brought some other dream into physical reality.

Get off Your Pillow

In some ways, the "You and Money" course was like a time-release capsule; the benefits seemed to expand and grow with time. Certainly, it was about a lot more than money.

It started me down a path toward much greater awareness of what I was doing in life and why I was doing it.

Over the next three years, I took a lot of Maria's subsequent classes. My ultimate goal was to become a coach myself, and each workshop took me a step closer. There were also electives, from "Befriending Your Body" to "Life's Work and Purpose." The "Befriending Your Body" course was fascinating for me. Not only was I living with AIDS, but I realized that I had had several bodies in the course of my life—skinny kid, fat kid, awkward teen, young gay man, Rita Dayworth, and finally an adult gay man fighting to keep that body healthy—and that I'd had different relationships with each of them. Amazingly, I became much more open to intimacy. I became far more willing to let other people support me. I was able to be more vulnerable, and at the same time, I felt much, much stronger. Something had indeed opened up.

Those courses were also an opportunity to meet the most amazing, like-minded people. We had all been through "You and Money" and come out the other side. We'd learned that we actually loved the enrollment vultures and that they were doing the work of angels. I made many friendships in the Maria Nemeth world that are still strong today. It was an enriching, challenging time of development and personal growth.

◆ ◆ ◆

During those transformational months, it felt like the sap was rising. Like some big wave was coming. I was being challenged, in very subtle ways, to do more and be more. At times, I even found it uncomfortable. But it was always thrilling.

I was being confronted with the challenge of getting clearer about what my life meant and what I wanted to do with it. I had had a taste of my own personal power in my career, when I proved to myself and others that I was someone who could execute a plan and make it possible for others to do fantastic things under my leadership. But along with the deeper spiritual understanding that I was gaining, something new was emerging. It was becoming clearer to me, and more evident in my life, that I had a way of taking charge, a capacity for realizing my intentions.

I didn't know exactly what it all meant, but I had a sense of something powerful coming on the horizon. More and more, I remembered the words of my therapist, Barbara: "If you want to be a real Buddha, get off your pillow and take it out in the world."

I got off my pillow and onto my bike. My treasure map had been about riding from San Francisco to Los Angeles. That seemed impossible for someone with nine T cells, but I had learned not to let that sort of thing stop me. So I signed up for the 1997 AIDS Ride.

Back in the Saddle

I had been exercising and riding my bike again even before "You and Money," but training for the AIDS Ride gave me a new focus. I had to take it seriously, or I just wasn't going to make it from San Francisco to LA. As I trained, my mind got clearer and my body stronger. I still didn't have many T cells, but I kept going. I'd feel good and strong one day, and then I'd have setbacks. The drugs would sometimes fail and leave me feeling awful, but I never gave up. It was a bit of a Lazarus effect, a phoenix rising from the ashes. I was getting very familiar with that phenomenon.

I was part of a group called Positive Pedalers and was chosen to bring forward the "Riderless Bike" at the beginning of the ride. It represented everyone who had died or was too ill to ride. That was a tremendous honor. My hair was very long at that point, and I blew it dry the morning the race started because I knew there would be TV cameras there. (I've always had a sense of occasion.)

The Ride was an amazing experience that I shared with more than two thousand other people who became like family over the course of seven days. I'll remember some of those moments for the rest of my life. When we rode through Capitola, near Santa Cruz, an older couple stood by the side of the road and washed people's sunglasses. Their grandson had died of AIDS, and that was their way of helping. It may sound like a little thing, but we really did need our sunglasses washed at that point—and somehow, they knew it.

Kids came out of schools and gave us finger paintings they had done, showing how they felt and thought about the race. That was incredibly moving. In King City, inland from Big Sur, the locals came around at night and warned us about the ticks, fleas, and spiders in the area where we were going to camp. Migrant workers came out of the fields and handed us broccoli because that's all they had to give us.

Most nights, there was entertainment—but if you had any sense, you'd get right to sleep. Just drop your bike, get your tent set up, go eat, and maybe take a shower if you had the energy. I had my own tent, thank God. My original roommate had been a guy I knew, and he bravely stepped forward the first night to announce that he snored loudly enough to wake the whole mobile city—so he was going to be in a motor coach. I felt like the angels were with me again!

Cycling accessories have evolved since I did the ride in 1997, but even back then, we had all sorts of amusing accoutrements like Butt Balm. We would pull into a rest stop, and there would be all these people gathered around in riding clothes, or drag, or leather, or red dresses, or whatever. In the center of the crowd was always a mound of Butt Balm! You just reached in, grabbed a handful, and stuck it between your legs. The first day, people were kind of shy about doing this. By the second day, we were all just slathering it on.

The Butt Balm mound was a place to gather and talk, like a water cooler, except that everybody had their hands down their pants. Male, female, it didn't matter. Another technique was to stuff ice bags or packs inside your spandex shorts. Anything to keep going. (I understand that today they have very genteel little packets instead.)

One day had been especially hard for me, despite the ice in my pants and all the Butt Balm. I was closer than I'd ever been to saying, "Okay, I just can't go on." At the end of the day's ride, I usually set up my tent before I ate or cleaned up or anything—but that day I was just too exhausted. I dropped my tent and headed toward the food. When I came back, my tent had been set up for me. There was no one around, and I had no idea who did it. A lot of people just hung around, looking for ways to support riders, watching for ways they could be of service. My Tent Angel was probably one of those people. I went to bed in a place of utter gratitude. That little event lifted me up and allowed me to pedal on.

On the sixth night, I decided to stay in a hotel so I could take a shower and get a good night's sleep. I wanted to look and feel good when I held my bike over my head at the end of the Ride. I was exhausted and exhilarated, and when the time came, my bike felt as light as a feather in my hands. It was one of the most thrilling moments of my life.

Listening to the Call

I had achieved the goal I had set for myself in that first workshop, but whatever had been awakened in me still wasn't satisfied. There was more for me to do. I knew there had to be. What was I going to do with the rest of my life, as long or as short as it might be?

I wasn't going to find it by attempting an even bigger physical feat (there was not enough Butt Balm in the world), so I decided to pause and step outside of my normal routines, to look inward and try listening again to what was brewing.

I had learned about a Vedanta retreat center at Olema, out in beautiful western Marin County, near Point Reyes, my special spot. It had a meditation hall, miles of stunning walking trails, and a spiritual library. It sounded like just the place to do some soul-searching.

I booked three days at the Olema retreat in the beginning of January. It was the perfect opportunity to reflect and integrate the last year and prepare for the one ahead. How I spent the time there was up to me. It was a silent retreat, which was fine, and I was to bring along everything I would need, including food. It was interesting to drive up to Olema through the beautiful western Marin countryside in my Mercedes, and then immerse myself in this very simple, ascetic environment. I thought about what that might mean, then decided it didn't have to mean anything at all.

When I arrived, I went immediately to my room. I unpacked and laid out all my nurturing things and reflection tools with me—candles, meditation bells, sage, journals, and recordings from past readings. I settled my mind and set my intention to spend the next three days listening to and being open to this feeling that was swelling up in me.

I woke up the next morning and wrote in my journal, putting down all my thoughts, however they came, until I felt I had cleared my mind. I made lists of what I wanted to bring with me into this new year and what I wanted to leave behind. After that, I took off on a long, long walk until I was tired—and then returned to the journaling and reading and list-making. I did that for three days.

I tried to write to figure out what it was that I felt was coming on the horizon. I'd be dishonest if I said that, though the AIDS was now somewhat under control, I didn't think about my own death during these three days. I started to think about how, whenever it came, I wanted to be as present in my death as I was waking up every morning. I want to experience it fully, to the point that I thought about what I would do once the signs were there, how I would approach the final moments—with clarity, grace, and ease, surrounded by the people I loved. Should things be ending soon, I was ready.

But I was still here. And if I was still here, I was going to really be here, in the present. I was going to do things.

· · ·

On my second day at the retreat, a monk invited me to a Tuesday evening meditation group. I and four other people sat in a room, singing along to a very old, harpsichord-like instrument, the only time we were encouraged to be vocal. Then the monk asked a question about the meaning of life, and before I knew what I was doing, I blurted out an answer immediately. The monk looked at me and said tersely, "Thank you, Tom. Some are still in the exploration phase," basically asking me to be quiet and listen. At that moment, I knew this trip, and all the other work I'd done to that point, was worth the effort.

I would return to Olema many times after that initial trip, and each time followed a similar pattern: I would spend my days outside and then go inside to study and meditate. In the late afternoon and evening, and sometimes early in the morning, I would work on my intentions. The place and the patterns remained the same, but I was different each time, and each time it gave me whatever I needed in that particular moment.

The clearing work I did out there was a precursor to the next big change in my life—which was already on its way.

A Turning Point

Between the workshops, retreats, and the fact that I woke up every day with the knowledge that my health could take a turn at any moment, those years in San Francisco were all about learning to see life as a bigger picture and myself as a very effective force within that picture. I came away from these explorations with a stronger faith in myself, in the oneness and wholeness of all things, and in my capacity to grow and contribute even when I was very sick.

And I was still very sick, with my nine little T cells. I was stable but not actually suppressed. Most people probably thought I was going to die and considered it a miracle that I was still walking around. I would alternate between dying and doing well, vomiting and doing the AIDS Ride. I had been told that this was what my life would be like from now on—as long as it lasted.

I had financial stability because I was on disability, and that created a little cocoon around me. Most people told me just to relax, be happy, take the money, and run—but I kept thinking of the Peggy Lee song "Is That All There Is?" I yearned for something more or something different. After all the workshops and all the silent miles I walked in the forest of Olema, I kept coming back to the feeling that something needed to change. I wasn't going to meditate or workshop my way to an answer. I needed to act.

I didn't know what was next, but I suspected it wouldn't happen if I was on disability. I had a feeling that I had to step out into life more and expose myself to more of what was out in the world. Everyone assured me that I was wrong, that what I had was enough, that I should be content and keep things stable and still. When I mentioned going off disability, even Mary said, "You can't do that. You're going to kill yourself." They weren't spreading gloom and doom; they just thought my situation was terrific, given the circumstances, and that I should hang onto it for dear life.

But I knew in my heart that I wasn't where I wanted to be. I had already come further than anyone ever thought I would, simply by remaining alive. And now I wanted more.

Never be afraid to acknowledge
that you want more out of
life. Get off your pillow and
keep growing. There's always
something to contribute.

SIXTEEN

Back to Work

OING OFF DISABILITY IN 2000 WAS DIFFICULT but not in the way I was expecting. I thought the biggest challenge would be making the decision to do it. I was not expecting the effort involved in convincing the disability people to let me go! My situation was complicated by the fact that I was still technically an employee of MCI, which, by this point, had been bought by WorldCom and technically no longer existed. When I approached the insurance company to end my benefits, they couldn't find me in their system! There had been years of medical ups and downs, disability reviews, and somehow—possibly because I just kept keeping on—I had simply been filed away and forgotten about. It took them two weeks just to find my records.

It's expected that insurance companies will harass you and subject you to horrific reviews in their attempts to get you off their rolls. What most people don't realize is the other side of this dilemma. If *you* want to go off disability, they actually make it very hard. You have to do vocational training, and they leave you eligible for benefits for months or years after you're supposed to be gone. They actually force these benefits on you, as I found out when I was assigned a special rep whose view was essentially, "You poor baby, you won't last long out there. We're going to give you two years to fall back on if you get sick again, even though your policy says one year." They were worse than my friends and doctors.

Once this Kafkaesque situation was resolved, I set up a lot of job interviews, hoping for the best. I was fortunate to be in a very hot job market and to be around a lot of tech startups, where people were making things up as they went along—an approach I was very used to by that point.

Tech 101

More daunting was the fact that I had missed the whole tech revolution when I was on disability, so I knew there would be a steep learning curve when it came to technology. I was using a computer that belonged in the Smithsonian, and I had never seen an email job application. Still, I had a feeling I could catch up.

Just as I had done as a drag queen, a waiter, a hospital unit coordinator, and a customer service star at MCI, I would put one foot in front of the other and solve each problem as it arose. I was a smart guy, loved a challenge, and had done a lot of successful catching up in my life. This would be no different.

Plus, I did know a whole lot about customer service—and that would be enough to get me in the door. Two other factors working in my favor were that I had done very well at MCI and that I was technically still an employee there—so I didn't have to explain an eight-year absence from the job market.

♦ ♦ ♦

My big moment came one day as I was walking around Union Square and got a call from iPrint.com, an online company that sold self-designed printing materials, offering me the position of director of Customer Service and Satisfaction. I could hardly believe it! I said yes immediately and could barely keep my feet on the ground. I just wanted to capture that wonderful feeling and hold it to me. I pulled it into my solar plexus to anchor and savor it and kept it there for a minute as I felt my feet come back down to earth. I realized that this was a very special moment and felt so grateful.

My first thought, as I recovered myself, was that a whole new life was opening up for me. My second thought was, *I have no clothes.* I looked around, saw a Men's Wearhouse down the street, went in, and bought three suits.

My first day on the job was a whirlwind of meeting people and getting used to being in a 2000-era San Francisco office. So much had changed. All around me there was an enormous amount of tech talk. I kept thinking, *I have no idea what you people are saying!* But I just breathed deeply and said to myself, *I can do this. I just need to learn my way through it.*

I knew that my personality would take over and help me out until I could figure out what those people were saying—and I knew my brain would pick up the technology very quickly. Hopefully, quickly enough that no one would even know where I had started out. Either that, or I might look stupid every now and then. But that was okay; I could manage that. I'd lived with imposter syndrome all my life, and I knew how to act the part. Rita Dayworth only came out for Halloween during those years, but she was always inside me.

Working at iPrint was very exciting and a lot of fun. I learned the technical aspects that I needed to know and brought all those new tools and tricks together with what I already knew about customer service. I had always worked very hard and had always reached the goals I had set for myself. When I didn't, it was usually because I didn't feel worthy and got in my own way. I was not going to let that happen here.

I realized during that first foray back into the business world that I, too, had changed a lot in the time I'd been away from work. At MCI, it had been all about making money, getting ahead, climbing the corporate ladder, doing better than the next guy, and covering up that I was an imposter—a drag queen, waiter, stoner, and hospital worker posing as an executive. And I had become an up-and-coming executive at that.

But I had just spent almost ten years, and actually, many years prior to that, growing personally and spiritually. One of the reasons I was back at work was because of what Barbara had said about Buddha getting off the pillow.

I was grounded in a different way and had different priorities now. I was a lot more interested in getting to know who people were and in being of service where I could.

That was convenient, because I was in customer service and training people to serve customers.

Good Stress

There was no such thing as easing back into things. I was working at least sixty hours a week at iPrint, but somehow, it was a good kind of stress. Everything was going well, and I was thriving. I didn't have time to think about T cells or anything else. Occasionally, I would get sick and have to hide it—but for the most part, I started feeling better. There was something about being back in the game and needing to give my all that was very good for me. It worked like a tonic. My morning practices were shortened, but I learned to make them happen in other ways. I could meditate walking down the hall and do my journaling by thinking things over as I drove to work.

iPrint got a bit ahead of itself with its IPO and ran smack into the post-2000 recession about a year after I joined them. Luckily for me, I had made friends within the company who put me in contact with another startup, InLeague, a payroll and benefits company. (Think ADP on steroids.)

Not only did I know a lot more about technology when I parted ways with iPrint, but I had connected with a lot more people who wanted to support me. I felt a lot less like an imposter when I started at InLeague.

I was hired as the vice president of Customer Care, did a combination of customer service and HR, and quickly became vice president of human resources. we had 265 people working for us at one point. I liked that because I was able to effect change. I could use all the relationship and communication skills that I'd learned during my last decade in the world of personal growth and coaching—some of which I'd learned from the enrollment vultures!—and felt like I was not only expressing a deeper part of myself but also giving more to the people on my team.

In 2001, when 9/11 happened, the InLeague investors freaked out and decided they could no longer fund the company. As a result, I had to fire most of the employees (and on my birthday, no less). I stuck around for a few more weeks as the remaining skeleton staff dropped one by one. All alone in the office on my last day, I processed the paperwork to lay myself off. As I left the office to turn in the keys to the building manager, I looked out at the empty room and the over two hundred staplers, hole punches, and tape dispensers. I helped myself to a tape dispenser and still use it to this day.

Naturally, it was a time of great fear—and that would become a lesson for me. Sometimes, when we think we've mastered something, when we think we have it all together, we are tested once again. Fear was doing that to me the day I walked out of the InLeague offices. I went from being on top of the world to thinking, *What will I do? What will I do?* I no longer had disability benefits or health insurance, and the drugs I needed cost $100,000 a year. There was COBRA, but it wasn't enough, and it wasn't going to last long. Luckily, I was able to get back on Medicare because I had gone back to work on my own. Another benefit of having taken action.

The Gift of Flexibility

My reentry into the arena of work was a bit bumpy, but it taught me so much. I was astonished at how much I had changed and how different it felt to be back at work after all that time away.

When I was sick and on disability, I had focused *inward* on maintaining my health, deeper personal exploration, qigong, coaching, meditation, and other spiritual pursuits. Going back to work focused me *outward* into the corporate world, but all the inner work I'd done over those years came with me.

· · ·

I had been told that you couldn't apply spiritual principles like "Do unto others..." and "Follow your bliss..." in business settings. But just as I had done all my life, when someone told me I couldn't do something, I thought to myself, *Oh yeah? Watch this!* With the skills I had sharpened through coaching, I found a way to make good business decisions, use spiritual principles like manifestation and letting go, and use "soft" interpersonal skills at the same time. It made me feel good, and I know it supported other people in doing a good job and feeling good about themselves—even if the companies themselves did not wind up being successful.

My tool chest was so much bigger, and I was more adept at moving around in it. I could go inward or outward—or both—as needed. I was an executive who wielded some power in these companies, but I could also go inside and see intuitively when a different set of personal skills would work better in a situation.

It wasn't confusing at all. In fact, I loved going in and out, like a wave. That flexibility helped me access more of life, of myself, and of other people. It was a case of bringing forward what I'd learned in the past and using it to support what was happening now.

Suppression and Stability

One day during this early back-to-work period, I went to my regular doctor's appointment. To my amazement, I suddenly had two hundred T cells! I nearly floated out of the exam room. This was a huge milestone because it meant I could stop taking additional drugs that would keep me from getting those nasty opportunistic infections.

As my health got better, I was coming back into my body and felt very tactile. Smells, tastes, and touches were more vivid. At the same time, I was running around at work, sixty hours a week. I believe the "good stress" of work, of being out there and doing something I enjoyed and did well, was literally improving my health. I clung to those two hundred T cells!

In all my years with Mary Romeyn and all the drugs and trials I had access to through her, we came to learn something very important about my HIV. I had become what's known as a "salvage patient," someone for whom disease-suppressing treatments have failed. For us, the protocols were aimed at keeping us stable and not changing anything too drastically, because at least we were still alive.

At some point, I managed to get into a salvage therapy study. You never really knew what would happen with these studies because different combinations of drugs had different effects on different people and at different stages of the disease. This particular trial involved a course of four drugs plus two other drugs that I was already taking. If this combination failed, we would drop one and add another. It did fail, so I ended up taking a seven-drug regimen that was a combination of things that I'd done and these new drugs, plus another that acted as a potentiator.

The result was: I got suppressed! And have been ever since. Being suppressed means that you have a very low level of HIV in your blood and that it's not replicating itself. Lower levels of the virus mean that you have a minimal chance of infecting others and that you can stay healthy more easily. Being suppressed is not a cure, but it certainly is a goal—especially when you start out with the kind of T cell count I had. If you were suppressed and had a healthy T cell count, you were in good shape. I had been salvaged from being salvaged.

An Old-Fashioned Startup

For as much as I appreciated all the lessons in flexibility, I realized that the unpredictable world of startups did not mix well with my requirements for health insurance. I needed a good job at a stable company that was not going to go away. Enter Walmart.com.

I had actually gotten an offer from Walmart before my last job but turned it down. Walmart was a good old boy, old school, very conservative company. And I was me. Luckily, the recruiter had taken a liking to me and happened to get in touch again just when I needed it. Thanks to her, I was hired at Walmart.com as the director of Customer Service.

I had to laugh a little because, really, *me?* At Walmart? Again, the imposter syndrome reared its head—maybe for a slightly different reason this time. I started the job wondering what I was even doing there.

But I quickly learned that Walmart and Walmart.com were two very different entities—and their differences were reflected in the nature and location of their offices. Our Walmart.com offices were at Oyster Point in San Francisco, in a high-end building with huge windows and breathtaking views. It was known as "The Crystal Palace" at Walmart.

Walmart proper was headquartered in Bentonville, Arkansas, in a building that had no windows at all. There were many supposed explanations for this. Some said it was because they were in Tornado Alley. Others said that founder Sam Walton believed people were more focused and productive when they couldn't look out the window and daydream. Still others said that Sam was just too damn cheap to put in windows. We will never know.

These differences were just the beginning. When you start a new job, the first thing you find out is all the stuff they didn't tell you during your interview process. At the welcome dinner to meet my corporate team, I learned a lot about the relationship between Walmart and Walmart.com.

The cultures were entirely different. Aside from working in a building with no windows, the Walmart people had very cramped quarters and had to take out their own garbage. They had to share a room if they traveled with a co-worker of the same sex, and they couldn't keep their miles if they traveled for the company. In fact, if they went to the counter at Delta Air Lines, which was the only carrier Walmart used, and tried to upgrade, the Delta people had been instructed to tell them, "You're a Walmart employee, and this is grounds for termination." The rules applied to everyone, even top management.

Walmart.com was very different. Like every other company in Silicon Valley, you didn't have to share a room. You could keep your miles when you flew. You had a nice office in "The Crystal Palace," and somebody else took out the garbage.

The Walmart people didn't know much about what a tech company was, didn't like what little they did know about it, and considered Walmart.com a tiny gnat buzzing around their giant supercenter. Walmart.com didn't want anything to do with Walmart because all those nonexempt employees would wreak havoc on their compensation plan. Plus, they might have to go to Bentonville, Arkansas, someday.

The main concern for me, however, was the shake-up that had taken place just before I arrived. The customer service operation at Walmart.com had been entirely outsourced, and Walmart proper hated outsourcing. The people responsible for the outsourcing were now gone, and I had been brought in to get rid of all these dreadful outsourced customer service call centers.

Not surprisingly, I would wind up being the go-between, the person who had one foot in each camp. I knew I didn't want to become the battlefield where this culture war was being fought, and I was determined to build my own little bubble inside the company so I could go my own way, without too much interference from either side. It was a seesaw, but I had pretty good balance.

◆ ◆ ◆

The morning after the welcome dinner, someone from HR showed me to my office. I sat down at the desk and suddenly got a distinct whiff of "Poison" perfume. It was overpowering—and everywhere! There was nobody in the office, so I realized that the smell was coming from deep within the drapes, the carpet, maybe even the glass in the windows. With my heightened sense of smell because of all the powerful medication I was on, the perfume certainly lived up to its name. The office was going to have to undergo a serious de-Poison-izing.

This was on a Friday. They cleaned the office and shampooed the rug over the weekend, and proudly presented it to me on Monday—but it still reeked. Meanwhile, I had discovered the source of the scent. My predecessor, who was a larger-than-life customer service executive at that time, was apparently known for wearing lots of jewelry and lots of "Poison." She had left months before—but the scent still hung heavy in the air.

After some additional shuffling I didn't even request, I settled into a very nice office with an even better view.

Seeing the Liability as an Asset

One of the first steps in my mission to undo everything my predecessor and her team had done was to embark on a whirlwind tour of these call centers and the corporate headquarters in Bentonville, Arkansas.

First stop, the call center in Hattiesburg, Mississippi.

The three hundred employees at the Hattiesburg call center were frightened of being shut down if we withdrew our business. The holidays were coming, and they didn't know if they'd be losing their jobs. Of course, our mandate was exactly that—to withdraw our business from outsourcers and have our own call centers. I was going to have to call on all of my prior HR experience to handle this situation.

While I was getting familiar with the Hattiesburg center and its people, I was also spending time in Bentonville and learning more about the Walmart corporate culture.

Everyone who lived in Bentonville worked either at Walmart or at Sam's Club, also part of the company. It was very family-oriented, overwhelmingly Christian, very 1950s, and extremely friendly on the surface.

The code words used to grease any social or business situation were "I appreciate you." People were always saying that to one another, even when they just passed one another in the hall. "I appreciate you!" Everyone was very interested in whether I was married and where my wife was. They had an employee store where you could buy everything at a discount—but I learned later that they only stocked items that didn't sell in the regular stores, so they would have been discounted anyway. Still a great deal.

The more I learned about the Walmart culture, the more I saw how easy it would be to build my own little world and stay under everybody's radar. My ability to speak Southern gave me an enormous edge. I could slip between the two sides without either of them noticing me too much. I just had to keep my mouth shut about all the great perks at Walmart.com that the folks at Walmart didn't have—and when I was back at "The Crystal Palace," not talk too much about attending and even testifying at the Black church in Hattiesburg.

· · ·

I explored other options for call center locations, including shuttered Walmart stores in tiny towns all over the country that desperately wanted the business. Then, at two o'clock one morning, I had a brilliant idea. There was already a call center in Hattiesburg. Sure, it was owned by an outside company, but *what if we just bought that center and Walmart-ized it!?* We could keep three hundred wonderful people from losing their jobs. They were already trained, and we wouldn't need to go through the headache of hiring and training all new people. There was no downside!

Plus, those three hundred people would all love me. The town would love me. I'd have a party. It would be wonderful!

I took this idea back to Walmart. I hadn't yet crunched the numbers, but I knew intuitively that it would work. Their number-crunchers crunched the numbers, and it turned out to be even more brilliant than I had imagined. We were going to save huge sums of money, and I would be a hero.

But, for reasons having to do with conflicting compensation structures, Walmart.com didn't want to take on the Hattiesburg folks as employees; it made more bookkeeping sense for them to be a part of the Walmart structure. The Walmart people didn't want anything to do with that plan, largely because it came from Walmart.com. Basically, nobody wanted my little Hattiesburg call center. It was a great idea. It saved money, made people happy, and created a more efficient system—but Walmart and Walmart.com kept squabbling about it. Finally, my boss Jeffrey told me, "Tom, if you believe in it, go ahead and do it." I really did believe in it, and I knew my head would be on the chopping block if it didn't work.

Since Walmart.com, in the person of Jeffrey, had given me a green light and nobody seemed terribly interested in the details, I just proceeded to set up the Hattiesburg center exactly the way it should be done—and put it on Walmart's books rather than Walmart.com's. I spent months planning everything out, structuring every aspect of it, and created my own little world down there in Mississippi. It became a huge cross-functional project at Walmart.com.

Now, getting anything done at Walmart was very complicated. Every time you negotiated a contract, you had to have eight people sign it. If any part of the contract changed, you had to go back to the beginning and get everybody to re-sign it. Again, the Walmart Way. At first, I pretended I didn't know about this rule. I was, after all, an employee of Walmart.com. But I got caught and had to start abiding by it.

I once ran into Lee Scott, the CEO, in the hall. He asked me, "How's everything going?"

"Well," I said. "This contract process you've got; it's really slowing me down." He started laughing, and I said, "It's not funny to me!"

He said, "Ah, don't you understand? We have so many contracts here, and so many people trying to get us to do things, that if you can get through this process, *the project probably needs to get done!*"

I remember thinking that I could have had the project done already if it hadn't been for that rule—and I found many crafty ways to get special considerations for the Hattiesburg center by flying under the radar. The fact that Jeffrey trusted me so much helped a lot. And the fact that I had to keep running back to Bentonville for all those signatures kept me connected there. That turned out to be very important.

I learned to "walk the halls" in Bentonville. That meant talking to everybody who was going to be in the meeting *before* the meeting took place, just to make sure you had them all on your side. I would walk around "I appreciate you"-ing people and getting them to cave before the meeting even started, so that they wouldn't have to do it in public.

In the end, we bought the call center, and everything went according to my plan. It was a huge success for the company and for the town, and everybody involved was a winner.

I threw the party I'd planned, and everybody in Hattiesburg showed up—even the mayor. A Gladys Knight song, "Our Love," played in the background, and that became our theme song. Of course, I was standing over in the corner, mouthing the words as Rita would have done—when the mayor wasn't looking. It was the perfect song because the story of that center was all about coming together.

I gave a speech that had them all laughing, smiling, and carrying on. Everybody in the room knew what I'd done—but really, it was just treating people the way I would want to be treated.

That's really the secret to customer service and life.

The only people who weren't entirely clear on what had happened at this call center were some of the Walmart folks whom I had circumvented. I'd told Jeffrey about it to make sure I wouldn't get fired—but a few people in Bentonville were quite surprised when evidence started surfacing about the new setup in Hattiesburg. There is only so much you can do to keep a call center with three hundred employees under the radar.

Some people were upset that I hadn't done things the usual way and grumbled about it.

But the success of the plan was soon undeniable. Hattiesburg became known as a state-of-the-art call center, a showcase, and eventually the Walmart folks came around—even though the center had been touched by Walmart.com and might have cooties.

The Walmart Corporate Ladder

At the same time as I was putting together the Hattiesburg call center, I was representing Walmart.com at corporate meetings in Bentonville, running the rest of customer service, managing my staff back in San Francisco, keeping everybody happy, making sure that everybody knew what they needed to know—and did not know what they *didn't* need to know.

One of my many tasks was to assess the current state of customer service. It was not good. At the 1-800 center, the abandonment rate (the percentage of calls that you do not answer because customers hang up before you can pick up) was 50 percent. A good rate would be 0 percent to 5 percent because sometimes the baby cries, a caller changes their mind, or something else happens to make them hang up before you have a chance to answer.

I asked people, "Do you realize that when you don't pick up the phone, all those people you didn't handle today are going to call back tomorrow—along with all the people who were already going to call you tomorrow?"

The reply was blank stares. I later told the president about this, and he laughed. Then he sighed and told me what was really happening.

"We know that every customer who sets foot in a Walmart store spends an average of $40.37. If we don't answer the phone, they'll probably just go to the customer service desk at their local Walmart. They might be mad, but they're going to be in the store. And if they're in the store, they're going to spend $40.37. Why should we answer the phone?"

I was stunned, thinking about how brilliant this was—and how backward. How was I going to change the world of Walmart customer service to actually serve the customer? And right on the heels of that thought, I realized that if I hadn't known about the $40.37, there were probably a lot of other things I didn't know. Clearly, I had many more rocks to turn over at Walmart—and indeed, I uncovered a lot of disasters when I started poking around.

Luckily, there was also a place to take these problems. Walmart had an Executive Business Training (EBT) committee, a group of about twenty executives to whom you could bring difficulties, challenges, or just situations on which you wanted some advice or coaching. Whenever an issue bubbled up, the best way to solve it was to get it before this committee. Not only were you likely to get a great solution, but you would catch their attention.

If they accepted your project, they would take it on as their own. They would bring in specialists, interview experts, hold cross-functional meetings, and get high-level coaching on the issue. It was a six- to eight-week process, during which you simply went away and did your job.

The process for getting your project accepted was, of course, very complicated. You had to work your way up through several smaller committees, and then hopefully be selected to present your issue to the EBT. You had only twenty minutes for that presentation, and some people were asked to leave by their third PowerPoint slide. Plus, you were supposed to be a vice president to even make a presentation.

The issue I brought to them was basically the terrible state of customer service in customer service centers around Walmart. Turned out there were more than one could count. They wanted customer service to be as efficient as everything else in the company. It had become increasingly clear to me that customer service outside of our little Hattiesburg center was completely inefficient. People were doing extremely backward, archaic things that would never support their business in the future.

When the day of our presentation arrived, the imposter syndrome raged within me. What was I doing there, standing in front of the largest corporation in the world, making a presentation in this secret meeting, and not even being a vice president? It was a song I'd heard many times before, and by then, I knew to just keep going because the only way through it, was through it.

Our presentation was forty-five minutes long, but nobody stopped us, and we got the attention of many, many people. We made the cut, and the improvement of customer service became a priority for the EBT.

My star was rising, and I was being given more and more responsibility. The wheels turned very slowly at Walmart, but I could see that they had been set in motion and were heading in the right direction. I later discovered that, through this project and some other things I did, I had basically gotten onto a trajectory to potentially become vice president of Customer Service at Walmart.

I was on everybody's radar, especially CEO Lee Scott's.

Culture Clash

Ultimately, though, I was never going to feel at home at Walmart. The culture was all about fitting in, and I couldn't see myself going back to the survival tactics of Church Tom. I had worked too hard to get to this point of acceptance in my life. I loved many aspects of working at Walmart. It was a fascinating job at a huge company, and I was able to carve out my own little empire where I could express myself, be creative, and put together something wonderful for people. I was totally consumed by that job. One day, I was working on my BlackBerry and was so into it that I walked off a curb, tripped, and fell right into traffic. They all honked their horns, but I just got back up and kept going—and working.

I did very well there, learned a great deal, and met some wonderful people. But in the end, I was not destined to stay at a conservative, family-oriented company—and I was certainly not destined to live in Bentonville. That was what they wanted me to do, and I was going to have to do it in order to move up.

One day, I was sitting at my desk in "The Crystal Palace," a bit bored because I wasn't traveling, looking out my windows at the bay, and thinking about what I wanted to do about Walmart. They were talking seriously about moving me to Bentonville, which was definitely not it. (I had actually sworn off Bentonville temporarily because someone had started inviting me to use the new Walmart gym—and I was not about to enter a locker room filled with Walmart employees.)

As I sat there, the phone rang. It was a recruiter who wanted to talk to me about a company named Palm. I thought, *Hmm, maybe I should talk to them.*

Flexibility is one of the most important skills you can master to survive and thrive. But don't become so flexible that you lose your backbone.

SEVENTEEN

Around the World, and Home Again

I N THE YEARS SINCE MOM DIED, DAD AND I HAD BECOME very close. I visited him every chance I got, even once I went back to work. He continued living alone in the house we'd moved into when I was twelve and continued to be loyal to the memory of Mom. He was still very handsome and caught the eye of any number of little old ladies in Jacksonville Beach, but there would only ever be one woman for him.

Aside from the awful routine he'd endured for nearly thirty years as a result of his radical prostatectomy—the catheter and the leg bag, changing them every day and night—he was still in decent health at more than eighty years of age. And then, something strange happened. His PSA (prostate-specific antigen) score went up dramatically. The prostate cancer was back.

By this point, we had dispensed with the formalities and the charade of saving face, and he told me about it right away. I was working for Walmart at the time and flew out at the next possible opportunity to be with him and help him decide what to do next.

Not that there was much to decide; at the time, the standard, one-size-fits-all remedy of Western medicine was a drug called Lupron, a synthetic hormone administered via injection. Nothing else about your condition or medical history mattered. If you had this condition, *you got Lupron*. Dad would soldier on with this medication for years, and while it did keep the cancer itself in check, it was difficult to watch it ravage his system. One of the side effects was osteoporosis. Dad's bones were already frail from all those years of working construction, and Lupron made them even more fragile. Once again, as had happened decades before, he grew breasts and lost his fingernails. Eventually, his knees got so bad that he could hardly walk, but like my mother, he was very resistant to using a cane or walker.

Lupron can also affect your teeth, but Dad didn't have many teeth. He had lost them in the Navy and gotten a partial plate through the VA when he was in his thirties, though he rarely wore it. If it broke or peeled away, that was that. He just said, "Who cares? I'm not spending money on dentures. I'm saving it for hard times."

This was one of the many times I said to him, "You made it. These *are* hard times."

The Reluctant Fixer-Upper

Although he was becoming increasingly frail, Dad was still determined to live alone in the house—a house that was fine for an able-bodied person but not workable for someone who was as compromised as he was and refused to even use a walker.

I spoke to my good friend Noreen, who was ninety at the time, and said, "Noreen, he really should be on a walker. He's going to kill himself."

She looked at me and said, "Honey, it's a real simple solution, but you're going about it all wrong. Buy the walker, leave it in the house, and go home to California. By the time you get back, he'll be using it. And it'll be on *his* terms, not yours."

That's exactly what happened.

◆ ◆ ◆

I knew we had to make the house safer for him and said, "Dad, we can do some construction ourselves, so you can get around more safely. We can put up guardrails, ramps, and hold-ons." He refused to spend the money, and he wouldn't let me spend mine. He took great pride in knowing how to fall, he said, a skill he had learned in the Navy. I rolled my eyes.

I knew that he would continue to say that he couldn't afford to do anything, no matter the evidence to the contrary, so I just started fixing up the house. I put up iron pipes in the laundry room to act as railings. I also put up some tacky wrought iron bars so he could get up and down the stairs and out the door. He fought me on all of it, but after the first few times he used them, he called to thank me, tell me how helpful they had been, and say how sorry he was that he'd been so difficult about it.

Around the World in Twelve Days

The trips to see Dad and keep fixing up the house, combined with all the traveling I was doing for work, meant that I spent a great deal of time on the road in the mid-2000s. But the San Francisco–Hattiesburg–Bentonville triangle I was doing for Walmart was nothing compared to the routes I would take all over the planet with Palm.

When I started at Palm in 2005, it was hot stuff. My position there was director of Global Service Operations, reporting to a vice president. It was customer service, but it also involved product readiness, training, quality, and basically anything that touched a customer.

My position had been vacant for nine months, so there was a lot of catching up to do. Palm outsourced all their customer service to centers all around the globe, so instead of trying to reconsolidate customer service as I'd done at Walmart, I would be working directly with each of these outsourced call centers, or "partners" as we called them, to train and maintain consistent quality. They were all overseas, scattered around the world, so there would be an enormous amount of travel involved. Using these outsourcers was a low-cost way to do things, but it required a ton of oversight.

On top of that, Palm was also putting in a pay-for-service model. Instead of just calling up someone in tech support or customer service for help, you could buy various levels of help. Support cost a certain amount of money under one plan, another amount under another plan, and the customer service reps had to be familiar with each plan and its features, plus all the devices, which were kept in the centers.

As if this weren't challenging enough, Palm was actually the result of a merger between two companies—Handspring and PalmOne—and it felt like two separate companies under one roof when I got there. That led to a lot of confusion, competition, and dysfunction. There was always a whirlwind of activities, and nobody was completely grounded in what was happening. We were all spinning plates.

I had a corporate staff of about fifty people at headquarters in Milpitas, down on the southern end of the San Francisco Bay, but my primary focus would be to oversee our call centers all around the globe. On my sixth day of employment, I was told I would be leaving on a twelve-day trip around the world with my boss, Dan, and Kristen, a senior manager in Technology.

The three of us would be meeting all the people who'd be reporting to me. I would repeat this world tour at least quarterly for the eighteen months I worked there. We were scheduled to leave in two days on November 1—the day after Halloween.

* * *

As usual, Rita made her annual appearance. Because of all the job interviews and traveling to and from Dad's, I had done very little Halloween prep before this. Normally, I'd wear my high heels around the house for a few weeks before an appearance, just to get a little practice and toughen up those toes. This proactive blister care was really a must, but it simply could not happen that year.

Well, Rita had a fabulous time and completely put out of her mind that the next day she was leaving on a jet plane for a twelve-day world tour with a group of people she did not know, including her boss, and meeting all the people who would be reporting to her—or rather, to her alter ego, Tom.

It wasn't lost on me that perhaps Rita was so ready to let loose because Tom was feeling nervous about the major career move he had just made.

(I often wondered if anyone noticed I had a mustache before our trip but was clean-shaven the day we departed.)

I remember getting up the next morning and not being able to put on shoes. I wrapped my feet in Band-Aids and gauze, gritted my teeth, and crammed my feet into a beautiful pair of business shoes that I had bought for the trip.

Palm treated us like royalty when we traveled, protecting and watching over us with wonderful hotels and drivers, but there wasn't much they could do about my feet. I remember lagging behind everybody as we ran to the gate at the airport and begging, "Please God, I'll never wear a Springolator again. Just help me get through this."

Our first stop was London, and I nursed my feet enough to get to the first meeting. People were walking around and doing presentations. I tried to sit as much as possible, but I couldn't sit all the time. We were off to lunch, then meetings, then dinner, and everybody walked quickly with the "chop chop chop" business gait. Not only was I in agony over the Rita blisters, but I was getting new ones from the work shoes I hadn't broken in. I had no choice but to keep up. Between the heels and the pantyhose, I don't know how women do it.

We left London and went on to Amsterdam, which I made a mental note to come back to; the people there were wonderful. Next, it was on to India, which was quite a culture shock. I had been warned about the poverty in India and how I might react to it. I've since known many people who tolerated it for work and never strayed from the hotel and chauffeured car service—but in fact, I loved India.

I think my personality allowed me to morph, blend, and cross cultural lines that not everybody felt comfortable crossing. By that point in my life, I had adopted that philosophy of flexibility. I just breathed it all in, then let it out, and rode the wave of whatever happened around me. That's how I lived, and it was a great way to travel.

Some of it wasn't pleasant. We were being driven around in expensive cars, surrounded by crushing poverty. Children tapped on our windows every time the car stopped, begging for food or money. Others played in the gutters and sewers, against the backdrop of gleaming buildings built by global companies and elegant hotels full of international travelers and businessmen, like myself.

"Those People"

The first time I visited the centers in Chennai, Hyderabad, Bangalore, and Mumbai, I was very aware that I was a white man from America, traveling to a country where the supervisors in the customer call centers I was managing earned more than the local doctors. A lot of people at the companies I've worked for looked down on call center workers and discounted the crucial role they filled for us. It would be my goal to make sure they knew that I honored their work and honored them.

This was sometimes an interesting position to maintain when faced with the Indian caste system. Naturally, I am all about fairness, in how I treat people personally and in how people are recognized and promoted in organizations that I am a part of, and I noticed some things at one of our Indian centers that did not sit right with me. I brought up my observations with the American expat who ran the center, who opened my eyes to the fact that the caste system was still in effect in Indian society—even in our call centers, if you looked under the surface.

"We try to manage away from it. But it still exists," was her explanation.

I was immediately offended by it, but I had to accept that certain things were within my influence and others were not my place to dispute. At least, not outwardly. My priority was to make sure my customers were cared for and that the best people were doing it, so I did what I could to mitigate unfairness wherever I could. Learning when to push against the culture was an art, and it required every bit of diplomacy and emotional intelligence I had.

· · ·

My next stop on that initial world tour was the Philippines, to the call centers in Manila and Cebu. Here, too, technology was a way out of poverty and chaos. People with bachelor's and master's degrees were hoping for a job in the call centers because they were the best-paying jobs in the country. Once again, I was reminded that this work was not to be dismissed or taken lightly.

Our call centers were in places that were not only very different from the United States but very different from one another. Manila and Cebu, for instance, were both in the Philippines—but Manila was a very urban environment and Cebu was basically a beach community. A very high-end beach community, but nothing like Manila. I went to Boracay and Bohol, where there were monkeys all around and rickshaws and pedicabs everywhere. Each one was covered with pictures of the Virgin Mary. I was fascinated and had to find out what that was about. Apparently, all the drivers had covered their pedicabs with pictures of nude women and other things that were quite risqué. The women in the community had gotten together and put a stop to that. Since this was a very Catholic country, what better way to cover up those naughty pictures than with images of the Virgin Mary?

The women allowed them to keep their other decorations—and, of course, their fringe. All the drivers competed to create the most flamboyant pedicab. It reminded me a little of a drag bar, only with straight men. And monkeys running around.

From the Philippines, we went on to Singapore, and then another place or two, and finally headed back to the States. Then I was off again, this time to Brazil and Argentina to do it all over.

· · ·

Finally, I had some time back at headquarters and threw myself into the work of getting to know the people there and growing my staff. One of the first things I noticed was how disparagingly corporate looked at the people who worked in our call centers. They definitely didn't think of them as part of the company and often spoke of them as "those people." But these were valuable, dedicated, productive people to me. When I visited them, they were amazingly gracious and generous.

The more I worked with them and got to know them, the higher my esteem. They always stepped up and did what they were asked to do, and I developed wonderful relationships with them. They had a great spirit and a great sense of fun and loyalty. They would decorate their centers for the holidays, had parties and contests that they invited me to judge, and I handed out awards to top performers. Of course, I loved this kind of *esprit de corps*. It was inspiring to watch people have a good time and support one another.

Taking Care of Dad

The "good stress" that I had attributed my HIV suppression to was surely at an all-time high during the Palm years. And I was thankful for it. I like to think that it created a positive feedback loop—my health was good, I had the energy and stamina I needed to travel and get to know my co-workers all around the world, and strengthening those relationships in turn filled me with gratitude for all that I had.

Plus, my dad and I got closer than we had ever been in those years after Mom and Bubby were gone, and he needed more and more help. We started sharing confidences that had never seemed possible in our relationship before that, and I got to know and understand him in a new way. It wasn't that I didn't appreciate him before, but his basic goodness, integrity, and generosity just became clearer as we got to know and trust one another more. I learned things about him that I'd never known. I think it was that way for him, too.

At night he would sit in the tub, letting his poor aching joints warm up in the hot water, and we would talk. I think the water soothed him enough that he would go into a sort of trancelike state. Memories would bubble up from the distant past, and he would share them with me. One particular night, he told me that his friend Bryant, who was a deacon in the Baptist church, had baptized him! In that very bathtub! I was astounded because my father had never had any religious beliefs, or at least had never spoken of them. He didn't speak against God or religion; I think he just believed that sort of thing was for other people. And the old joke among his friends in town was that if you ever saw Vic LeNoble walk into church, you should watch the rafters, because either they were about to fall down, or he was there to fix them.

I was perfectly fine with my father being baptized, even in a bathtub, and why not by Bryant? But I was having a hard time wrapping my mind around the image of my father in a bathtub with one of his boyhood friends baptizing him. I chuckled. Maybe even giggled. And then we both laughed out loud about it.

Later, we talked about what it had meant to him to be baptized. He didn't exactly use these words, but I pieced together that, although men in his generation didn't talk much about feelings, or transformation, or death—or really much of anything—he had felt a certain peace about life after that baptism, a certain forgiveness for anything he might have done wrong. I found that very moving and a little surprising. It was one of many times I had the feeling that Dad felt he had done something wrong at some point in his life—but I never found out what that was.

◆ ◆ ◆

In addition to his physical problems, which got worse after he took a bad fall in the tub, Dad was starting to experience some normal mental decline. For instance, we'd had a Sears air conditioner in the front window forever. It was old and inefficient, but Dad didn't want me to replace it because, in his mind, it kept people from looking in and had the added value of making people think we were poor so they didn't "report" us and push us into a higher tax bracket. And one time I came home, I noticed that there was a pot on the stove that had clearly been burned to the bone and could have set the house on fire. Dad had just left it there and not even cleaned it.

As willing as I was to put in the work to adapt the house to his needs and come out to visit as often as humanly possible, I had to admit that the time had come, and Dad needed full-time care. I braced myself and brought it up with him. "Dad," I said. "There are really just two choices. One, you go into assisted living. Two, we fix up the house, and somebody stays here with you twenty-four seven. But there is no third option."

I expected a lot of resistance, but he surprised me. "I've been thinking about that," he said, "and I think you're right." I was astonished and thought about how hard a time he must've been having to have come to that thought on his own.

He opted for assisted living but, naturally, didn't think he could afford it. I had to show him, practically on a spreadsheet, how he could afford it—and if he couldn't afford it, then *we* could afford it. He wanted to share a room to save money, but I put my foot down. Like he did for me when I started my freshman year in Gainesville, I made sure he had his own room.

I went into action, and by the time I flew back to San Francisco, we had a place for him. I came back the next weekend to move him into HarborChase, "Celebrating Senior Living!"

Accepting Help

The move was hard, but we both knew it was the best option. As we were packing, Dad decided that he wanted to take his one remaining gun with him. He had gotten rid of all the other guns because he knew I didn't like them, which I thought was very sweet, but he had one stored away in a metal file cabinet. I said no, and I think he understood why he could not take a gun to an assisted living facility.

There were three levels of care at HarborChase: Independent Living, Assisted Living, and Memory Care. When Dad moved in, he was still somewhat ambulatory and was still driving. Despite having just left the house he'd lived in for about forty years, he adjusted quickly to his new living situation. Everybody at HarborChase loved him, and they were amazed that I came all the way from California to see him every month. Some residents had relatives who lived down the street and had never visited them at all. Whenever I was there, I made it my business to get friendly with the staff. I wanted to make sure that Dad was never mistreated and that he got the best care and service possible.

It was a whole new way of life for both of us. Little dramas were always popping up that would require my attention. There was one period where Dad was convinced that people at HarborChase were stealing his belt. His eight dollar belt from Walmart! I argued with him but finally realized, *Tom, you can't fight this. You have to outsmart it*. I went to Walmart, bought six of the same belt, and put them in strategic locations around his room. We never talked about stolen belts again.

Dad still had the old Caprice Classic I'd given them for Christmas about ten years earlier, which by then was really faded and had several serious dings. The tinting was even peeling off the windows. He would occasionally sneak out of HarborChase in it and drive around town, which was strictly against the rules. He said he only drove around "the Beach," so it was all right because he knew those roads very well.

Apparently, he got confused one day and was pulled over for driving through a construction zone—which, frankly, could have happened to anyone. My dad freaked out when the cop stopped him, because he had never been in a wreck and never even gotten a ticket. Nothing bad had ever happened to him involving a car and a cop (unlike his son, who had hung a car over an embankment in the parking lot of a bar while dressed as Santa Claus, loaded to the gills, wearing three-inch red and green eyelashes, in July).

The cop said, I'm sure very kindly, "Let me take you home, sir. You can have somebody come back and get the car tomorrow. It'll be fine." Dad didn't want to leave the car, but this was the police telling him to do something, so he did it.

About eight weeks after this incident, he got a letter from the DMV telling him that he needed to come in and take a driver's test because he was a senior citizen. Dad was convinced that somehow his former housekeeper Denise had come back from Georgia and turned him in, so she could make money chauffeuring him around. I tried to tell him it might have been because of his little incident at the construction site.

He studied up, took the written test, and then learned to his horror that he also had to take a driving test! Now, the DMV was in a shopping mall and conducted its driving tests out in the parking lot. Dad would argue that this was why he failed the test. It wasn't a normal driving situation, with streets and corners; it was an obstacle course with *cones*. He missed passing the test by one point, and they refused to renew his license.

It's scary for anyone to face losing their driver's license and, therefore, their independence. My dad had been driving probably ever since he could see over the steering wheel. His father had owned one of the first garages in the Southeast, and Dad could fix cars in his sleep. He did not intend to be without a driver's license.

Dad stared at the guy and said, like the Terminator, "I'll be back."

The guy said to him, "Well, sir, you can take the test as many times as you want. You just have to pass it."

My father went back, and he got the thing he had missed right—but he missed something else. He tried, and failed, again a third time.

"Then let's take the test again!" Dad said.

He passed it on his fourth try, and they gave him a license. It was good for about twelve years, which was ridiculous, but Dad clung to that license like a badge, long after he stopped driving. It was his way of saying, "I am okay, even in the presence of really not being okay."

We kept that 1996 Caprice Classic around for years, even though Dad stopped driving not long after he succeeded in passing that driving test. I remember being out with him one day in this dented and peeling car, with knobs falling off and Scotch-taped back on, and a broken gas gauge so you never knew how much gas you had. Out of the blue, my father reached up and started stroking the dashboard. I looked at him when we stopped at a light and asked, "Dad, what are you doing?"

He looked up at me and said with a smile, "She looks just like she did the day you gave her to us, doesn't she?"

Hot, Hot, Hot

Palm held a huge sales conference in 2006 at the Fontainebleau Hotel in Miami Beach. I reported into sales, so I was invited. One of the theme nights was "Hot, Hot, Hot," and there was a friendly rivalry among the attendees about who could be the most outrageous. When it was my turn, I came in wearing a business suit and stripped down to a T-shirt and polka dot boxer shorts with little "Hot" stickers all over them, dancing to Gloria Estefan's "Conga." Some people acted horrified, but I think they were secretly thrilled. I did not tell them that I had a bit of an advantage, since this was not the first time I had danced and lip-synced to a female recording artist.

But my proudest moment was when it came time to present my report on the status of customer service around the world. Instead of standing up and delivering a lot of numbers, I showed them a video. I had asked each service center to prepare something. They were not to hire anybody or produce anything slick or professional. They were simply to get somebody to hold a camera while people answered three questions: What does Palm mean to me? What does working for Palm mean to me? What does Palm customer service mean to me?

I got submissions from all over, and we put together an incredibly moving piece showing our call center workers as faces, not just numbers. They spoke clearly and simply about what customer service was and what it meant to them, and their appreciation for Palm and for the life it offered them was palpable. One woman was also an anchor at the local news station. She made only two dollars an hour there, but she made four dollars working at the Palm service center.

When it was over, I didn't speak a word. There was complete silence in the auditorium. The people on screen had said in twelve minutes, quite eloquently, that what they did was important and that we could all learn from them. Very quickly, corporate folks stopped talking about "those people" and began treating them as part of the team.

* * *

Palm was a great experience for me. It was a time of real learning and stretching. I spent about 70 percent of my time on the road, and aside from that first trip's toll on my feet, it didn't wear me out at all. It felt wonderful to have an important position and to do a great job at it. It felt even better to develop the relationships I had with those extraordinary people in the centers. I was so proud of them, and they were proud of themselves.

But the corporate leadership situation at Palm left something to be desired. The reason my position had stayed vacant so long could have told me something. They were afraid of hiring the wrong person and afraid of how that person might fit into some of the politics and dysfunctional dynamics at headquarters—or not. Palm itself was having some ups and downs. People were in flux, always leaving or deciding to stay, coming on board or jumping ship. There was a lot of drama.

My generation is all about climbing the corporate ladder, and I was seeing a lot of rungs crumble before my eyes. People around me were being promoted, but I wasn't—and I wasn't feeling very appreciated, either. I knew it was all politics, but I was getting pretty fed up.

As always seemed to happen at these times, the phone rang. It was a recruiter, and she wanted to talk to me about a company called Facebook. I got recruiting calls at least once a week, but they were rarely of interest to me. I was always courteous and returned the calls, and I would often brainstorm with them about people from my network that they could call. Somehow, I'm always doing human resources, whether or not it's part of my job. It couldn't do any harm, and at minimum, I was building some good karma.

I had no idea what this Facebook thing was, so I went back about my business. The next thing I knew, I got a call from Jeffrey, my friend who had been my boss at Walmart and had since left to become a venture capitalist in Silicon Valley. I told him about the Facebook call, and he said without hesitation, "I think you should talk to them. Do it for me."

I had known Jeffrey for a long time, and we'd gotten closer over the years. He had never asked me to do anything, and he had never steered me wrong. I did some detective work on Facebook and was fascinated by what they were doing and by social media in general. I had a sense that something important was happening there.

Back at Palm, my boss gave me a tremendous performance review—but still no promotion. He said I was doing a fabulous job, but that the promotion was going to someone else: a "great guy" who just happened to have the right friends in the right places. And I would be reporting to him.

I was feeling vulnerable and was ripe for poaching, so I agreed to take the interview and see what Facebook was all about.

The signs that it's time to move on don't always feel like a push out the door. Sometimes the sign is that there's nothing compelling you to stay.

EIGHTEEN

Facebook and Beyond

M Y FIRST CHALLENGE AT FACEBOOK, BEFORE I
even began working there, was finding the office. The
address was a sandwich shop on University Avenue in Palo
Alto—but to get to the Facebook office, you had to go through an
unmarked door on the side of the building and then up a dark staircase to the second floor.

I was dressed in a business suit. I figured this was a job interview, and it was common courtesy to dress appropriately. I carefully
picked my way, step by step, up this dark staircase. As I entered the
office and my eyes adjusted to the light, I realized that the walls of
the office were covered in graffiti murals of women with huge breasts.
They were everywhere, closing in on me!

All around, I saw a bunch of kids sitting in chairs and milling
around in T-shirts, shorts, and jeans. Beer cans, pizza boxes, and bottles of liquor were strewn about. Every single individual in sight was
young enough to be my child.

The recruiter, Sandra, who was a bit older than everyone else
but nowhere near as old as me, came out to greet me, and we spoke

for a minute about how delighted we were to see one another. The whole time, I was thinking I should probably take something off. She briefly introduced me to Dustin Moskovitz, one of the co-founders, and I remember thinking, *I am having zero luck making a connection with this guy*. Dustin was the epitome of an early internet tech guy— young, extremely smart, and not the best communicator at the time.

Sandra deposited me in a not-so-clean room with a couch, a TV, a chair, and a window that opened to the roof. Mark Zuckerberg, the founder, appeared a few minutes later wearing his signature Adidas sandals, gym shorts, and T-shirt. He was very personable. After he introduced himself, he flopped down on the couch, kicked off his sandals, and curled up in the sofa. Then he patted the couch, indicating that I should come sit next to him, and I thought again, *I really need to take something off*. So I took off my jacket.

Mark looked at me and said, "I haven't interviewed many people before, and I don't know anything about customer service. Could you just talk to me?"

At that moment, three things became crystal clear. First, the ball had just been tossed into my court. Second, since he didn't know anything about customer service, I could say anything, and it wouldn't make any difference. Third, this talk was not about customer service— it was about whether or not I would fit in at the company and whether or not he and I got along.

I looked very different from everybody there, but the prevailing wisdom in Silicon Valley at that time was that you needed a few "gray hairs" around any company for some modified adult supervision—so my suit and hair (gray*ing* but still mostly blonde at the time) were not complete disqualifiers.

About that time, people carrying laptops started to crawl through the window from the roof. I interrupted myself to stare at them, and Mark said, "Don't worry. The engineers go out there to get fresh air while they code. They'll just pass by us for a few moments." Which they proceeded to do, jumping through the window to the couch, and then bouncing like cats away to wherever they were going.

I finished the interview with Mark, hooked my coat over my shoulder, and waved goodbye. I descended the stairs in a vaguely out-of-body state, feeling much as I had the time I smoked opium on the beach in high school many, many years ago. The experience of being at Facebook was surreal. I kept asking myself, "What the hell just happened?"

A New Frontier

Next thing I knew, I got a phone call from Facebook wanting me to meet with a man named Matt Cohler. Matt was known as the Vice President of Everything, but his official title was Vice President of Product Management.

Matt and I met at Coupa Café, which was becoming famous because Facebook people hung out there. He was a brilliant, gifted guy with a magical brain for business. He asked me some questions, and I realized very quickly that, although this man understood much more about business than Mark did, once again the conversation was really about whether I would fit with Facebook. Could I work with these people?

While we were talking, a gentleman in a business suit walked up to us. He was carrying a briefcase, and Matt introduced him as Chris Kelly, Facebook's new general counsel. Chris and I would later work very closely, and he eventually became Facebook's chief privacy officer.

Well, Facebook and I started talking about money and stock options, and I was trying to wrap my head around the idea of working at a startup again. Startups want you to take stock options in lieu of a higher salary because they typically don't have a lot of money at the beginning and also want you to be invested in the company's success. But I was coming off Walmart and Palm, which were publicly traded companies and more likely to compensate you with money. My head started to spin, and I realized I had better reach out to friends and contacts who could help me negotiate all this. Stock was nice, but I had bills and care to pay for.

The Facebook folks were very focused on my taking more stock and less salary. As these negotiations started to get a little more hardball, suddenly Sandra the recruiter was gone, and in her place was super-recruiter Robin Reed, a well-known, high-powered figure in the Valley.

Facebook was starting to get famous, and people were beginning to smell success in the air. Robin had been brought in to help with the recruiting and closing. Robin had placed Meg Whitman at eBay and had just landed Facebook as a client. I was one of her first projects at Facebook, and she was intent on showing them how valuable she was. Very quickly, in Robin's hands, my relationship with Facebook went from "Let's keep talking" to "Here's our final offer. We need to know by such-and-such a date." I had an ultimatum.

All the while, I had been engaged in my normal decision-making process, my columns of pros and cons. What if this happened? What if that happened? I wrote free-form words about each alternative, as if I were white-boarding and brainstorming with myself. Then I put it aside, came back to it, put it aside—and at some point, the answer usually jumped right off the page.

All My Children

Since my first interview with Mark, Facebook had moved a block down the street into part of the second floor of what was at least an office building, not a restaurant. Soon, we would take over the whole second floor in a negotiation that was conducted along the lines of, "We're Facebook, and we're buying out your lease!"

The office was a huge open space, with a conference room and one office way back in the corner. My first thought was, *That must be my office.* After all, I was senior director of Customer Operations. But no, the seat chosen for me was just *outside* this office, on the periphery of the open bullpen.

I took a deep breath because I'd had luxurious offices at MCI, Walmart, and Palm. It turned out that the office would be occupied by Catherine, who was the new controller and needed to be behind a door that she could lock.

Musical chairs was the order of the day at Facebook. You never really knew who would land where. Cath did start out as controller but eventually managed HR activities. When Robin and I were negotiating my contract, there was some discussion of my being director of HR. We talked about me doing it alone, then about Cath and me sharing it, then about Cath doing it alone. But when she started, Cath was controller, and we got along very well. She was another "adult in the room," and we became friends.

The other person in our little area outside the conference room was Melanie, the director of Marketing. The three of us seemed to have a bit more seasoning than most people running around the office.

Not only did I not have an office, but I didn't have a desk. The room was filled with tables that appeared to be from Ikea, with three or four people sitting at each table. I shared a table with Christina and Meredith, two of the seven people who reported to me. There was nothing on these tables except computers. No phones, no papers, nothing.

I sat down and thought, *Okay. I used to have an office. I'm now sitting in this big room, with people who report to me.* I leaned back in my beautiful Aeron-like chair and asked myself, *What the hell have I done?* Then I decided, *I'm here, so I'm going to do a good job.*

I leaned over to Christina and asked, "Where is the phone?"

She responded, "Phone? We don't use phones. We don't want to talk to anybody. We do everything by email."

Hmm. I had been hired to run customer service for Facebook, and everyone there thought they could avoid having to talk to anybody on the phone. It's true that you can offer service that doesn't involve being on the phone, but based on what I had learned about Facebook and where it was going, I knew that we were going to have to talk to people on the phone—if only the crazed parents of people who used Facebook! But that was a battle for another day.

My first week was spent getting to know those who reported to me. They were all brilliant, very green graduates from the likes of Stanford or Harvard or Brown—and they all had their dream job. They had been hired from all over the place, but I noticed right away that they all seemed to know one another. Even the people who'd been hired that day seemed to know the *other* people who'd been hired that day. They were all connected in some mysterious way. Then it hit me. I harkened back to what I had been doing at their age. My style and preferences—and my costumes—may have been different from theirs, but we had done the same thing. That's what people that age do, and that's how they all knew one another.

The Facebook culture was all around me, so I learned quickly. The first week I was there, I asked an engineer to print something for me. He was old enough that I had replaced him as the oldest member of the Age Diversity Club, but this guy pointed out to me that *nobody printed anything* in the world of tech. I was the first person who'd ever asked him to print anything, he explained. I realized that the average age at Facebook was about 23.9—and that was with me skewing the numbers.

Facebook was very much a hack culture, in which the ability to hack computers was valued over almost everything. Not hacking in the malevolent sense but taking programs apart and putting them back together so that they worked better. Hackers were the most prized employees. They commanded the most prestige and the best salaries, even if they were eighteen years old and unable to make eye contact with another human being. If you were a good hacker, and you broke into Facebook's code, they'd hire you rather than press charges against you. I wasn't used to thinking of hacking as a good thing and, of course, wondered what people outside Facebook would think, but I got over it.

Like most startups, everything at Facebook was catch-as-catch-can. Whatever came along that you could do to help, you did— between beer bong parties and some shenanigans that I thought I had left behind me thirty years earlier but apparently had not! Overall, it was energizing. If you didn't get your to-do list done today, you might as well toss it because you'd have a whole new list of to-dos tomorrow.

In those early years, Facebook was growing incredibly quickly, constantly acquiring new office spaces, and moving people around so fast that you could hardly keep up with it. People were sitting on top of each other, but nobody seemed to mind. They had the best jobs in the world.

At one point, all seven of my people were smashed together on a couple of couches and chairs over in a tiny alcove, right next to the elevator. Like the tables, all these couches seemed to be from Ikea. The legs fell off if you sat down suddenly, and we had only two of them for our whole team. We were waiting to be moved to a new area, but it wasn't happening, and we were in crisis.

I had an idea over the weekend. I would move out the couches and squeeze everybody together like kindergarteners around a couple of kids' tables. I was afraid they might feel they were being treated like children, but I decided, "So what? Just go with it!"

I got butcher paper and put it all over the tables, along with little boxes of crayons and stickers. When my team walked in on Monday, they were a little startled at first—but then a few people sat down and started drawing, and the others followed. They squeezed in so close to one another that they had to bump their chairs to get out—and it turned into something that they loved. We even called it the "kids' table." When our new space became available three weeks later, nobody wanted to move. We even folded up the butcher paper and put it up on the wall in the new space to preserve it.

The House Without Dad

When I wasn't managing the kids at Facebook, I was managing Dad back in Florida. And when I wasn't at HarborChase or gadding about town with him, I spent my time cleaning out and renovating the house. The whole process would take years. My parents had lived there for almost a half century and were not exactly neatniks or people who went through their stuff every year and threw out what they didn't need.

That process brought up a lot of childhood memories. The house was full of things I'd made for Mom when I was a kid, like a big wooden daisy key chain that I'd given her when I was eleven. Other things had material, rather than sentimental, value. Once I brought Jim Graddick with me because he was very knowledgeable about antiques and art. We salvaged three or four paintings that were solid black when we found them but were quite beautiful when I had them restored. One dated back to 1817. There were many things like that, left over from the days when Dad's parents had been wealthy.

Years earlier, we had closed up the Shack and just let it sit. It hadn't been inhabited since my grandma, Ma, went off to the nursing home. By the time Dad left for HarborChase, foliage had grown up all around the Shack, the roof had cracked, and everything inside was ruined. My mother's azaleas and amaryllis—in fact, the whole backyard—had gone wild. It had a strange look—vines everywhere, the crumbling structure, and an enormous cocoon of ropes my father had strung between the cedar trees for the squirrels to play on. The whole place had gone back to nature, just as my father would have liked.

The bad news was that some neighborhood watch people had found a hypodermic needle out there and claimed that unsavory characters had been seen lurking around. A lot of people thought it was time to get rid of that broken-down Shack entirely. Nobody said anything to my father, but there was a movement afoot, and it was eventually condemned by the city.

My friend Celeste was my partner in crime when it came to cleaning out Dad's house and yard. We redid the kitchen, bathroom, and floors—and painted everything. Eventually, we emptied the whole house and sanded all the floors. I planned to keep the house as long as Dad was alive and I was coming to visit.

When I looked around during that process, I could get very sad if I let myself. My family had owned this land since the 1950s. Out in the front yard, there was a big rock Dad had brought home when they were excavating to build Disney World, with petrified miniature horses in it. The place where I grew up would someday be sold to strangers, and the whole LeNoble era would come to an end. Not right away but soon.

Tearing Down to Building Up

In the meantime, Facebook kept growing and growing. When I started, there were less than fifty employees. In the reception area, the signatures of the first one hundred employees were up on the wall. But people were coming and going so fast, those first one hundred names were not known to most people who now worked there.

I was getting more deeply involved and finding more and more things that needed to be built for customer service. I was growing my team so quickly that in fourteen months, I had one hundred people reporting to me. Most of them were right out of school and had no clue at all about customer service, but I had a lot of experience and had fun training them.

There was never a dull moment. Mark commissioned some artwork from David Choe, a graffiti artist who was already famous but is even more famous today because he was paid exclusively in Facebook stock—and not many graffiti artists have $200 million. His work was both erratic and highly sexual. He painted the elevator doors so that when they closed, it looked like two people coming together. When they opened, the people came apart. It fell to the two adults in the company, Melanie and me, to tell Mark that he couldn't do that. The elevator sex went away, but he replaced it with something that was just as edgy. Mark always did whatever he wanted to do. And really, what difference did it make? Kudos to him.

One of my big duties at the time was managing the construction of a new building to house my team. When we finally moved into our new offices, David Choe did some absolutely beautiful work there, too, and we took it with us to our next location when we expanded and moved again.

One of the best gifts of my years at Facebook was tapping into the culture of millennials. They'd had constant access to technology since they were born, and that made them different from any other generation. I had to learn about them in order to manage them and came to appreciate them in a way I would never have if I hadn't had daily contact with them. After all, if I had had children, these would be their peers.

Later on, I would give keynote addresses at several business conferences on what I had learned about this generation. One of the many things I found interesting about them was how different their relationships with their parents were from those of my generation. Their parents are more like friends, and that's one reason they tend to stay close to home.

*It's a more lateral relationship than a hierarchical one—
and that's how you have to manage them.*

*You can't train them from an authoritarian position. You can't throw
the book at them or tell them they have to learn anything. You have
to show them the value of relating to people in ways that produce
results and cooperation. You even have to show them the value of
being trained to do something! They need real-world examples and
illustrations of behavioral techniques—because until they see the
value of all that, they'd really rather be off working on their laptops.*

I loved the millennial challenge. I liked these kids, and I was good with that kind of training. It didn't work so well when we brought in outside consultants to do trainings or team building. Unless that person had the right approach, the kids' attitude was, "Okay. Wait a minute. I just graduated from Stanford. I'm pretty sure I know what I'm doing. Why are you trying to get me to talk to people and connect with them?" My job was to convince them to hang around long enough to see the value of learning some of these skills.

Meetings with Mark

Mark met occasionally with a group of us who were loosely thought of as "the leadership." It was fascinating to watch his mind at work.

He was absolutely brilliant, and sometimes, it was like watching five computers running at once. But he seemed to have trouble being present to a conversation, especially if that conversation was about something he didn't know well—like customer relations. You could tell he didn't really want to meet with us, but he knew he had to do it. He wasn't used to doing things he didn't want to do, so it was awkward for him. Still, I enjoyed those meetings, if only to watch his brilliant mind at work.

He told us he wanted feedback, and I think that, for the most part, he did—but there was a line that you didn't cross. You couldn't give him too much bad news or tell him too much about something he didn't like without creating tension in your relationship with him.

In the early days, Mark had what he called "fireside chats" with Facebook staff. That was a little confusing because, first of all, there was no fire. And second, it made no sense to do fireside chats with people who were twenty-one years old and just wanted to get back to their computers. He always made a point of inviting me to come to these chats, and I always attended. He told people they could ask him anything, and sometimes they did—but it was an odd setting and a very odd name and certainly not something that would happen at Facebook today. But they were a success and continued for some time.

Dealing with Dementia

Spending my weekdays surrounded by the brilliant minds of the Facebook kids felt all the more surreal because all my personal time was devoted to Dad, who continued to decline both physically and mentally. He fell and broke his hip, but there wasn't much they could do about it at his age and in his condition. The only "fix" would have been to cut him open and put in some pins, and it's very unlikely that he would have survived that. His body was just old and falling apart, and he had hardly been walking, even before he broke his hip. Now he couldn't walk at all. He was in a wheelchair with pillows stuffed all around him to make him more comfortable.

Dad would sneak out into the hall in his wheelchair to watch people and wind up either setting off alarms or wheeling himself out onto the sand around the building, which would cause the wheelchair to turn over and dump him out onto the ground. I was getting more and more calls in the middle of the night about his antics. It was actually fascinating to talk to the staff about him and to hear how he let these nurses do things to him—bathing and dressing him, helping him with his leg bag—that he never, ever would have permitted in his former life. I watched him surrender to so much, and it was just heart-wrenching. The nurses used humor to get through to him, and one day I discovered that he had been smacking women on the butt as they passed by—perhaps he'd been misinterpreting their tolerance. I had a talk with him about that, but he thought it was funny and just laughed.

Still, there were so many sweet moments with him. I'd come to visit, and we'd get in the car and go to lunch, or to our favorite places, and reminisce about Mom or my brother. He always wanted to know what was going on in my life. We'd talk about that, but over time, I could feel the distance and knew that my time with him wasn't going to last forever.

I became close with some of the HarborChase staff, and Dad seemed to have a special connection with one of the day nurses, P.J., who took a real interest and watched over him. I almost always spent time hanging out with the staff at the front desk, getting to know both them and the residents. I knew there would be a connection between how I treated them and how they treated my dad. I brought them little gifts and always participated in the Christmas drives and other events. I would listen to them complain because that told me what was really going on at HarborChase and what I might need to look into.

Dad eventually wound up in diapers because the leg bag that he'd used for decades got too confusing for him. Some people have some control over their bladders, but he had absolutely none. HarborChase had an issue with him using too many diapers and that being too great an expense for them. They were only going to let him have so many diapers a day, so I found a way to pay for the extra diapers and get some staff on board to make sure he had them when he needed them.

The weaker he became mentally, the angrier and more frustrated he got—which is typical. He was always telling people, "Take me to the beach!" They thought he meant the sandy beach by the ocean, but of course, to him, "the Beach" meant Jacksonville Beach. He just wanted to go home, to the place where he had grown up.

UTIs and Memory Care

One day, I got a phone call in California telling me to come quick because my father had pulled a knife on someone. Apparently, another resident, whom Dad didn't like, had taken "his" seat at the lunch table. Dad had taken the pocketknife I'd given him when I was ten out of his pocket and placed it on the table. Closed, according to Dad. They searched his room and found several screwdrivers, which, after the dining room incident, they considered weapons.

When I got to Florida, Dad was in the psych ward. I was livid. Dad had not been an ideal resident on that day, but what he'd done wasn't much weirder than a lot of things that went on at HarborChase every day—especially if you believed Dad that the knife had been closed and that he'd just laid it on the lunch table.

It wasn't long before we discovered that Dad had a raging urinary tract infection. He was prone to them anyway, and wearing diapers had probably aggravated that tendency. When older people get UTIs, they can become mentally unstable—hence the knife incident. The HarborChase people were telling me that I need to move my father out because he was a danger to the other residents, when in fact they had failed to prevent the infection by not changing him frequently enough, and then failed to identify the problem as a UTI.

As soon as the UTI began to clear up, he returned to his normal self. By that time, I was talking to lawyers and looking at other facilities for Dad. In the end, we all calmed down. I helped Dad understand why he couldn't have the knife, and I think they let him keep one screwdriver. Just in case he absolutely needed to tinker with something.

Goodbye, Gen Y

Back at Facebook, my legs were churning very fast beneath the surface of the water. I was trying to learn a new technology, keep on top of all the internal dynamics, and also be one of the gang to whatever extent I could, even though that seemed next to impossible. I had to learn where I was welcome and where I was not—and where, even when I was invited, I wasn't *really* invited.

When we hit five million members, we had a big party on a boat to celebrate. I remember there was a beer bong in the shape of a skeleton. Somehow, I wound up on my knees with beer coming down through this skeleton into me—and I don't even drink beer. Mark, his sister Randy, and everybody from the office just freaked out that I was doing that and gave me a big round of applause.

That kind of thing happened a lot. It wasn't all that much fun for me, but I tried to be a good sport and participate when it seemed like the right thing to do. Sometimes I felt like I was really part of it, and sometimes I didn't. Needless to say, my imposter syndrome was in full gear most of the time. Not that I was a very good imposter in that setting.

· · ·

For me, Facebook was the opportunity of a lifetime. I was fifty-five and got to work with a bunch of incredibly brilliant twenty somethings at the most cutting-edge company in Silicon Valley. I got to build my own little business within the company, which is something I always did and always enjoyed. I got to use a lot of tools I'd learned in my spiritual and coaching exploration and put them to work in a business setting. People were still saying you couldn't do that, but we did it at Facebook. We didn't call those tools coaching, or soft skills, or people skills, or even making people feel good about themselves—but we used them nevertheless.

The most rewarding part of my job was watching the young people who worked for me see what I did, understand its value, and start using those same tools themselves. I had learned so much over the years, and at Facebook, I could apply those tools in an environment where they hadn't been known before. And of course, it was such fun to be around young people—especially ones as brilliant as they all were.

Those years were also a time of great chaos, for Facebook and for me. Changes happened daily—big changes. New hires, people leaving, new offices, old offices, lots of money, and then more money. Huge, huge staff increases. With all that change, and with a large group of people whose gift was not interpersonal skills, there were bound to be challenges.

When my team grew to one hundred people, Mark didn't like the fact that we were bigger than the Technology team. We were trying to build our group out even further, and he didn't like that either. I think he was also uncomfortable with the fact that I knew how customer service was done in more traditional corporate settings and that I was a fairly large presence in the company. Plus, I couldn't write code.

None of that worked for Mark, and I began to feel some dissatisfaction from him. It may have simply been that I had not grown up professionally in the Facebook culture. I think I challenged that culture and Mark, as much as they challenged me. He didn't like any of that, and he was the boss.

· · ·

All the while, the company continued to grow exponentially—in users, employees, and earnings. There were all sorts of dynamics going on—some functional, some dysfunctional. I wasn't too involved with them, but at some point, I learned that new management was coming in and that I was going to report to them. Nobody said anything specific to me, but I was seasoned enough to understand what was going on.

There were a lot of big plans swirling around in those days, and nobody knew exactly where I or customer service might fit into them. Mark and I were talking about these possibilities, but things were on pause while we waited for further developments. He looked at me during one conversation and said, "Why don't you, like, go to Hawaii and hang out on the beach for a while until we figure this out."

That's not how I did things. My attitude, and my background, was more along the lines of: What is next? Give me something to do that I am good at doing, and I'll do that while we wait!

I said to him, "Mark, in my work experiences, there's no such thing as just hanging out. Doing that means you're not interested."

People at Facebook changed jobs all the time. They turned on a dime and learned each new skill or discipline as they went along. My skill was primarily around service and HR. I didn't want to do sales or other jobs that didn't interest me. That was yet another way I was different from everybody else. It became more and more evident that Facebook and I were not a good fit. They outgrew me, and I outgrew them.

As that reality set in, I decided to see a lawyer. I wanted our parting to be as amicable as possible, but I also wanted the best deal I could get. Hammering out the final agreement was a long, difficult process, and once it was resolved, that was it. There wasn't the usual two weeks' notice and farewell tour. In those days, when people left, they left. And that's what happened to me. I kept a few friends from Facebook, but my relationship with the company was just as a stockholder.

Because I had sensed which way the wind was blowing, I had already started interviewing, and by the time final documents were signed with Facebook, I had already accepted my next job.

. . .

Take a risk.

Bet on the unknown.

Expect the unexpected.

. . .

NINETEEN

Taranga

I N MY JOB AFTER FACEBOOK, ANOTHER BUSINESS STARTUP
called SupportSpace, I was the chief support officer and also took
on an HR role. I got to do more traveling (this time in Israel) and
explored an entirely new area of expertise—something I tried to do
with each successive job. But I was starting to have itchy feet.

Since going back to work in 2000, I had traveled the country and
the world, trained thousands of employees in customer service, and
developed close relationships that have continued to have a positive
influence on my life both personally and professionally. The company cultures were very different, but in each role, I called upon the
curiosity, initiative, and intentional focus that I'd built up over the
decades and that I'd learned to truly harness over the last fifteen or
so years.

I had left each job better than I'd found it, so in 2010 I thought
to myself, *Why not just start consulting?* When I began to think seriously about consulting, I already had a company from which to do it:
Taranga Enterprises, created during the Walmart years as a vehicle
through which to run my rental properties in Mississippi and Arkansas.

Consulting had always worried me a little because it didn't have the stability of being employed at a big company. My parents' Depression-era genes kicked in a bit when I thought about the mortgages or had dire visions of somebody pulling the plug on my insurance. But I didn't worry for too long because, right away, consulting jobs started flooding in.

The Wave

Taranga is the culmination of everything I've learned and done and taught over the course of my career in HR, customer service, training, organizational development, operational work, transitioning executives in or out, and especially, consulting and coaching.

I'm president and CEO, and work primarily with startups and coaching C-level executives. I've never marketed Taranga. It's all been word of mouth and usually starts with a visit to talk about what's going on in the organization. Most people begin the conversation with, "Would you just come talk to us?" If I warm up to the situation, I work with them—sometimes full-time, sometimes I just do what needs to be done and go away.

We often discover that the root of their challenges is very different from what they had thought, and the values of flexibility and focus are of the utmost importance.

The thing I love most about working this way is that I can bring in all the coaching, interpersonal, and spiritual tools I've gathered over the years and work with them in a way that lets people own them and make them their own.

I have always found magic in Taranga, on many fronts. Even before I started consulting, choosing the name was both a reflection of where I was at the time and a preview of what was to come. A long time ago, when I started teaching qigong, I was trying to come up with a name for what I did. I had put together a series of exercises that involved breathing in, breathing out, and a few other things that I called the Wave Series. I wanted to brand it, so that I could spread the word.

An old friend told me the Hindi word for wave: taranga. I loved the way it sounded, so I used it. Everything I did was like a wave, a flow, an in and out—from qigong, to coaching, to my own health and finances, to my relationship with the divine.

I later learned that in Hawaiian folklore, Taranga was the mother of Maui. Maui had appeared to be stillborn, so Taranga wrapped him in a cradle of her hair and lifted him out of the nest, so that he wouldn't be destroyed, as was the custom. She gave him a chance to make it on his own. That became a metaphor, in my business, for not throwing out things that may at first seem defective or unwanted. Rather, we look at them from a different angle, in a different light, and find something beautiful.

That's what I'd done with AIDS, in business, and, really, with every challenge I'd ever faced in life. Let's look at this apparent problem as a challenge, a way to grow. Embrace it, see what we can make of it, set an intention, and keep going.

Vic

It wasn't a driving factor at the time but going into business for myself while my father was still around to witness it turned out to be incredibly meaningful. Even though our roles had long ago reversed, he was still my father, and I know it filled him with pride (and not a little relief) that I was going to be okay.

Now that I no longer had to travel for work or put in days at the office, I spent more time with Dad as his condition continued to deteriorate. Sometimes I'd find him locked in the bathroom with the wheelchair. I could see how he might have forgotten how to unlock the door, but I wondered why nobody had come in and found him.

I could no longer get Dad in and out of the car, so we used the HarborChase van when I took him to his doctor's appointments. It was a typical tourist bus, except that it had "HarborChase" on the side so you knew who you were!

This is how we got to the doctor's office on the day I almost killed my father. The appointment went fine. We said goodbye to the doctor, got out the front door, and I was wheeling him down the concrete sidewalk when all of a sudden, the wheelchair veered off sharply onto the gravel "lawn" that is everywhere in Florida. The tire got stuck, the wheelchair came to a screeching halt, and my father flew out of the chair like a bullet and landed on his head. I was afraid that, after all I'd done to keep him alive, I had killed my father.

About this time, the van drove up. They scooped up my dad and loaded him in, then loaded in the wheelchair. We arrived safely back at HarborChase, got him ensconced back in his room, and started monitoring him for a concussion. Dad had no recollection of any of it—the van, the doctor, the fall, *any* of it—nor did he have a concussion. He was just getting more and more confused.

He would do typical sundowner things like leave the TV on all night, but he always knew me—and when he saw me, he just lit up. He was like a kid who had waited all year for a piece of peppermint candy, and now he had it. But he was not fully in touch. There was a cloudiness about his perceptions. At one point, he thought there were *two* of me. I think he thought I was both me and my brother.

The more confused he got, the more agitated and upset he got—
and the more trouble he caused. He began to require a lot more
attention and care, so I started providing extra nursing assistance
for certain shifts.

At some point, it became obvious that Dad needed to move from
the Assisted Living unit into the Memory Care unit—the next step
up in care at HarborChase. I thought it might be a huge ordeal for
him, but again, Dad didn't offer any resistance. He accepted the
move and saw it as an adventure.

I remember vividly the day we moved him to Memory Care. I was
worried about everything. We saw an old antique typewriter sitting
somewhere in the Memory Care unit with "Victor" written on it, and
I thought, *That's got to go. You've got to move that or cover it up, or he'll
have it all taken apart by noon.*

He said to me, very good-naturedly, after about a week, "I guess
you put me back here with all these crazy people." In fact, I did hear
a lot of the Memory Care residents talking just like my grandmother
had talked when I was a kid.

Dad adapted well, better than I'd thought he might. Memory
Care was very different from Assisted Living. The residents clearly
had no idea where they were or what was going on. Dad would come
out and socialize a bit, but his memory was gone and he could barely
move. The poor man was miserable.

Shortly after Dad had settled into Memory Care, I got another
phone call. He was in the ER with another UTI. But this time, it was
very severe, and his kidneys were shutting down. The ER doctor had
a long list of heroic measures and invasive procedures that she could
do to save his life—and she thought we should get started on them
right away. I said, "No, no, no, we're not doing any of that." I had
talked often with Dad about various options and possibilities, and I
knew that he didn't want that kind of heroics.

She insisted she could make everything better, and I said, "You're going to make him better so he can sit in a wheelchair, not knowing who he is, pee all over himself, and be in pain?"

I got Dr. Mark Messinesse on the phone. The Messinesses had been our neighbors, and my father had held Mark when he was a baby. Mark was the only person in that family to go to school. He became a doctor and then came back home to take care of everyone. He and my father had connected over astronomy, which was Mark's hobby.

We discussed the procedures the ER doctor had wanted to do, and Mark asked me, "Is this what you want?"

"Mark, you know this isn't what I want or what Dad wants. We're not going to do it."

"Are you sure?" he asked.

"Of course, I'm sure." You always question decisions like that, but Dad didn't want to do anything extreme, and at that point, neither did I. Mark agreed to honor our wishes. As soon as I could, I got on the plane and went to my father's side. When I got there, I called hospice.

Hospice and the Hawk

Word got around that Dad was near the end, and many people showed up to say goodbye. One was his friend Mary Jo, who had been his secretary and a confidante for over forty years. Another was my dear friend Celeste. And of course, Liz, Mom's best friend and my second mom.

The hospice nurses came and went. There was nothing to do, really, other than to keep him comfortable. We were not going to turn him over in the bed. All those rigid, painful bones had frozen solid. We couldn't move him even an inch without getting an extraordinary pain reaction from this man, who was only partly conscious.

I lay in the bed with my father, as I had with my mother and my brother, and just talked with him about whatever my intuition prompted me to say. His eyes were mostly closed, but I would go on and on for hours. I gave everybody else their time with him, but I slept in his room on a little pallet on the floor, even though the house was only five minutes away.

At one point, he roused himself and tried to tell me that he'd done something that he'd been ashamed of all his life, and for which he was afraid he would be punished. Then he stopped talking. I'll never know what that was, but I'm glad he had a chance to say at least what he said and that he felt safe saying it to me.

On Thanksgiving morning, Mary Jo came in and told me, "You've really got to go take a shower, Tom, and get something to eat." I thought I'd go clean up, eat, and pull myself together. Instead, I just took a quick shower and went right back.

Dad was looking more and more peaceful as time went on—and strangely, younger and younger. It was rather amazing. At one point, I was gazing out the window and saw a hawk land on the fence outside Dad's room, only about twelve feet away from us. I pointed it out to Liz, Celeste, and Mary Jo, and they thought it was beautiful. The hawk sat there on the fence for about five hours. Hawks don't usually sit like that. They might rest on your fence a moment while they look around for food, but they don't sit for hours at a time.

In some spiritual systems, the hawk is considered a conduit or messenger between us and the universe, or between us and God. The message is about going back or going home. I looked at this hawk and felt very much supported in letting my father go. It was almost as if there were an energy field around me and the hawk and my dad. We were cocooned together, and nothing was in there except us. Our little cocoon was vibrating with life and death, and the abundance of all of it.

As the day and the night went on, I watched my father's breath and talked to him. I remembered that when Mom died, I was very, very sick. She was beside herself, worried about who would take care of her baby after she was gone. Her other baby was already gone, and she wasn't going to be able to take care of me. I'm sure my dad made a deep soul contract with her to take care of me. I wanted him to know that he had fulfilled that contract, that I was okay, and that he had done a great job.

The next day was a Friday. I kept thinking that the day before had been my last Thanksgiving with my biological family and that I was about to be the only one left.

I looked out the window, and there was the hawk again, sitting on a post, keeping watch. I lay in bed with my dad and held him. I talked to him about Mom. I told him it was really okay to let go and that wherever he was going would be better than this. I was fine. We were all fine.

Around sundown, Dad opened his eyes and looked at me. It seemed to go on forever. I tried to gather in everything that was in that look. The hawk flew away, just before Dad took his last breath.

· · ·

After that experience, I never questioned that we did the right thing by letting him go. I knew absolutely that this was the right place and the right time. I knew, even with all the ups and downs we'd had, that he loved me and I loved him.

This man's life was over. The man who had been my father, my grandfather's son, my grandmother's son, my mother's husband, my brother's father. Something new was beginning for him, and I had no idea what that was.

Dad's Celebration of Life

Dad's rule was no funeral, no obituary, no nothing. You might accept the ashes when they got delivered, but no more. Still, I wanted a celebration of his life. And really, how was he going to stop me? (Although, when I stood up to give my eulogy, I did start by saying, "I could get hit by lightning while I'm standing here talking to you. If I do, you know it's Vic.")

I did the same kind of Celebration of Life for him that I had done for my mother—in the same chapel, with the same minister, and the same wonderful, nostalgic scents wafting through the church, probably from generations of candles and flowers and incense.

The church was full. I'd set up pictures of him and placed the things he loved all around the church. I had a little step ladder on which I put all his photography equipment. In another area, I set up his tools. I found a place for everything I thought was special to him or interesting or heartwarming for others. Then I had another area devoted just to him, to the stages of his life, and a little bit about us, his family.

I learned a lot about my father after he died from people who attended the Celebration of Life. They told me stories about things that had happened when he was young and more recent stories about kids he had helped get out of trouble. Listening to those people talk about Dad after his death gave me a whole new perspective on his life.

Everybody's Ashes

In keeping with the family tradition of no funeral when you're gone, everybody got cremated.

After Mom died and before Dad moved to HarborChase, I had told him to move her ashes from the little table between their armchairs to the cabinet underneath. Some time later, I was visiting and made some comment about Mom's ashes. We opened the cabinet to find them, and they were gone! My father's mind was slipping enough by that time that it was entirely possible that he had done something with those ashes and forgotten about it. Or that when Liz and I had reorganized the house we had put them in some "special" and now-forgotten location.

I called Liz and asked, "Where did we put Mom's ashes?"

She panicked. She couldn't remember what, if anything, she had done with them. "Oh, my God," she said. "What did we do to Mary?" She wanted to jump in the car and drive three hours to our house. I tried to stop her, but she refused.

Finally, I said, "At least wait until the sun comes up tomorrow."

Dad and I had been up half the night, looking everywhere for those ashes. He kept saying, "Where's Mary? Where's Mary?"

I walked around the house, trying to open myself up to some universal force or channel or *anything* that might tell us where those ashes were! And suddenly the words came through my mind: "Closet, closet, closet." I remembered the closet where Dad stored all his hurricane paraphernalia, mostly big trash bags to wrap around the plastic garbage cans he used to protect his pictures and guns. I had an eerie intuition or memory that Mom's ashes were stashed in that closet "for safekeeping"—and there they were.

Peace was restored to the land. Liz didn't have to drive three hours. The ashes went back where they belonged, in the little cabinet under the table. The crisis was over, and all was well with the world.

Once Dad had been cremated and his ashes arrived in the mail, I thought, "Okay, now I have both Mom's ashes and Dad's ashes." During the final clearing out and cleansing of the house, I'd come across a bookcase where I put things that I didn't quite know what to do with. It became my "free space," and God knows there was precious little of that in the house. I put Mom's and Dad's ashes, side by side in their two little boxes, on this bookcase and told them, "There! Talk among yourselves. I'll be back." And I jumped on a plane to California.

The next weekend, Celeste and I continued cleaning out the house and the yard. I was digging through the big shed one day and finding things like a broken eight-track cassette player—that I'm sure Dad intended to fix one day—and things so old and grimy that I could hardly even tell what they were. Deeper and deeper into the piles of "keepsakes" I went.

Suddenly, I looked up and saw a box sitting on a shelf. It didn't look like it belonged there. I looked up at this box and thought to myself, *I believe this might be my brother's ashes.*

Very likely, UPS had delivered them one day, and my father had signed for the package. Knowing that my mother would be distraught, he had hidden them in the shed—no doubt planning to resurrect them one day but probably forgetting about them or not wanting to upset my mother by bringing them into the house. So there his ashes stayed, along with the broken eight-track recorder and all the other debris, in the Florida heat and humidity since 1985.

I dusted him off, spoke a little greeting, and brought him over to the bookcase with Mom and Dad.

"Hello, folks. Talk among yourselves. By the way, if anybody's upset about where you've been staying, I have nothing to do with this. I am just the help."

But that was not the end of it. Once Celeste and I had cleaned out the shed, we had to contend with the second shed in the backyard, which contained everything that had been in the Shack when it was finally torn down.

I started digging through this shed. I found old briefcases and papers and things that even a hoarder would have thrown away decades ago. In the process, I discovered a strange little box, kind of leaning up against some other, larger boxes. It had no paper around it, but when I opened it up, I realized, *Hmm. This is my grandmother!* It was Ma, my father's mother, who had lived in the Shack after we moved to the bigger house and whom I had cared for as a teenager.

I could easily imagine my dad putting Ma's ashes in the Shack with all her other belongings before all the foliage grew up around it, then moving the ashes along with all the other Shack contents over to this second shed.

"Hello, Ma. How are you?" I said. "Let's take you into the house and put you with the others." My last words to the little group on the bookcase before going to the airport were, "Talk among yourselves. I need to go back to San Francisco and see a therapist. And oh, again, if anybody's upset, Dad's the one to talk to. I've had nothing to do with any of this."

· · ·

The next weekend I was back in Florida, still working my way through the second shed. I came across what looked to be a decorated metal can, like a cookie or candy tin that your mother might have filled with goodies and given the lady down the street at Christmas. I opened it up, and inside was a little burlap bag containing some gray stuff with hard chunks in it. I showed it to my dad's best friend, Jack, who was a veterinarian and happened to be visiting that day.

"Jack, what is this?"

"That's a tooth," Jack replied.

We realized this was Pa, Ma's husband, my father's father, who died when I was ten, almost a half century earlier. Teeth, bones, burlap. I closed it all up and said, "Hello, Pa." I dusted Pa off and put him on the bookcase. "Hello, everyone. Talk among yourselves. And by the way, I need to go away for a while. Please behave. I'm closing this door now. You have a party or whatever you need to do. See you soon."

A few weekends later, Celeste and I had the house almost ready to go. When all was said and done, we had cleared out two tons of scrap metal and filled two thirteen-foot dumpsters with stuff from the house, including many books from the nineteenth century that multiple book experts had told me would be worth a fortune if they had not been left out in the heat and humidity.

The final step was to transport everything that I wasn't throwing away from Florida to California. I rented a huge storage container that would be loaded onto a truck and driven the three thousand miles to San Francisco. Everything had been packed into it except the ashes. I couldn't figure out what to do with them. I couldn't fly with five people's ashes in my luggage, but I didn't want to pack them away in the container and have them bounce around in there for days as the driver made his way across the country. Finally, I decided to pack them away in Dad's cedar chest from the Navy. It's a sacred box, after all.

I placed all my relatives reverently into the chest, put some papers over them so if a cop or state trooper opened the chest, Everybody's Ashes wouldn't be the first thing he saw, and slowly placed the chest into the container. When it arrived in California, it would be stored in an industrial area south of San Francisco that also boasted many, many cemeteries. My relatives sat in a storage facility right next to one of them for a year and a half. I was okay with that because at least they weren't being pummeled by Florida hurricanes and, in fact, they were as close to a burial as they'd ever been. Plus, they were all together. I said to them, "In my opinion, group, things are looking up."

In 2011, I bought a new house and loaded everything from the storage unit into a van and moved it in. Even today, as you walk out my back door into the garage to get in the car, pressed up against the stairs is the cedar chest that contains Everybody's Ashes. I say hello frequently.

The bottom line is that my family is all together again, with me, in my new home—and really, ever since their deaths, things have never been better for them.

Don't fight the wave.

Ride the wave.

TWENTY

A Final Surprise

O NE OF THE MOST VIVID RECOLLECTIONS THAT has remained with me from the big cleanup after Dad's death was coming upon all his photography supplies and accoutrements. He had collected cameras old and new over the course of his life, and I still have them all.

But the pictures. My goodness, so many pictures. Thousands, certainly. I knew he had captured all the big and small moments—holidays, school plays, Mom's retirement party, their road trips, every meaningful occasion—for which I am so grateful. But as he was learning and experimenting and testing out different cameras and equipment over the years, snapping photos of objects and plants and people for no particular purpose other than to practice, I don't think he ever got rid of any of the resulting prints.

I found boxes filled with photo after photo of the same thing, with his notes on the back: "Out of focus," or "Too far away," or "Wrong light." And he had kept them all. At first, I silently cursed his hoarding tendencies for leaving me so much junk to sort through. Then I realized that he had his reasons. It must have made him feel good to be able to see his progress, the fruits of all his effort and hard work. The "best" shots may have been the ones to make it into the frames, but the others were never discarded. They all were part of the story.

* * *

For so much of my early life, I was trying to figure out who I was. Not only that—that there was such a thing as the right way to be. Once I felt I could never be that, it became about trying to hide or losing myself completely—in drugs, in drag, in success...For a time, I wondered whether each one of these was a stage I was meant to pass through and leave behind on the way to some more meaningful, "truer" destination. And you could say that I've lived many different lives in one, which would be accurate, but it wouldn't be the truth as I've come to understand it.

One of the most memorable things I've learned during my many periods of searching and self-reflection comes from my coaching work with Maria Nemeth. She first introduced me to the very simple and elegant principle that life, or the self, is like a holographic image on a piece of glass. If you were to shatter the glass, each individual shard would retain the holographic image in its entirety, though from a slightly different perspective—not unlike my father's stacks of pictures of the same object.

I know now that each of those moments, those different lives, contained all of me. We are all the things, all the time. And though one or another aspect of ourselves might take center stage at any point, we are still showing all of ourselves to the world. I used to work so hard to hide so much from everybody. Now I don't hide anymore. Because you can never be an imposter in your own life.

Would I have reached this way of thinking had I not been confronted with my own mortality at the young age of thirty-five? I can't really say. My diagnosis of full-blown AIDS certainly accelerated and amplified my journey toward peace and healing—that was its gift. But I like to think I would've gotten here eventually.

· · ·

By the summer after Dad's death, I had settled into a new rhythm of life. I was now the only LeNoble left, living by myself out in San Francisco. There was no one left in Jacksonville Beach to take care of. (They were all in my house!) No more lots to clear out. My work was now all consulting, and with no fixed office to report to, my time and space were completely my own.

I kept up with my usual exercises and spiritual practices, filled my days with client work, made frequent trips to Maui, and enjoyed the gift of time with the friends around me. Though I lived alone and worked by myself, I was once again living in abundance.

Sometime that summer, I had a routine doctor's appointment. By then, going to the doctor was like brushing my teeth: something I did all the time, a normal part of life that I didn't think much about. Because prostate cancer—which my father had had (twice), as did both grandfathers—has a strong hereditary component, we always did a prostate-specific antigen (PSA) test to screen for it. I was absolutely shocked when my test came back at 10.8, which is very high. My levels had always been at zero or very, very low.

They immediately did a biopsy, which was perhaps the least fun procedure I have ever endured—and I have endured a lot of procedures! The technology has surely improved since 2012, but at the time, they took the equivalent of a TV remote, placed it up your rectum, pressed it on your prostate, and took twelve tissue samples.

A familiar feeling arose as I waited for the call with the biopsy results. I had played this waiting game so many times in my life by then. I was pretty sure what the result would be—and I was right. I had two tumors in my prostate gland. My father's illness and death were fresh in my mind, along with what prostate cancer had done to him thirty years earlier. I had some dark thoughts about what this diagnosis might mean for the rest of my life. What would my sexual function be? Would I have to wear diapers? Or worse—a leg bag?

And, would I live?

· · ·

Before I could jump into my usual course of action—explore all the alternatives, investigate everything and everyone, make decisions about what to do—I had to sit with what had just happened.

I had already been told three times that I had six months to live, so I was not unfamiliar with the idea of death—but this was different. I had just been diagnosed with an illness that had killed three men in my family. I knew the medical ropes better than most people and was confident of my ability to negotiate the world of doctors, hospitals, surgeries, and alternative treatments. But now I had cancer.

I went through all the usual stages of grief, which I was able to do rather quickly by that point in life, and started to consider the way I would approach this new, upsetting situation.

I thought back to when I'd been so sick with AIDS, and my morning sunrise ritual of meditating, chanting, journaling, reading, and spinning the energy. I remembered when I had my hip replaced, working with the rock and taping it to my hand for the surgery, watching the videos of the operation, and talking with my hip and being part of Maureen's healing group. I remembered my Healing Wheel. I'd now been HIV-suppressed for a long time and not even my massage therapist could tell I'd had my hip replaced. I knew I could heal myself, but this would be a different kind of journey.

There's a point where it's so easy just to say, "This is too much. Take me. Let me gather all the people who will wring their hands and commiserate, and let's put an end to this." There was a point after this diagnosis that I asked myself whether I was up for this fight again.

But right on the heels of that, I thought, *Why not just be a little more inquisitive about this? Why not, in the middle of feeling bad, let myself experience the horror of it—but also be curious about what it means? What can I learn from this? What is it here to teach me? How can I reach out and grow from it?*

I knew I'd done better with AIDS when I took that attitude. I had lived when everybody had expected me to die. I could probably survive this—if I chose to do so.

Pick one. Live or die. Just pick one and move forward toward that choice, for as long as you can.

When I was very, very sick with AIDS, there were many times when I chose to grab for life rather than throw in the towel. I chose to live because it would give me *time*. And time gives me *experience*. We're all going to die at some point, but if I can be exposed to more people, more places, and more experiences before that happens, then I grow. I become *more*. I become deeper within myself, closer to whatever God or the universe, and richer in who I am.

So, with prostate cancer, as with AIDS, I chose to live.

It was time to trade business suits and heels for a hospital gown.

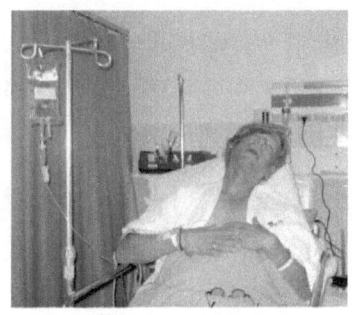

◆ ◆ ◆

I knew the doctors were going to tell me, more or less, what they'd told my father decades ago, with a few improvements: cut it out, radiation, chemo, no sex ever again, and little or no urinary control. They had better, fancier ways of doing those things and slowing the cancer down, but that path was still unacceptable to me—and I let them know it.

I knew how to challenge medical people in a way that was strong but not confrontational enough for them to write me off. I knew how to intrigue them and invite them to look at the problem in new ways, rather than alienating them or making them think, *This guy is a lunatic.*

I began to learn everything I could about the treatment of prostate cancer. I didn't discard anything until I'd given it a good look because sometimes the treatment that seems the weirdest, or the farthest from "reality," could spark a new thought and lead to something else.

The other key for me was, as always, to look beyond the finite and the physical, toward the energetic and spiritual. By then, I had experienced how much stronger, wiser, and more powerful we are than we realize. When we open up to infinite realms and possibilities, we almost always expand. To me, that's where the real gifts, and healing, lie.

So I found people who were really, really good at the finite and the physical, which freed me up to work with the infinite.

◆ ◆ ◆

After interviewing many doctors and having many tests, I saw that I had three choices. One was to have needles pierce through my perineum and deposit 120 radioactive seeds into my prostate gland. Over time, the seeds would kill the cancer and then eventually die themselves. Then there was radiation. I knew enough about radiation, and had seen enough of it, that it seemed like a very poor choice. The third option was a radical robotic prostatectomy, a new surgery that caught my attention.

I chose that. There was a handful of doctors who did this procedure, which involved removing the prostate in as minimally invasive a way as possible. Normally, I don't let anybody touch me who hasn't done the procedure a thousand times. But with this robotic surgery, the choice was a little more complicated. Several doctors knew all about prostate surgery, but the robot was new, and they were all just learning to use it.

It turned out that the two doctors who were the gurus when it came to this surgery, both with over one thousand cases, were in California—one in Los Angeles and the other right here at UCSF Hospital. I did my usual research and due diligence and determined that Dr. Peter Carroll at UCSF was the natural choice.

Now it was time to set a date for the surgery. I looked at my calendar, found out what Mercury was up to over the next few months, and scheduled my robotic radical prostatectomy for September 11, about a month and a half away.

I had a little time and space to think. What would my life be like after the surgery? The main concerns after prostate surgery are bladder control and sexual function. Lately, I had been feeling more open toward love and relationships in general and had even started corresponding with a man I'd met online. It felt new and different to start getting to know a person this way, and I was intrigued by where it might go. But would I ever be able to have sex again? I just wasn't ready to let go of that part of life.

There were no definite answers. The range of outcomes was wide, and I wouldn't know where I fell on it until I got there.

◆ ◆ ◆

The day of the surgery came. Pola and Mary Romeyn were both there with me for support. The robot (and Dr. Carroll) must have done a good job, because I woke up from the surgery feeling good and was doing very well. My tumors were gone, my levels were good, and the next day I got up and was walking laps around the unit. They expected I'd stay in the hospital anywhere from three to five days to recover, but I went home on the second day. The nurses had told Dr. Carroll that I was asking to unplug the IV pump from the wall so I could plug in a power strip for my laptop and other devices so I could get some work done.

"You can stay here if you want to," Dr. Carroll told me. "But, clearly, you're doing okay."

I went home with my leg bag (which was temporary, thank God), and Celeste flew out from Florida to stay with me. The first ten days were a blur of catheters, leg bags, and keeping everything clean and infection-free. Sometimes I'd be fumbling with some catheter or other and would call out to my dad, "What do I do here?" And he always gave me an answer.

As far as urinating and having sex, Dr. Carroll told me that sometimes things came back as soon as they took out the catheter, sometimes they came back a year later, and sometimes they never came back at all. I had a lot of apprehension about the future, not to mention short-term apprehension about infection, sleeping at night, and a host of other things.

After ten days, I went back to the doctor, and his wonderful nurse, Cindy, removed the catheter. I had absolutely no control whatsoever over my bladder and left with a diaper that was sopping wet by the time I got home. I was terribly deflated.

That was my lowest point. I allowed myself to have a pity party for a few minutes. Then I simply decided I would seek out the best pads and diapers. I tried them all and found a really, really good pull-up in a little place down in the Mission where nobody spoke English. That kicked off my healing process, and things started to look up. There would be no Rita for Halloween that year, but it didn't stop me from thinking about how I might incorporate and accessorize those diapers. (Was this so different from the foot cast?) No matter the costume, the show would have to go on, for Rita and Tom both.

Thanks to a very gifted physical therapist whose specialty was post-prostate surgery somatic therapy, I started to see some gradual improvement in my bladder function, but I still had very little control. It would be a while before I could discard those pull-ups. Over the next year, they said, things might improve—but for now, this was what I had.

Their best guess about sexual function post-surgery was that it would return over time to where it had been, maybe a little less. That was better than I'd expected, based on what was happening with my bladder, and I decided to approach it as one more thing to move through as patiently as I could.

◆ ◆ ◆

My prostate surgery was in September of 2011. By January, I was still wearing those terrific pull-ups but looking forward to the day when I would graduate to the big ugly pads, then small ugly pads, and then nothing. But in January, I still had zero control over urination. It went when it wanted to go.

Nevertheless, I decided that I'd recovered so well and been so stressed out by the slings and arrows of life, that I needed to go away to Maui and recover. All I wanted to do was forget about the surgery, forget about the cancer, and *go out on a boat*. The ocean was calm and blue, and I wanted to go snorkeling!

I asked around and came across this thing called snuba, which is a combination of snorkeling and scuba but less complicated, and you don't need to be certified. You breathe through a hose connected to a tank of air on the surface and can descend as deep as twelve feet, so you can swim among the fish instead of looking down at them.

I found a little boat that took small groups of people on snuba outings. They provided the equipment and a little light lunch. It looked wonderful, but what was I going to do about the pull-up?

A plan came to mind very quickly. I would take my towel and my belongings and my camera onto the boat, wearing the pull-up. When it was time to go into the water, I would sneak into the bathroom, slip on my swim shorts, fold the pull-up into my towel, and leave it in a neat pile with the camera and all my other things. When we came back out of the water, I would simply reverse the process. I would grab the towel, sneak into the bathroom, switch out of the swim shorts into my regular shorts and the pull-up, and be on my way.

I arrived early and settled into a nice little spot to sit on the boat and greeted the other people as they came aboard. We got to chatting, and I had my little towel beside me and my plan in place—so I was quite enjoying myself. I watched the birds, looked out over the water, and took a few pictures. Then we pulled out of the harbor to great cheers from everyone on the boat and were on our way.

Everything was going beautifully until we hit a section of choppy water and, to my surprise and horror, I started to feel seasick for the first time in my life! The instructor started giving a little lesson on the snuba basics, but all I could concentrate on was trying to keep my breakfast down. Soon enough I'd forgotten entirely about my clever plan for the towel and the pull-up or anything other than getting back on dry land. The only part of the training I heard was something about hand signals to use if you were in trouble.

The instructor assigned me a partner, and through my seasick haze, I tried to smile at him. My situation must've been written all over my face because a crew member reassured me that we were just going through a rough, windy patch, and in just a few minutes, the sea would be calm again. The next thing I knew, everything was, indeed, calm. I still felt a little sick but better and opened my eyes just in time to hear the instructor yell at me from the water, "*It's your turn!*"

I jumped up, ran over to grab my snuba gear, wrapped it around me, slipped into my fins, stepped down onto the little stairs, and fell backward into the water. Only then did I remember my plan to switch out of the pull-up. The instructor swam over to me and my partner and handed us our hoses. Then he put these weighted belts around our waists so that we could go down to fish-level, and off he swam to the next set of partners.

I sank down under the water, a little worried that my lungs probably weren't as strong as they should be in order to snuba, but I was determined to handle whatever difficulties arose. Now, I normally don't weigh too much, and after this cancer surgery, I weighed even less. I started slowly sinking deeper and deeper, and then it felt like the weights were pulling my pants off. What to do?!

I remembered the hand signals and started waving my hands and arms wildly, trying to signal two things. One: "I'm going up." And two: "Help!"

I popped up to the surface, and the instructor swam over with a concerned look. I told him the belt was too loose and falling off me. He checked it and said that nothing was wrong, but he tightened it up a bit. My poor partner was treading water over to the side. We were attached to one another, so he had to go wherever I went. Poor guy.

I went down again, and the same thing happened! I felt the weighted belt slipping off me, taking the pull-up with it. I started to panic, did the hand signal again, and popped back to the surface. The instructor came back over, and now he looked a bit irritated. He checked the belt again, said I was good to go, and sent me back down. "These weights are not going to fall off you! Okay?"

My long-suffering partner still hadn't had a chance to snuba, so I was determined to make it work. I shifted the weights and put my body in a different position, and that seemed to do the trick! I was snuba-ing!

Suddenly, I tipped over in the water and felt like I was being pulled up...by my pull-up. It had soaked up so much water that it was acting like a life preserver, dragging me to the surface! Up I went again, hand signaling all the way. And along with me came my very sad and frustrated partner.

The instructor swam over, and I told him, "I'm done with this. I can't do this anymore." I handed him my belt and swam back to the boat.

Fortunately for me, most of the people were out snuba-ing except for a few folks who had stayed on the boat to prepare the food. But as I approached the boat, some of them had stopped to see what was going on. And I could sense everyone's eyes on me from the water as I started to climb the little ladder to get back onto the boat.

I steadied myself on one of the rungs and leaned down to take off my fins. At that moment, I realized that my very full pull-up—and my shorts—were down around my ankles. I was mooning the people out in the water, and the ones on the boat got a little bit of a show as well. I reached down as nonchalantly as I could to grab my shorts and this very full, cumbersome pull-up, all the while trying to hold onto the stairs so that I wouldn't fall back into the water. I struggled until I finally got my flippers off, took a few deep breaths, and somehow climbed back into the boat.

The first thing I saw there was my cute little towel, neatly folded with no pull-up inside it. I went into the bathroom, tried to wring out the wet pull-up (which didn't really work), put it back on, and wrapped myself in the towel. I tried to act casual while we waited for the group to come back on board. When everyone ate their burgers and hot dogs, 1 (a vegetarian) snacked on chips and tried to ignore the Pacific Ocean in my pants. It wasn't the most comfortable party.

At long last, we got back to the dock and said our farewells. 1 walked to my car, still soaking wet, desperate to get home and put on a new pull-up. 1 covered the seat with a dry towel and off 1 went.

1 had a little bit of a drive ahead of me, and as my nerves calmed down, 1 convinced myself that there was plenty of humor to appreciate in the situation. There were no costumes or accessories, but they still got some show! And a good vacation story to take back home with them. My ego was a little bruised, but Lord knew I'd been in worse predicaments.

As 1 drove past all sorts of markets and restaurants, 1 started to notice how hungry 1 was and wondered whether 1 should stop for something to eat.

Tom, you have no control over yourself, 1 thought.

At that point, 1 figured, *I'm wet and wrapped in a towel. Who cares? The worst that can happen is 1 get wetter.*

So 1 stopped at a fish restaurant for lunch. I had the most delicious sandwich I'd ever tasted, wrapped in a towel and sitting on a bench overlooking the ocean, probably peeing all over myself. 1 know Dad would've loved it and been laughing.

You never know what's coming next, and you never will. Life's like that. So pull up your diaper, get back in the boat, and enjoy the ride.

Final Bow?

Well, now you know everything.

In this book, I've revealed some of my deepest secrets to the world. And because I always try to be of service to people in everything I do, I hope that, even in some small way, this book has been of service to you.

If nothing else, I hope I've shown that being yourself, loving yourself, and dropping all the forms of drag are the keys to living the life you were meant to live.

It took me a little while to get to that point. Before I could drop all the drag, I had to try on a couple of different versions, both the good and the bad. Some people believe in the cruel irony that life's wisdom comes to us only when it's too late to use it: *"If I'd only known at twenty what I know now, I would have done things differently!"*

I'm so grateful I'm not one of those people. I wouldn't have skipped any of it.

* * *

My Life in Business Suits, Hospital Gowns, and High Heels ends when I was fifty-five years old. As I put pen to paper, I'm seventy. I assure you the last fifteen years have been just as eventful as the first fifty-five. And I'm grateful for every day. For in life, just as anything is possible, nothing is certain.

So remember to take what life presents. Let it mold you, shape you, teach you. Take what you've learned—even the terrible gifts—and use it to create the life you're meant to live.

Otherwise, you're just sitting on your pillow.

Acknowledgments

To my parents, Vic and Mary LeNoble—thank you for the greatest gift of all: life itself. You taught me compassion, integrity, and how to love with my whole heart. That compass has never failed me...even when my GPS has.

To Donna Daniels, for introducing me to Pola, a soul connection that rerouted the course of my life in the most extraordinary way. Pola, you are my sister, best friend, confidant, and healer. Never forget: We were born to be alive. I'll love you forever...and then some.

To Carol Costello—this book exists because you said, "Let's do this." Your guidance, expertise, and no-nonsense magic turned scattered stories into something sacred. Without you, this would still be a stack of sticky notes and wishful thinking.

To Mary Romeyn, MD—you scooped me up when I was barely hanging on. You kept me breathing and believing. We saved lives together, including mine. What we've shared goes far beyond medicine or words on a page. Thank you for being one of my life's great lights.

To Maria Nemeth, PhD—thank you for cracking open the door to what's possible and then gently pushing me through it. You gave me the language of transformation, the tools for service, and the gift of friendship. You are a lighthouse in a foggy world.

To Alessandra Lusardi—you made this book happen. Your craft is a gift and you shared it with me freely, generously, and with abandon. Let's do it again. And again. And again.

To Natasha Adamo—my twin flame in this lifetime. We finally found each other. Your brilliance, precision, and fierce love elevated this book in ways only you could. You're not just a master of your crafts, you're the unicorn I never knew I needed.

To Kacy Wren and Rose Conway, for joining forces and riding shotgun as this book made its way into the world. Thank you for your wisdom, grace, and patience (especially with my "miracle grow" emails). You've carried this story with such care.